THE ULTIMATE GUIDE TO
GREEN
PARENTING
ZION LIGHTS

'A science-based account of the ways we parents might be more green, and raise healthier children in the process.'
Bill McKibben, author and co-founder of 350.org

'A comprehensive, informative, and indispensable green guide for parents!'
Raffi Cavoukian, singer, author and founder of the Centre for Child Honouring.

NONONSENSE LIFE

Bill McKibben, 350.org, author of *Deep Economy*
'A science-based account of the ways we parents might be more green, and raise healthier children in the process – I was especially glad to see the detailed chapter on why one wants to vaccinate one's children. The whole book is written with a view to the larger society, which is good, since that's the society our children will have to live in.'

Raffi Cavoukian, Member of the Order of Canada, singer, author, founder of the Centre for Child Honouring
'In the climate-change era, our children need green parenting – and this well-researched book shows how to do it. It offers easy-to-read, science-based options for greening the family. Kudos to Zion Lights for this comprehensive, informative, and indispensable green guide for parents!'

David Bond, Director of Project Wild Thing
'*The Ultimate Guide to Green Parenting* is a refreshingly clear-headed and well-researched practical guide to environmentally friendly parenting. Zion Lights is a wise, calm voice for new parents. She debunks the myths, and reminds us what is really important: children need care and time – not tonnes of stuff – to make them happy. Finally, a crystal-clear case for what many have suspected for years: green parenting is not for sentimentalists. It is the smart way to think about bringing up children if you care about their (and your) happiness.'

Jay Griffiths, author of *Kith: The Riddle of the Childscape*
'A book of glorious clarity, offering parents the great tool of evidence-based wisdom.'

Tim Gill, writer on childhood
'There's no such thing as the perfect parent – or the perfect environmentalist (I speak from personal experience). But by doing a better job of caring for the planet, we can also do a better job of caring for our children. This is the argument of *The Ultimate Guide to Green Parenting*, and it makes a clear, thought-provoking and persuasive case.'

George Marshall, author of *Don't Even Think About It: Why Our Brains Are Wired to Ignore Climate Change*
'As if being an ethical parent was not challenging enough, we are plagued by self-appointed pundits playing on our insecurities. So hoorah for Zion Lights, who applies the latest research evidence to even the most intractable myths around sleeping, diet and vaccination. The result is an indispensable guide loaded with sound advice.'

Natalie Bennett, Leader of the Green Party of England and Wales
'More and more parents are thinking not just about what they can give their children as individuals, but about the kind of world they are creating for them. Zion brings together the latest peer-review science, looks at it practically and calmly, without being judgemental or preachy, simply helpful. I hope many parents will find this useful and reassuring.'

Dr Marc Bekoff, Professor Emeritus of Ecology and Evolutionary Biology at the University of Colorado, author of *Rewilding Our Hearts*

'Zion Lights' new book is a must read for people of all ages and all cultures. **The Ultimate Guide to Green Parenting** is a very practical, fact-filled, wide-ranging, and easy-to-read book and parents, teachers, and youngsters will learn a lot about how to make "the best and most sustainable/green choices" for themselves and for future generations. Topics range from green birth to travel to diet to toiletries and I continued to be amazed by the breadth and depth of Ms Lights' latest work. I learned a lot from this forward-looking book and I hope it enjoys a wide readership. We really cannot continue to live as we do and expect the very best for our children and theirs. I often wonder what the world will be like for youngsters when they're my age or even half my age, and this book made me hopeful that the future of our challenging, demanding and rapidly evolving planet could indeed be a very bright one if we pay close attention to the choices we make and if we serve as good models for current and future generations.'

Scott Cooney, Adjunct Professor of Sustainability in the MBA program at the University of Hawai'i, author of *Build A Green Small Business*

'Zion's book cuts straight through the noise and presents the best available science on green and naturally healthy parenting. The best part is that it's done in a practical, humorous and easy-to-read way that any parent concerned about the environment and about their children's health can understand.'

John Cossham, compost expert and children's entertainer, winner of the Oxfam Carbon Footprint Competition in 2008

'I enjoyed reading **The Ultimate Guide to Green Parenting** so much I didn't want to stop. Parents like me have been waiting for this sort of sensible and wide-ranging book, and I'm just disappointed it wasn't published when my teenagers were babies. I believe it will appeal as it's based on sound science, and is well researched and referenced. Zion Lights outlines the available evidence where there are debates about a subject. I particularly enjoyed the chapter on travel, as, although it's a parenting book, much of the content applies to all of us, whether parents of young children or not.'

NONONSENSE LIFE

THE ULTIMATE GUIDE TO GREEN PARENTING

About the author
Zion Lights is a writer with a passion for science and the environment.
She writes for and co-edits *Juno* magazine and is a blogger for *The Huffington Post* and *Green Living Ideas*. Zion is active on social media and can be contacted via her website zionlights.co.uk or via the Twitter handle @ziontree

Acknowledgements
It goes without saying that my thanks go out to the superb New Internationalist publishing team who put this book on the shelves, and the many dedicated scientists who have studied and continue to study the important topics covered in this book. Gratitude is also due to the fantastic community that I am fortunate to be part of, particularly John 'Compost' Cossham, John Stumbles, Dave Wilson and Hannah Wainwright-Dumont for their invaluable support.

Thank you also to everyone who provided feedback on chapter drafts, to Andrew Glynn for being the best friend a writer can have, and to my partner Aaron Cleland for constant ideas-bouncing and for putting up with a sleep-deprived zombie after endless hours spent writing and researching. Finally, thank you to my children Arwyn and Raven, who made me a green parent, and for whom I labor to make the world a better place.

NONONSENSE LIFE

THE ULTIMATE GUIDE TO GREEN PARENTING

Zion Lights

New Internationalist

NONONSENSE LIFE
The Ultimate Guide to Green Parenting

First published in the UK in 2015 – and this US edition in 2016 – by
New Internationalist Publications Ltd
The Old Music Hall
106-108 Cowley Road
Oxford OX4 1JE, UK
newint.org

Illustrations, including front cover: Ruth Walton

Series editor: Chris Brazier
Design: Juha Sorsa
Layout: Avocet Typeset, Somerton, Somerset

Printed on recycled paper by Versa Press, Peoria, Illinois, US.

Library of Congress Cataloging-in-Publication-Data.
A catalog record for this book is available from the Library of Congress.

ISBN 978-1-78026-324-3
(ISBN ebook 978-1-78026-325-0)

Contents

Introduction

It's not easy being green. It's also not easy being a parent, which means that being a green parent can be very tricky indeed. I was an environmental activist before I became a mother, but I was so overwhelmed with all the information that was thrust at me as a new parent that consciously being green simply dropped off the map completely for a while. Should I use cloth diapers or disposables? Is there a way to get around needing a car when you have children in tow? And what on earth is palm oil anyway?

Thankfully there are some simple answers to many of the questions a green parent might ask (though no manual for being a parent generally, unfortunately), and some more complex answers that can be explained to the sleep-deprived modern-day parent with a little effort. I'm an editor, journalist and science writer so research is at the core of everything I do, and by keeping on top of the latest science on how to bring up a baby and child with minimal environmental impact I can attest that it *is* possible to make the transition to being a green parent with comparative ease. The answers are out there, they're just hidden between overflowing laundry baskets and sleepless nights.

If you're reading this book, you're probably already interested in being green, and almost certainly already a parent (or about to become one), so I won't trouble too much with the semantics of what 'being green' means, but just say that doing the 'green' thing here means being as environmentally friendly as possible, while considering your child's everyday personal health as well, and taking into account social-justice issues to some degree, because no-one is an island and humans and animals are part of the environment too. Even if you're new to this, it's entirely possible, with a little helping hand, to form new, green lifestyle habits, so long as you're prepared to take baby steps to begin with (and pardon the pun).

The way you use this book is up to you. You might want to choose one chapter, covering a particular subject, and focus on 'greening' your lifestyle choices as far as practically possible there. Or you might prefer to take pointers from different chapters and make it up as you go along. Whatever works for you.

Some topics, like childbirth, are surrounded by fear and misinformation because parents are lied to by both sides of the debate: in this example, the medical professionals[1] and the alternative birthworkers (doulas). Other areas discussed don't get the research funding that they require so the science available is less rigorous, which can lead to emotionally invested people and groups filling in the gaps and skewing the results of the data that is available. I have tried to be clear where I can see that this is the case.

Many people, myself included, want to know the actual science behind the claims and are fed up of being lied to by researchers with vested interests. When I became a parent I searched for a book like the one I have written with desperation, but I always hit the 'use common sense' and anecdotal/theory-based chapters of books and gave up on them. Therefore, I do not make up theories that aren't supported by science, or mislead readers by misinterpreting studies or leaving out vital details. Where the research is unclear or conflicting, I say openly that I am offering personal advice. This is mostly regarding green issues where there is no data available to use but my personal experience as a mother of two may be applicable and useful.

This is a science-based book that highlights a green approach. What you do with this information is up to you. If it reduces your carbon footprint in any way, I'm happy with that (and so are your children, and the planet). By sharing this vital information, I hope that you are able to make informed choices and prepare for parenthood, or alter your approach, as you feel necessary.

Now, a note on population. I'm sure you already know that climate change is a real and serious issue, and that population growth forms part of the debate.[2] However, this book does not discuss population growth. Science tells us that birth rates go down to sustainable (or lower than sustainable) rates when women have access to education[3] and birth control. For more on this topic I recommend watching acclaimed statistician Hans Rosling's TED talk[4] on global population, which demonstrates succinctly that lifting people out of poverty leads to their having far fewer children and is more effective than any lifestyle change. This is one of the main reasons for my argument that green issues are inseparable from those of social justice. Fix those issues and the birth rate will fall, but we still need to reduce the amount of greenhouse gases that we are putting into the atmosphere.

Besides, I don't believe this book will actually make people go out and have more babies (it's not *that* sort of book!). I'm working from the assumption that those of you who already have children have decided to reduce your carbon footprint, but need some guidance, or you've already decided to have a baby and want to minimize your environmental impact as much as possible. There's good news in that area, as doing the green thing will not only help to save the planet and help to protect your child's health, it can also give you a parenting framework to refer to, save you money and probably make you happier in the long run too.[5] For example, eating more nutritious foods can improve your health, and cycling or walking (exercising) instead of driving can improve happiness levels long-term.[6] A UK study from the University of Sussex also found that spending more time outdoors makes people happier.[7] These topics are covered in detail later in the book.

Thankfully, there is a burgeoning demand and market for accessible, scientifically accurate information on health and environmental matters. If you uttered a sigh of relief while reading that sentence, it's you I am writing for. If you're simply 'sci-curious', delve in and see whether you like what you read. There's no dogma here, only evidence.

This book will allow you to make the greenest choices for your family, without breaking the bank or having to buy lots of shiny new 'green' things. It offers sound science to back up its arguments and product recommendations, and, where none is available, I will let you know. It has taken me a lot of research and hair-pulling over the years to sift through all the misleading advice given to parents about being green, and now I'm going to share the relevant information with you, to enable you to make the best choices for your family and also for the planet. Since it is not always possible for people to do the greenest thing every time, I will discuss different possibilities to help you do the best you can. I hope this ultimate guide to parenting that won't cost the Earth will save you from tearing your own hair out!

1 World Health Organization, nin.tl/WHOonpharma **2** Harvard College Global Health Review, nin.tl/femaleeducation **3** 'Education acts through several pathways to decrease birth rates among women in developing countries. Economically, income increases by at least 10% for every additional year of school,' from nin.tl/femaleeducation **4** Available to watch at: nin.tl/RoslingTEDtalk **5** According to research titled 'Mind the Gap: why do people act environmentally and what are the barriers to pro-environmental behavior?' nin.tl/mindthegappaper **6** nin.tl/scienceofexercise **7** thejournal.ie 20 Jul 2013, nin.tl/seaplussun

1 The science of green parenting

The need for science rather than anecdote... Minimizing brand exposure: managing screen time... Minimizing material wants: raising low consumers... Is there a green parenting style?... Sensitive/responsive parenting... Birth bonding vs sleep training and 'cry it out'... Does sleep training work?... Co-sleeping and bedsharing... Breastfeeding after infancy... Babywearing: what is it and why do it?

Why science? Many people, with the best intentions, like to give parents advice about raising a child, including parents, non-parents, health visitors, friends, celebrities, bloggers and next-door neighbors. Unfortunately, much of this advice can be completely wrong or based on archaic ideas and practices that have since been disproved or debunked. Some of this advice can even be damaging.[1] In addition, some parents say that they advocate using 'common sense' or 'intuition' in raising their children, but what do those things mean? How is intuition classified, when it differs so greatly from one person to another? Some people do the 'common sense' thing only to find out it was wrong later in life, which is why it is altogether better to be guided by the latest scientific research. In order to learn how to filter the good advice from the bad, I believe that new parents need science-based evidence in their corner. You'll find it in this book.

We have moved into new territory in the parenting realm – from extended family and community support to the more isolated nuclear and post-nuclear family. This perhaps explains the myriad conflicting information available to new parents today. We constantly question whether we're doing it right and whether we're doing enough, which suggests that there is a lack of support available to parents, and also that we lack natural confidence in our parenting. There is also the issue of isolation – given that we no longer grow up in extended families and close communities, our own baby can sometimes be the first we have ever held.[2]

There are plenty of anecdotal tales out there and there is much dubious 'science' created by individuals with blogs and the ability to set up their own surveys – as well as plenty of books by parents who have found their own rhythms and want to shout them to the world. I'm not saying that they're wrong. But being told that breast is best, for example, or that co-sleeping is dangerous (it's not), is not useful advice when you physically can't breastfeed (which is extremely rare but does happen) or your baby simply won't sleep alone. The parenting approaches discussed in this chapter include key areas like breastfeeding, babywearing and co-sleeping, but some flexibility is allowed for within each approach.

Parenting is rife with new worries. We all want the best for our children, and for them to be healthy and happy, but there's no manual for raising children in the 'right' way, only a plethora of conflicting parenting ideologies. One thing we can be sure of as green parents is that we're looking ahead to our children's futures, and we may be inclined to read and digest anything that tells us how we might be able to reduce what we consume and our reliance on material parenting aids. But most parenting books, blogs and gurus have little science to back them up and we can get lost in a quagmire of supposition or anecdotal arguments.

IThe US and Canada are consumer-based societies,[3] which makes it difficult (though not impossible) to raise our children in any other way. Festivities and holidays are promoted through catchy advertisements and shop displays months ahead of the actual events and companies spend huge amounts of money competing to sell us their sometimes identical brands, which has a significant impact on our purchasing habits. For example, research that compared the soft drinks Pepsi and Coca-Cola found that the two drinks are 'nearly identical in chemical composition, yet humans routinely display strong subjective preferences for one or the other.'[4] It concluded that: 'This simple observation raises the important question of how cultural messages combine with content to shape our perceptions; even to the point of modifying behavioral preferences for a primary reward like a sugared drink.' This study found that personal preference for one of the drinks based solely on its brand image had a dramatic influence on the choices people made and even on the way their brains responded to the idea of the favored brand. In fact, in blind taste tests, most people actually preferred Pepsi to Coca-Cola when they didn't know which brand was which, but when the drinks were labeled their brains actually *changed preference to Coca-Cola based on the idea of the brand*.[5] Some researchers consider this to demonstrate that branding is a case of mind over matter.

So how do we protect our children's brains from this powerful consumer-culture materialism and branding?

Not every society is based on consumerist principles. A friend of mine was shocked when she returned from Cuba, where only one type of toothpaste was available in shops, and was confronted by the wide choice of toothpastes in a standard supermarket aisle. Too much choice can be paralysing and even for the conscious consumer it can take a lot of time to research ethical brands and take into account the many different variables. For a deeper look at the difficulties that having 'too much' choice brings us, watch American psychologist Barry Schwarz's interesting TED talk on the topic.[6]

We need to move away from consumer culture not just in the planet's interests, but also for the sake of our own mental health. One study found that materialistic people are more likely to become compulsive purchasers as adults, gamble, have more debt, have more frequent financial problems, and experience lower marital satisfaction.[7] Other research found that 'Fifty per cent of children from affluent households said their lives were harder... They talked about "too muchness": too many activities, too many consumer choices, too much to learn.'[8] The lesson here appears to be: buy less, do less, and learn to be happy with a smaller lot. But, in our busy culture, the idea of doing less with our children might be a difficult thought to accept, so where to start?

Minimizing brand exposure: managing screen time

Never underestimate the power of advertising, especially to children[9], who have yet to develop the critical thinking skills that allow them to pinpoint biases in what they see: one study found that children under the age of eight believed everything that adverts told them.[10] However, it's impossible to eradicate your child's exposure to brands altogether, and perhaps not desirable to do so either, as the technological world is here to stay and children need to learn tó think for themselves about what they see, through critical eyes, rather than be switched off to television advertising influences altogether.[11] This is especially the case since adverts also seep into daily life by other means (such as outdoor billboards, peer pressure at school), and continue well past childhood.

One easy and obvious thing a parent can do is limit the child's exposure to clever marketing campaigns and tactics through screens (television, iPad, phones) at home. There will still be other marketing influences to contend with, but keeping adverts out of your home, where your child is heavily influenced from birth, will go some way to reducing the power that marketing companies have over your children's lives.

Scientific research supports managing children's screen time in two ways. One, the way digital media are used can healthy if managed right. Remember that screens other than TVs now show videos, such as personal phones and other portable devices, so we now have to be more vigilant about what our children are exposed to from a young age. For the home television there are often settings that allow adverts to be at least muted while they are on. The American Academy of Pediatrics (AAP) recently updated its guidelines from advising zero screen time for children under two to an approach that is 'science-driven, not based merely on the precautionary principle' – in other words, not based on scaremongering about screen time.[12] This decision takes into account various factors, including the fact that children need to watch appropriate content, experience plenty of positive interactions and unstructured free play, and so on. I recommend reading all the points the AAP makes on this matter, one of which is the following: 'More than 80,000 apps are labeled as educational, but little research validates their quality.[13] An interactive product requires more than "pushing and swiping" to teach. Look to organizations like Common Sense Media[14] that review age-appropriate apps, games and programs.'

Two, organizations like the American Psychological Association (APA) advocate teaching children 'media literacy'.[15] Media education can help children become less susceptible to the bad effects of watching violent television, as studies have shown that children who receive education on the way media works display less violent behaviour after watching violent programs.[16] So the key here is to ensure that you have a dialogue with your children about what they are exposed to on screens, to teach them to question what they see in adverts, and think critically about marketing techniques.[17] Spend time watching adverts with your children and discussing their meanings and messages, exploring how realistic they are, how you are able to identify their aims, why specific images or soundtracks are used, how they make your child feel, and so on. For those who wish to take this further, The Media Literacy Project is a company that trains people to become 'media literate',[18] while computer-science researcher Jonathan Mugan's book *The Curiosity Cycle* is an excellent resource for more practical information on this topic.[19]

As a parent or guardian you also have some power over what your child is exposed to outside of the home. Many schools in the US have succumbed to budget shortfalls, and according to an article in *TIME* magazine there is little parental resistance to this.[20] If you notice that your child's school is compromising in this area, the first step is to speak to your child about this, as a form of media literacy awareness. You can also speak to other concerned parents, and think about addressing these matters with the head of the institution. Perhaps community-led events might be organized for fundraising purposes instead. Teachers may also dislike the presence of advertisers in their classrooms and can be asked to join a campaign if the headteacher chooses to ignore parental concerns. Campaign for a Commercial-Free Childhood is a good starting-point resource.[21]

In summary, if you can, adjust your parenting approach to reduce brand exposure and therefore the impact of marketing on your children. As your child gets older, focus on teaching media literacy so as to help raise children who are aware of their material wants and not at the whim of every clever marketing campaign that targets them throughout their lives. This is an organic way of counteracting our society's consumer culture.

Minimizing material wants: raising low consumers

In addition to tackling brand exposure and media literacy, there is another parenting approach you can incorporate to encourage or discourage materialistic behaviour in your children. This is to do with the way you buy your child material products and whether you control the way these items are used by your child.

A recent study found that using material goods as punishments, rewards, or to show affection causes children to be more materialistic.[22] It's natural for parents to want to bring their children joy and one way of doing so is by buying consumer goods for them such as toys and games. Equally, when you really need your child to co-operate it's easier to get your way by using material goods to enforce disciplinary measures – for example by taking toys away until your child co-operates, or committing to buying a desired toy to reward your child's accomplishments or good behavior (in the non-parent world, this is also known as bribery). The study's authors call these tactics 'Material Parenting', where material goods are used to express love and parental warmth, or to shape children's behavior.

Of course, doing this now and again is not going to harm anyone long-term. What we're discussing here is a pattern of behavior that is repeated over a child's lifetime. In their efforts to make their children happy and shape their behavior through the use of material parenting, some parents are unintentionally paving the way for their children to become materialistic adults. Studies show that materialistic people consume more than others, and the research presented here suggests that children who receive many material rewards during childhood will be likely to continue rewarding themselves with material goods as adults.[23] On an environmental level, materialism has been found to be associated with less concern for the environment.[24] The higher consumption levels of high consumers contribute to greenhouse-gas production and climate change, depletion of natural resources, and environmental pollution. The researchers conclude that: 'Our findings suggest that material parenting may be setting the stage for long-term overconsumption and consequent environmental harm.'

So what can we do instead?

Study author Marsha Richins says: 'The best gift you can give your child is the gift of your time, and the gift of your love, and the gift of your attention.'[25] She says that when we focus more on spending time together and less on material goods, we raise happy, secure kids who don't need material things to feel fulfilled.

It can be hard to break habits and you may be using material parenting because

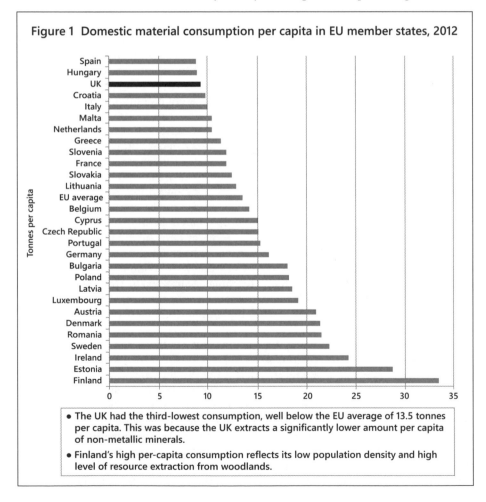

Figure 1 Domestic material consumption per capita in EU member states, 2012

- The UK had the third-lowest consumption, well below the EU average of 13.5 tonnes per capita. This was because the UK extracts a significantly lower amount per capita of non-metallic minerals.
- Finland's high per-capita consumption reflects its low population density and high level of resource extraction from woodlands.

you were raised in this way yourself, but you can teach yourself new habits through using specific tactics to break them. For a start, choose specific ways of rewarding your children that involve experiences and spending time together rather than material objects – for example a specific day trip, baking together, reading a book, drawing or coloring together, playing a board game, or simply sitting and talking together about a specific topic. With punishments, try to look at the root of the misbehavior to head it off before the need arises to remove the problematic material item from the situation. It may even be that your child is too developmentally young to follow the rule you want him or her to stop breaking, for example if s/he has been given a personal phone or computer game before being able to regulate personal screen-time. Through trial and error you can find what works for you and your children and through repeatedly using the same tactics you can eliminate the need to rely on material parenting altogether.

Is there a green parenting style?

We know that green parents aim not to be material parents, but what other options are out there? Parenting styles that people follow in the US and Canada include, believe it or not: tiger parenting and elephant parenting, helicopter parenting and free-range parenting. These examples are almost polar opposites in their approaches, which is not at all useful if you want to draw on different parenting styles to create one that works for you, or if you are a new parent who has no clue what any of them are. Without delving into the various methods, it's worth pointing out that they all have their critiques, and most of these prescriptive styles have little, if any, scientific evidence to support them. One exception to this is attachment parenting.

The study on material parenting uses the term 'parental warmth' to mean: 'a parenting style reflecting nurturance, acceptance, or responsiveness to a child is of central importance to the child's wellbeing',[26] as studies have observed a relationship between parental warmth and curbing children's materialism.[27] The focus on parental warmth is closely aligned with the definition of attachment parenting (AP), a term coined by pediatrician Dr William Sears,[28] who states: 'By becoming sensitive to the cues of your infant, you learn to read your baby's level of need. Because baby trusts that his [sic] needs will be met and his language listened to, the infant trusts in his ability to give cues. As a result, baby becomes a better cue-giver, parents become better cue-readers, and the whole parent-child communication network becomes easier.'

Attachment parenting is often critiqued as a fad yet in billions of homes around the world, parents use 'attachment parenting' principles to raise their children and have done so for many generations. In much of the Western world people have generally moved away from some of the key AP principles in – evolutionarily speaking – relatively recent years, from breastfeeding to formula-feeding, from co-sleeping to cots, and so on. Technically, these new approaches are actually the fads, and science is overwhelmingly in favor of some of the 'old-school' methods.

Some people extrapolate from this to argue that we should follow hunter-gatherer techniques for child-rearing because they got everything right. As anthropologist Jared Diamond points out in his book *The World Until Yesterday*, this is not necessarily true. Although some hunter-gatherer societies do follow AP principles such as breastfeeding for many years, parenting sensitively, and bedsharing, other traditional societies have strong punishment regimes, including physical violence, and some even practice infanticide. Diamond is outspoken throughout his book about this vital point, but the media tends to ignore it, as demonstrated by the recent *Newsweek* headline 'Best Practices for Raising Kids? Look to Hunter-Gatherers'.[29]

In addition, Diamond speaks in favour of things practiced by certain hunter-gatherer societies such as cradle boards and swaddling, yet both these examples have been found by scientific research to be potentially damaging to physical development by causing hip dysplasia.[30] Again, therefore, we need to look beyond the theories to the scientfic evidence.

Although no research has been done into attachment parenting as a whole, some of its key principles are supported by science to varying degrees. These key areas are bonding, breastfeeding and babywearing, but sensitive, responsive parenting is the method underpinning all of these ideas, so let's start with that.

What is sensitive/responsive parenting?

In the late 1980s, during America's crack-cocaine epidemic, a team of researchers led by a neonatologist named Hallam Hurt studied children who were born to addicted mothers.[31] They expected to find certain patterns relating to health issues in the children born to addicted mothers. Instead, they found significant differences in IQ levels in both drug-affected and drug-free families. These differences apparently came down to nurture: whether or not their parents spoke to their children affectionately, hugged, kissed and praised them, and answered their questions, was directly related to IQ levels. Children who were responded to more and were exposed to emotionally stimulating experiences early in life had higher IQs, and as teenagers they had more developed brains when they'd been nurtured more at the age of four – regardless of parental drug abuse.

In contrast, a famous study of the brains of Romanian orphans found that children who were left to cry in their cots from birth and denied any chance of forming close bonds with an adult acted like feral animals in many ways.[32] They were mentally underdeveloped, particularly in the part of the brain (the orbitofrontal cortex) that enables us to manage our emotions, to relate sensitively to other people, to experience pleasure and to appreciate beauty. This study is often used as an example in favour of attachment parenting, yet it is an extreme example of neglect that shows nurture has a significant impact on how a child's brain develops, and is not relevant to most parents.

A strong case for forming close attachments comes from psychoanalytic psychotherapist Sue Gerhardt in her book *Why Love Matters*. Gerhardt explains that emotional experiences in infancy and early childhood have a measurable effect on how we develop as human beings, and argues that who we are is inscribed into our brains during the first two years of life in direct response to how we are loved and cared for. The stress hormone cortisol plays an important role because in normal amounts cortisol is fine, but if a baby is exposed for too long or too often to stressful situations (such as, potentially, repeatedly being left to cry) their brain becomes flooded with cortisol, which leads to the long-term issue of either over- or under-producing cortisol whenever the child is exposed to stress. Too much cortisol is linked to depression and fearfulness, and too little is linked to emotional detachment and aggression.

This can be summarized as the ability to regulate emotion. Babies cannot regulate their stress response without help, as they learn to do it through repeated experiences of being calmed down from their distress by others. Through positive interactions, the baby's brain learns to produce only beneficial amounts of cortisol, and they learn to emotionally regulate themselves over time.

Therefore, sensitive parenting, which means responding to a baby's needs, leads to good development of the baby's cortex, which in turn enables the growing child to develop self-control and empathy, and to feel connected to others. Gerhardt says that through research and her line of work she has found that the infant and toddler years are the most important for brain growth, whereas children who are adopted several years later are less likely to recover from the effects of childhood trauma.[33] However, guilt is a well-covered area for the conscious parent and it doesn't help anyone, so I want to be clear here that it's unlikely that your child has experienced actual trauma, or at least any trauma that you can't parent him or her through successfully, and if your child is older and you didn't use AP you haven't ruined your child's life. There is a section at the back of Gerhardt's book on 'repairing the damage' that might help to reassure worried parents in this regard and point you in the right direction for change if you're seeking it.

A recent study by the University of Montreal found that parental behavior may also play a role in the link between verbal frustrations and aggression.[34] The study used a large and representative population sample to study infant aggression, which is often put down to natural frustrations over slow language development. This study debunked that idea – it found that aggressive behaviors in toddlers are *not* linked to language delays. Instead, the researchers found a link between affectionate parenting and low aggression levels, and good language development in children.

Finally, a study examined the association between attachment quality and mother-infant interaction at night.[35] The main finding was that mothers of securely attached infants had night-time interactions that were generally more consistent, sensitive and responsive than those of insecurely attached infants. In secure attachments, mothers generally picked up and soothed infants when they woke and fussed or cried. This study suggests that, at least in terms of attachment security, it is not simply whether the infant wakes or whether the mother responds to the infant's fussing or crying during awakenings, but rather, for those mothers who generally do respond, whether the response is sensitive, consistent and in tune with the baby's needs. This is perhaps a very succinct outline of what sensitive parenting means.

Now allow me a moment of supposition. If we raise children who can't care for each other or their own mental health, who have problems regulating their emotions as adults, problems with empathy and relating to other people, and with dealing with stressful situations, it seems likely that these traits might reflect the way people care for their immediate surroundings and the state of the planet in general. There's no science to support this idea, but it's worth considering in the context of the climate catastrophe we are facing as a planet and our apparent inability to halt the destructive behaviors that are driving it.

Birth bonding vs sleep training and 'cry it out'

Can sleep training be a facet of sensitive or responsive parenting? 'Cry It Out' (CIO) is a type of sleep-training coined by Dr Richard Ferber[36] and advocated by some parenting authors and people from older generations who argue that children should be left to sleep (and cry) alone for increasing periods of time at night in order to learn to 'self-soothe' – in other words, to put themselves to sleep. They argue that this practice is harmless in the long term.

Parents sometimes turn to sleep training in order to have some (perceived) control over how their babies sleep. Others follow the CIO rule blindly, however, without reading the arguments by Ferber *et al*, who generally state that babies under six months of age should **never** be left to cry because they may be ill or need feeding, and are too young to respond to behavioral training anyway. For example, Alan Sroufe, a professor emeritus at the University of Minnesota Institute of Child Development, says that CIO is inappropriate for younger babies because they have not yet developed object permanence – the ability to understand that mum and dad still exist when they're not in baby's line of sight.

Methods like CIO stand in polar opposition to sensitive parenting, because they involve ignoring a baby's needs by failing to respond to its cries. While some childhood experts, like Sroufe, argue that it won't threaten a secure attachment with your baby if you let him or her cry at night a few times, other experts, like Gerhardt, argue that regular unresponsiveness poses a risk of causing potentially irreversible damage to a baby's brain through raising cortisol levels and neglecting the immediate need for emotional regulation.

Further, Harvard Medical School researchers Michael L Commons and Patrice M Miller examined childrearing practices in the US and in other cultures and concluded that the practice of putting babies in separate beds and rooms and not responding quickly to their cries may lead to incidents of post-traumatic stress and panic disorders when these children reach adulthood.[37] Commons and Miller say that instead of letting infants cry, parents should keep their babies close, console them when they cry, and bring them to bed with them, where they'll feel safe. Commons said: 'Parents should recognize that having their babies cry unnecessarily harms the baby permanently... It changes the nervous system so they're overly sensitive to future trauma.' The Harvard researchers' work is unique because it takes a cross-disciplinary approach, examining brain function, emotional learning in infants, and cultural differences, according to Charles R Figley, director of the Traumatology Institute at Florida State University. It should, therefore, be taken seriously.

One argument people use in favor of sleep-training techniques is that babies will become independent children who are capable of self-soothing. However, Commons and Miller say that this is on the wrong track: physical contact and reassurance will make children more secure and better able to form adult relationships when they finally head out on their own, as borne out by the research. Another study on this topic that is worth mentioning is the 'Middelmiss' study, which found that, after a few days of separating the mother and baby from their usual night-time routines using sleep-training techniques, the baby continued to have high cortisol (stress) levels but stopped showing 'behavioral stress during the sleep transition', so they *seemed* at ease when they stopped crying at night, but were in fact very stressed – the very opposite to the desired outcome of 'self-soothing'.[38]

Some babies simply don't naturally sleep through the night, but many parenting experts and books are aimed at helping you to get your baby to do this. One study looked at night-time sleep awakenings and family characteristics and found that of 1,200 infants of varying ages, the majority (66 per cent) of babies, labelled Sleepers, slept through the night by six months of age, waking up just once or twice per week.[39] However, babies labeled Transitional Sleepers (34 per cent of the infants) had seven reported nights of awakenings per week at six months, then two nights per week at 15 months and one night per week by 24 months. Transitional Sleepers were more likely to be boys, scored higher on the six-month difficult temperament assessment, and had more depressed mothers at six months old. So it's more common for babies to sleep through the night by six months, but perceived 'sleep issues' are not uncommon: babies like to wake up at night.

However, sleep-deprived parents can become desperate to sleep more, and are sometimes persuaded to try CIO by an often-quoted but poorly conducted Australian study that aimed to determine long-term harms and/or benefits of an infant behavioural sleep programme at the age of six.[40] The study concludes that: 'behavioral sleep techniques have no marked long-lasting effects (positive or negative). Parents and health professionals can confidently use these techniques to reduce the short- to medium-term burden of infant sleep problems and maternal depression.' However, a valid and important criticism of this study points out that it looks at two very different groups of sleep-training methods: parents using the Ferber method of CIO; and parents using an alternative technique called 'extinction with parental presence' where babies are not left alone to cry but are gradually taught that the parent will leave the room but return again, usually repeatedly for longer periods each time.[41] As a result, this research is not very useful for assessing effects of the Ferber method of leaving a baby to cry alone.

Does sleep training work?

A 2012 study[42] from Philadelphia University was reported by the *Daily Mail* newspaper as advising mothers to let babies 'self-soothe'.[43] In fact, this study simply documented the natural development of sleep patterns in more than 1,000 babies between the ages of 6 and 36 months. The study did *not* advise on whether babies could be taught to self-soothe themselves. It merely reported that babies' 'signaling' (crying) on waking up at night is a developmental course, with most babies naturally waking once or twice a week by the age of six months but then learning to settle at the age of three, and with just six per cent of children waking every night at the age of three. The authors of the study discussed how self-soothing might work – but they neither researched it nor recommended it. In addition, this research found that: 'Infant-mother attachment measures were not related to these sleep awakenings.' Babies sleep when they want to sleep; controlling this is only in the parent's mind.

In fact, a *British Medical Journal* study[44] of babies between 6 and 12 months old found that those who underwent controlled crying for two months slept better *according to their mothers*. However, when the study finished after four months, the sleep-trained babies slept no better than those who hadn't been trained.

Although many studies have reported *initial* increases in infant sleep duration, and/or reduction in night waking, many other studies[45] have found that these benefits do not continue long-term, and *none* have been found to have an effect lasting six months or more after the sleep-training methods were originally used, or found to 'improve' babies' sleep. This means that the initial improvement, or 'benefit' of using the sleep-training method disappeared over time, and since outcomes were the same for the group of babies who had been 'sleep-trained' as for those in the control group who had not, this suggests that babies either do or do not learn to settle themselves to sleep at night regardless of any sleep-training methods that are used.

What can you do?

Unfortunately, it's normal for bedtime problems and night-time wakings to persist into toddler and preschool years.[46] In the meantime, you can try to nap or at least rest when baby naps in the daytime, until s/he begins to sleep for longer periods of time at night. You can also have a solid bedtime routine, as one study found that the use of a consistent bedtime routine contributes to improvements in several aspects of infant and toddler sleep, bedtime behavior and maternal mood.[47]

Co-sleeping and bedsharing

These terms are often used interchangeably, but to be specific co-sleeping is generally used to refer to having baby in a 'side crib' or on a mattress next to your bed, while

Side crib

bedsharing means having baby in bed with you. The UK National Health Service recommends that a baby should sleep in the same room as its parents up until six months of age, although this is not recommended if either parent is a smoker.[48]

Bedsharing and co-sleeping can be effective methods of sensitive, responsive parenting and bonding. Mothers have been found to get more sleep when they bedshare,[49] are more in tune with their babies, and are likely to breastfeed for longer.[50] In fact, some researchers have proposed a new word to encapsulate this concept: 'breastsleeping'.[51]

La Leche League International states that bedsharing safely involves following the 'Safe Sleep Seven'[52] principles, which are:

If a mother is:
1   *A non-smoker*
2   *Sober*
3   *Breastfeeding*

And her baby is:
4   *Healthy*
5   *On his/her back*
6   *Lightly dressed and unswaddled*

And they:
7   *Share a safe surface*

Then the baby's risk of SIDS [Sudden Infant Death Syndrome] is no greater than in a crib, and any breathing hazards have been hugely reduced.

The AAP currently advises against bedsharing,[53] but the evidence used to support this advice is significantly flawed because much of the research into bedsharing incorrectly includes all cases of parents sleeping with their babies, whether they are *intentionally* sleeping in a safe bed, or *accidentally* falling asleep on an unsafe surface like a sofa or armchair.[54] So, the AAP recommends the arrangement of room-sharing without bedsharing, of having the infant sleep in the parents' room or on a separate sleep surface near the parents' bed, based on data implying that this is safer than bedsharing. However, it acknowledges that: 'this arrangement is most likely to prevent suffication, strangulation, and entrapment, which may occur when the infant is sleeping in the adult bed'. This conclusion is incorrect because it confuses SIDS with other sleep risks including wedging, entrapment, falling and strangulation, while at the same time stating that SIDS deaths are *unexplained*: '[SIDS] is a cause assigned to infant deaths that cannot be exlplained after a thorough case investigation that includes a scene investigation, autopsy, and review of the clinical history.' Unsafe sleep surfaces and dangers to breathing are *known* causes of infant deaths but not causes of SIDS. Also, SIDS deaths are rare.[55]

The problem here is that while healthcare professionals continue to recommend that parents do not bedshare, many parents end up doing it anyway without taking safety measures first. The AAP states that 'Parent-infant bedsharing is common. In one national survey, 45 per cent of parents responded that they had shared a bed with their infant (eight months of age or younger) at some point in the preceding two weeks. In some racial/ethnic groups, the rate of routine bedsharing might be higher.' One study found that: 'While no mothers intended to bedshare with their infants immediately after delivery, 60 per cent reported bedsharing at some time at one month after discharge and 9 per cent at three months. Only 19 per cent of mothers reported receiving information about infant sleeping practices from their physician and 22 per cent from their nurse.'[56] Instead of concluding that many mothers are going to bedshare at some point whether they intend to or not, and advising on safe sleep practices from the beginning, bedsharing is blamed as the problem instead by researchers who wrongly conclude that: 'Interventions aimed at teaching new mothers about responding to infant cues and ways to manage a fussy infant may minimize the rate of bed-sharing.' This suggests an inherent bias on the part of the researchers, perhaps because they approached the study with the view that bedsharing is to blame for SIDS (it's not).

Another shoddy study, by the University of Glasgow, found that 'the largest risk was associated with couch sharing'[57] – but sleeping on a sofa is *not* an example of intentional bedsharing as it is not at all safe. In addition, important variables were not taken into account, for example whether the parents were intoxicated (more babies die in their sleep on New Year's Eve in the US than any other time of year, which suggests that intoxication plays a large role in the baby-parent sleep debate,[58] and that more parents need to be made aware of this correlation regardless of where their baby usually sleeps).

This is by no means all of the research on the subject but it does give a general idea of how incorrect assumptions in research can lead to flawed conclusions.

Now on to the more thorough research. In their review[59] 'Why babies should never sleep alone: A review of the co-sleeping controversy in relation to SIDS, bedsharing and breast feeding', Dr James J McKenna and Thomas McDade state that: 'Co-sleeping... especially with an actively breastfeeding mother saves lives' and 'is a powerful reason why the simplistic, scientifically inaccurate and misleading statement "never sleep with your baby" needs to be rescinded, wherever and whenever it is published.'

A study[60] by the Alaska Division of Public Health examined 13 years of Alaskan infant deaths that happened while bedsharing and found that: '13 per cent of deaths occurred while bedsharing; 99 per cent of these had at least one associated risk factor, including maternal tobacco use (75 per cent) and sleeping with an impaired person (43 per cent)... 60 per cent of mothers reported no risk factors; the remaining 40 per cent reported substance use, smoking, high levels of alcohol use, or most often placing their infant prone [face-down] for sleeping.' This indicates that advice to parents on safe bedsharing would almost certainly reduce instances of baby deaths. The research concludes that 'Almost all bedsharing deaths occurred **in association with other risk factors** despite the finding that most women reporting frequent bedsharing had no risk factors; this suggests that **bedsharing alone does not increase the risk of infant death.**' [The emphasis is mine.]

In terms of effective preventative measures, something that is not being discussed enough is how the baby is fed. When a baby sleeps in a cot s/he is more likely to be formula fed, as one study found,[61] but breastfeeding a baby decreases the risk of SIDS. When we talk about SIDS, we really need to look at feeding methods and not just where a baby sleeps.

In addition to this, recent research has found that some babies have a genetic predisposition to SIDS,[62] which means that SIDS is probably unrelated to where the baby sleeps.

Co-sleeping or bedsharing may not be directly linked to having a green baby, but they are closely linked to the likelihood of a mother continuing to breastfeed,[63] and contribute to parental ability to be in tune with their babies.[64] By trying different sleeping arrangements you can hope to find one that works for you, without paying heed to the stigma that is associated with bedsharing. The better you sleep, the easier it will be for you to respond sensitively to your baby both day and night, and the closer you sleep to your baby, the easier it will be to keep breastfeeding and settle stressful upsets.

Breastfeeding after infancy

Breastfeeding your baby is one of the key principles of AP (and I look at this in detail in Chapter 3) but AP also supports 'extended' or 'long-term' breastfeeding. According to La Leche League, extended breastfeeding is defined as breastfeeding a baby past one year of age,[65] although WHO recommends breastmilk for babies until the age of two at least.

As well as being very eco-friendly, since no substitute milks or foods are required for a child who is still breastfed, it also has other benefits. In an article on the US National Public Radio website, anthropology professor Dr Katherine A Dettwyler, who has extensive cross-cultural experience in breastfeeding research, is quoted as saying:

'My research, and research by others on non-human primates and non-primate mammals, suggests that nursing large-bodied mammalian offspring for many years, until their first permanent teeth erupt (5.5-6.0 years in humans), is "natural" for humans in the sense of being what the underlying evolutionary, biological/ physiological norm is for us as a species. There is no research to suggest that normal durations of breastfeeding for humans as a species – 2.5 to 7+ years – lead to "harmful emotional dependency". There is some evidence that longer-term breastfeeding (along with co-sleeping in childhood) results in children who are more independent and score higher on measures of social competence.

'I would say that the benefits of long-term breastfeeding – as long as both mother and child want – are enormous. Long-term breastfeeding allows for normal development of the child's brain, facial structure, immune system, and emotional resilience to life's slings and arrows.'[66]

Unfortunately, as with bedsharing, there is much stigma attached to extended breastfeeding in North America, but if you're happy to keep breastfeeding your child then there's no need to stop because of social pressure. Join a support group and remind yourself of Dettwyler's words. You'll be continuing to build on the essential parent-child bond and you'll be amazing for doing it.

Babywearing
What is it?

The earliest clothes worn by humans are thought to have been strips of animal hide that were used to sling babies across parents' backs, as argued by Timothy Taylor, an archaeology researcher who says that the sling has been around for more than two million years (before modern humans existed).[67] This would have well suited our ancestors who had countless predators at ground level (think wolves, poisonous snakes), who were often on the move, and who needed to have hands free to forage frequently. In many cultures, babywearing is still practiced as the norm and pushchairs, prams and infant strollers are not available options.

Why do it?

There is research that has found that babywearing encourages a better connection between parents and babies[68] and also that babies worn in slings are happier and easier to soothe.[69]

The idea of 'the continuum concept' was coined by Jean Liedloff in her book of the same name where she argues that human beings have an innate set of expectations (called the continuum) that they have evolved to meet in order to achieve optimal growth. Although she is not always precise with her information, there is research to back up some of Liedloff's key points, which are presented in the following list and have been outlined with scientific research earlier in this chapter or later in the book. Babies benefit from:

- Immediate skin-to-skin contact with the mother after birth
- Constant carrying or physical contact with their parents and to some degree other people for several months after birth
- Co-sleeping until they choose to stop (usually around two years)
- Breastfeeding on demand
- Sensitive parenting
- Sensing (and fulfilling) elders' expectations that the infants are innately social and co-operative and have strong self-preservation instincts, and that they are welcome and worthy (but without making them the constant center of attention).

Do African babies cry?

There is an often-referenced myth that 'African babies don't cry' and this is somewhat rooted in the argument underpinning Liedloff's book. However, this is a massive generalization that fails to account for the many different cultures and traditions that are available across the vast expanse of land that is Africa. One writer explains that it is more the perception of crying that differs because, in her hometown of Kenya: 'The understanding is that babies don't cry. If they do – something is horribly wrong and must be done to rectify it immediately. My English sister-in-law summarized it well. "People here," she said, "really don't like babies crying, do they?"… It all made much more sense when I finally delivered and my grandmother came from the village to visit. As it happened, my baby did cry a fair amount. Exasperated and tired, I forgot everything I had ever read and sometimes joined in the crying too. Yet for my grandmother it was simple, "Nyonyo (breastfeed her)!" It was her answer to every single peep.'[70]

Anthropologist Jared Diamond, in his book *The World Until Yesterday*, reinforces this idea by stating that: 'The adolescent identity crises that plague American teenagers aren't an issue for hunter-gatherer children. The Westerners who have lived with hunter-gatherers and other small-scale societies speculate that these admirable qualities develop because of the way in which their children are brought up: namely, with constant security and stimulation, as a result of the long nursing period, sleeping near parents for several years, far more social models available to children through allo-parenting [when children are also parented by people who are not members of the immediate family], far more social stimulation through constant physical contact and proximity of caretakers, instant caretaker responses to a child's crying, and the minimal amount of physical punishment.'

We look more closely at the greenest options regarding babywearing in Chapter 8 on Travel. There is also more information on babywearing techniques and products in Chapter 7 on Baby Essentials.

* * *

Parenting is hard no matter what you do. Small people are demanding and we no longer raise them as communities but increasingly as couples and as single individuals when partners return to work. Your baby will cry, and sometimes may not be easily soothed. Your baby will almost certainly have periods of not sleeping properly. This is why it's important to grow with your baby and avoid following prescriptive methods that won't suit you or your child. This includes attachment parenting – there is no need to try to tick all the boxes, but the more of the key things you can do that are listed here, the better it should be for raising an emotionally healthy and greener baby. Keep the science in mind and use research to support your decisions. If it doesn't work for you, try something else. If you've been parenting in a different way and it works for you, that's fine, but if you want to change the way you approach it, baby steps are fine too. Good luck!

Summary

- Protect children from branding and marketing by limiting screen exposure at home, and teaching media literacy.
- Avoid 'material parenting': try to use time-based activities and experiences as rewards instead of possessions.
- Try to avoid giving punishments by heading off negative behavior before it strikes.
- Aim for parental warmth: responsive, sensitive parenting that is based on bonding activities.
- Avoid sleep-training techniques like Cry It Out and instigate a regular bedtime routine instead.
- Sleep when your baby sleeps – learn to nap, if you don't already.

- If you choose to continue breastfeeding, it's perfectly healthy for you and your child, so don't let anyone put you off.

- Co-sleeping and bedsharing are safe. Don't be put off by press reports, which often misrepresent research into these practices.

- Make your bed safe for bedsharing even if you don't plan to do it, in case you do fall asleep in bed with baby one night.

- Consider babywearing for closer bonding and as a soothing technique.

1 As Zoe Williams explains: *Guardian*, 29 May 2007, nin.tl/unscientific **2** Compared with, for example, many indigenous communities where it is normal for the older children to help with parenting the younger ones, as explained in Jared Diamond's book *The World Until Yesterday*. **3** 'Consumer society' is defined by the Cambridge Dictionary as 'a society in which people often buy new goods, especially goods that they do not need, and in which a high value is placed on owning many things'. **4** *Neuron*, 14 Oct 2004, nin.tl/cokepepsistudy **5** *Scientific American*, 2 Nov 2009, nin.tl/brainandbuying **6** Available at nin.tl/Schwartzonchoice **7** Marsha L Richins & Lan Nguyen Chaplin, 'Material Parenting: How the Use of Goods in Parenting Fosters Materialism in the Next Generation', *Journal of Consumer Research*, ejcr.org/publicity/680087.pdf **8** Barry Schwartz 'The Tyranny of Choice', nin.tl/tyrannychoice **9** For more information on the impact of advertising and consumer culture on children, read the book *Advertising to Children on TV*, nin.tl/TVadschildren **10** American Psychological Association, 23 Feb 2004, nin.tl/TVadsunhealthy **11** University of Michigan Health System, nin.tl/TVfamilyguide **12** aapublications.org/content/36/10/54.full **13** Hirsh-Pasek K Psych Science 2015,16: 3-34. **14** commonsensemedia.org **15** American Psychological Association Task Force report, nin.tl/adsandchildren **16** University of Michigan Health System, nin.tl/TVandchildren and livescience, 18 Oct 2011, nin.tl/noTVunder2 **17** University of Michigan Health System, nin.tl/TVfamilyguide and nin.tl/kidsshouldplay **18** Center for Media Literacy, nin.tl/medialiteracyintro **19** I look at the role of technology in raising children again in Chapter 10 on Entertainment. **20** nin.tl/TIMEcaptive **21** commercialfreechildhood.org **22** Richins & Chaplin, op cit. **23** Ragna Benedikta Gardarsdottir & Helga Dittmar, *Journal of Economic Psychology*, nin.tl/Icelandmaterialism **24** *Researchers World*, Oct 2014, nin.tl/greenpurchasing and American Marketing Association, Summer 2012, nin.tl/greenmaterialism **25** Care2, 30 Dec 2014, nin.tl/kidsmaterialism **26** See Kathy Vilcherrez Pizarro, *Scrib*, nin.tl/parentstyles **27** Chaplin and John 2010; Flouri 2004; Kasser et al. 1995 **28** Ask Dr Sears, nin.tl/attachmentbabies **29** nin.tl/HGkidsNewsweek **30** International Hip Dysplasia Institute, nin.tl/dysplasiacauses **31** Neurotoxical Teratol, Jan/Feb 2011, nin.tl/cocaineeffects **32** National Public Radio, nin.tl/childbrainshape **33** As argued in her book *Why Love Matters*, Routledge 2004. **34** University of Montreal nouvelles, nin.tl/toddleraggression **35** *Attachment & Human Development*, Jul 2009, nin.tl/nightattachment **36** nin.tl/Ferbermethod **37** *Harvard University Gazette*, 9 Apr 1998, nin.tl/childrenneedtouch **38** *Early Hum Dev*, Apr 2012, nin.tl/asynchronymother **39** *Developmental Psychology*, Nov 2012, nin.tl/nightwaking **40** *Pediatrics*, 10 Sep 2012, nin.tl/sleepintervention **41** *Parenting Science* 2014, nin.tl/Ferbermethodguide **42** *Developmental Psychology*, Nov 2012, nin.tl/nightwaking **43** *MailOnline*, 3 Jan 2013, nin.tl/Mailoncryingbabies **44** *BMJ*, 4 May 2002, nin.tl/infantsleepmood **45** Infant Sleep Information Source (ISIS), nin.tl/sleeptrainingresearch **46** American Academy of Sleep Medicine, nin.tl/nightwakings **47** *Science Daily*, 6 May 2009, nin.tl/bedtimeroutinehelps **48** NHS choices, nin.tl/NHSsleepadvice **49** Jama Pediatr, Nov 2013, nin.tl/infantbedsharing **50** According to UNICEF, nin.tl/babyatnight **51** nin.tl/breastsleeping **52** La Leche League International, nin.tl/safesleep7 **53** nin.tl/AAPadvice **54** US Lactation Consulting Association, nin.tl/infantsleeplocation **55** Ibid. **56** *Journal of Child Health Care*, nin.tl/bedsharingpractices **57** J Pediatr, Jul 2005, nin.tl/SIDSScotland **58** *Science Daily*, 15 Dec 2010, nin.tl/SIDSNewYear **59** *Paediatric Respiratory Reviews*, 2005, nin.tl/whycosleeping **60** *Public Health Rep*, Jul-Aug 2009, nin.tl/bedsharingAlaska **61** J Pediatr, Oct 2009, nin.tl/Brazilbedsharing **62** *Lancet*, 3 Nov 2007, nin.tl/SIDSLancet **63** UNICEF UK, nin.tl/SIDSguide **64** UNICEF, nin.tl/babyatnight **65** La Leche League International, nin.tl/LLLiextendedbreastfeeding **66** National Public Radio, nin.tl/breastfeedingat6 **67** *Guardian*, 4 Sep 2010, nin.tl/artificialape **68** Suzanne Zeedyk blog, nin.tl/buggiesandbrains **69** Cited in Deborah Jackson, 'Three in a Bed', Bloomsbury, 1989, p 67. **70** *InCultureParent*, 31 Dec 2010, nin.tl/africanbabiescry

2 The green birth

The cost of birth... Birth in a hospital obstetric unit... Birth in a midwife-led unit... Homebirth... Unassisted childbirth... Birth in a natural setting... Waterbirth... Birth trauma... Induction... Write a birth plan... Positions for birth... A note on men... Female birthing partners and continuity of care... Pain-relief options... Other birth issues to consider

A note for male readers: this chapter is written in a way that addresses the woman who is going to give birth. However, it will still be of use to you as a way of contributing to a safe, empowering, environmentally aware childbirth experience, and because you can play a vital role before and during the birth of your child. So please do read on.

What is the most environmentally-friendly way to give birth? Unfortunately the data on this subject is somewhat lacking, so we will have to delve into supposition for part of this chapter. One thing we can be sure of is that a woman's birth experience can have lasting repercussions on her physical and mental health and wellbeing. A disempowered woman who suffers from birth trauma is much less likely to make green lifestyle choices once her child is born than a woman who feels that her needs have been met and her voice heard during the birth experience, since negative 'self-conscious' emotions like shame, guilt, and embarrassment have been found to hinder individual ability to feel empathy.[1]

Research has found that when those attending to the pregnant woman during labor and childbirth communicate with her clearly and appear to respect her choices, this improves the way she feels about her birth experience.[2] In addition, a survey of mothers found that feeling in control impacts the way laboring women experience pain, creating a more positive birth experience.[3] Preparing for childbirth is perhaps key to a positive birth experience and to avoiding birth trauma and feelings of disempowerment.

Conflict in the birthing arena

There are some deeply conflicting views within midwifery and obstetrics, and much of this chapter may not sit well with people on either side of the polarized childbirth debate: on the one hand 'childbirth workers' (such as doulas) who support homebirths and no intervention, and on the other medical professionals who do not want women to give birth away from advanced medical equipment.[4] I've tried to take an objective position here that lies somewhere between the two and this will certainly not satisfy all practitioners but it should help parents who wish to prepare for childbirth.

The cost of birth

You may assume that a straightforward hospital birth in an obstetric unit (OU) is the most efficient setting for childbirth, since it is the most common route taken, but unfortunately this is not the case. While modern medicine has come a long way and the care provided for problematic births in the US can be exceptional, unnecessary interventions and interference in an obstetric ward actually increase the likelihood of problems during labor. In the light of this, a new report by Childbirth Connection, an American organization that promotes evidence-based maternity care, recommends that women's bodies should be trusted to labor without use of unnecessary interventions.[5] The report also makes the case for preparing mother and baby for birth through hormonal changes before the labor and birth process.

The most sustainable childbirth option is also the cheapest option: because, contrary to what many people believe, the economic cost of a hospital birth is much higher than for a homebirth, and, according to an article in British newspaper *The Telegraph*, a 'planned homebirth costs the NHS £1,066 [$1,700] compared to £1,631 [$2,600] for an obstetric-unit birth; £2,369 [$3,800] for a planned C-section and £3,042 [$4,900] for the emergency version.'[6] According to a study of 64,538 women, homebirth is also better value for money.[7]

According to Centers for Disease Control and Prevention, research that looked at home births in the US from 1990 to 2009 summarizes that: 'Home births have a lower risk profile than hospital births, with fewer births to teenagers or unmarried women, and with fewer preterm, low birthweight, and multiple births.'[8] Home births are also on the rise[9] (see Figure 1).

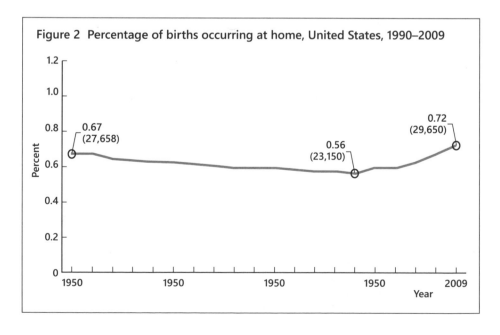

Figure 2 Percentage of births occurring at home, United States, 1990–2009

A note on birth rights

A Canadian study undertaken in 2012 found that there is a culture of medical professionals who pressurize mothers into having unnecessary interventions during labor, often without substantial scientific evidence.[10] The fact that hospital births make interventions more likely means that this chapter focuses on the homebirth aspect of birth, as this is the greenest option available to you in terms of impact on the environment and your mental health. Please use this information to empower yourself and ignore anything that isn't relevant to your circumstances: this is science, not dogma.

Birth in a hospital obstetric unit (OU)

Giving birth in an obstetric unit (OU) in a hospital is the standard way to give birth in the US but perhaps not in the world. There are two types of hospital birth, however, and the other option is a birthing center or midwife-led unit (MLU) if there is one available at your local hospital. It's worth looking into this as not all states allow MLUs – or midwives.

Giving birth in any hospital setting will have a higher carbon footprint than giving birth at home or in another setting outside of hospital, as hospitals adhere to high standards of cleanliness, which means that cleaning chemicals are used indiscriminately, that equipment is either cleaned or discarded after use, and almost all waste is disposed of through incineration to reduce risk of germs spreading, which is an environmentally damaging practice.

If you have circumstances that will certainly require medical intervention that cannot be undertaken elsewhere, then an OU birth is the best option for you, and what you can look at in terms of reducing your environmental impact and caring for your mental health is preparing for labor by going drug-free. It's worth bearing in mind that while every birth, just like every pregnancy, comes with certain risks, almost all of these can be identified by healthcare professionals beforehand, and unexpected problems during labor are rare. When you know you will have an OU birth for medical reasons, you're in a better position to prepare for this, and you have time to work with your healthcare providers to ensure that you have a birth experience that meets your needs.Some women dislike the hospital setting or feel that the situation spirals out of their control with one intervention or medical procedure leading to another and that they are unable to tell what is necessary and what can be avoided. During labor is not the best time to try to make big decisions about these things, but handing over control to medical staff is not a very empowering way to enter parenthood either and can sometimes do more harm than good – we will look at this issue later.

Hospitals have dedicated members of staff who work around the clock to give you the best care possible. Unfortunately maternity care is underfunded in many hospitals in the US and this means that staff can be overstretched and not always able to meet a laboring woman's needs.[11] OU hospital staff are also under pressure to monitor a woman's labor and to follow a list of interventions if things don't go to a timed labor plan.[12]

The risks of an OU birth

If the OU setting is your choice for giving birth or a choice that a high-risk pregnancy has already made for you, you might want to skip to the section titled 'The Birth Plan' now.

Libby Bogdan-Lovis of the Center for Ethics and Humanities in the Life Sciences at Michigan State University says that institutional strictures contribute to the problem: 'Insurance companies generally cover hospital birth, not home birth, they are more inclined to compensate doctors over midwives, they compensate doctors and hospital-based midwives for doing something over doing nothing, and the healthcare system's risk management approach backs those who can demonstrate that they did everything possible in terms of intervention... attempts to control birth are fraught with real medicalized risk and commonly lead to cascades of interventions.'[13] The Birthplace study followed over 64,000 women in the US and found that 'Interventions during labor were substantially lower in all non-obstetric unit settings' and concluded that 'Women planning birth in a midwifery unit and multiparous women [those who have given birth before] planning birth and home experience fewer interventions than those planning birth in an obstetric unit with no impact on perinatal outcomes.'[14]

Another thing that makes obstetric birth carbon-heavy is the higher risk of serious interventions such as episiotomies and Cesarean sections, which require longer hospital stays and further treatment (see Table 1), and the fact that lying in bed is a known risk factor for catching infections and developing blood clots.[15] To be added to this are the transport to and from hospital and the impact of the drugs that are more likely to be used in an OU.

A pressing problem in the OU birthing room is the wide disparity between the conditions that science shows are optimal for childbirth and what individual caregivers or the medical profession advocates.[16] Empowering yourself with knowledge beforehand is a good idea.

Birth in a hospital midwife-led unit (MLU) / Birthing center

From an evolutionary perspective, women's bodies are designed to give birth. When humans began to walk upright on two legs instead of four, women's pelvises changed to accommodate their babies and we evolved to give birth to them much smaller than before, so that their heads would still fit through our birth canals.[17]

Evolution does not get it wrong, but sometimes our human brains do, and we begin from the standpoint that lots of things might go wrong, so we must do our best to prepare for them all. This is essential in a few cases where the baby or mother need additional care, however it is not relevant for most women, as recent research shows.[18]

However, I am not arguing for a medicine-free birth with no aid from healthcare professionals (although some women do choose that path – see the section headed 'Unassisted birth'). What I advocate is somewhere in between both approaches, where the woman is empowered in her choices before and during childbirth, but she doesn't do it all alone. So let's start by looking at what works for laboring mothers.

The largest study on birth settings was well conducted, with expert researchers taking into account variables such as socio-economic status and using a large sample size of 17,000 women who were planning a home birth, 28,000 women planning birth in a birthing center (MLU), and 20,000 women planning birth in an OU.[19] The results were slightly better for homebirths.

Research released by the *British Medical Journal* in 2014 found that planned homebirths are less risky than planned hospital births, particularly for second-time mothers.[20] An Oxford study also found that planned homebirths and births at midwife-led units are more cost-effective than hospital births.[21] Unfortunately there is no such data relevant to the whole of the US as states vary so much in terms of healthcare.

If you have a medical reason that requires a doctor to be present during childbirth, then it may be that they are right, but even so some conditions can be treated in the comfort of your own home, so you may be able to reach a safe compromise that suits your needs as well as your baby's.

At The Farm Midwifery Center in the US, co-founder and long-term midwife Ina May Gaskin has successfully been delivering babies in a MLU/home-like environment with a minimum intervention rate since the 1970s. One study of work at The Farm offers this summary:

'Deliveries are conducted without analgesia [pain relief]... and great emphasis is placed on meeting the emotional needs of the family. Several family members and friends are commonly in attendance and are encouraged to take an active role in the birth....In the absence of signs of fetal distress, women are permitted to labor beyond 24 hours, occasionally for 2 to 3 days.'[22]

The abstract of this study states: 'the results suggest that, under certain circumstances, home births attended by lay midwives can be accomplished as safely as, and with less intervention than, physician-attended hospital deliveries.'[23] The same advice may apply to MLUs in the US, as they can provide a very similar setting to The Farm.

Homebirth

In the US, most homebirths are attended by midwives (see Figure 2 overleaf), whereas among hospital births, only seven per cent are attended by midwives.[24] Midwifery laws vary from state to state and in some places midwives are not allowed to attend homebirths. Therefore it is important to do your research before deciding where to give birth.[25]

The American Academy of Pediatrics (AAP) and the American College of Obstetricians and Gynecologists (ACOG) agree that hospitals and birthing centers are the safest settings for birth in the United States, 'while respecting the right of women to make a medically informed decision about delivery'. In the 2013 policy statement Planned Home Birth,[26] the AAP recognizes that women and their families may desire a home birth for a variety of reasons, and state that pediatricians should advise parents who are planning a homebirth that only midwives who are certified by the American Midwifery Certification Board should be employed. For low-risk women who have already given birth once or more, an MLU or homebirth is a very safe option, where interventions are far less likely to take place than in an OU

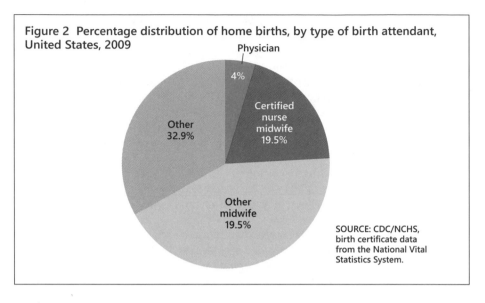

Figure 2 Percentage distribution of home births, by type of birth attendant, United States, 2009

Physician

4%

Certified nurse midwife 19.5%

Other 32.9%

Other midwife 19.5%

SOURCE: CDC/NCHS, birth certificate data from the National Vital Statistics System.

setting. It's not that non-OU options are unsafe for first-time mothers, though, but intervention rates are likely to be higher, perhaps due to lack of preparation and empowerment. Homebirth does have a slightly higher risk of complications than an OU birth for first-time mothers.

What will you need for a homebirth?

There is very little you need to buy for a homebirth. You can save up the following items well before your due date: old towels and sheets, plastic coverings or sheets for furniture (such as old bed sheets or shower curtains), and anything you might want to use for natural pain relief. Also stock up on eco-friendly sanitary pads such as Natracare brand pads, or buy or make reusable cloth pads (read more about this in Chapter 9). You may also find that a soft side light, a bucket and a birthing ball are helpful during your homebirth experience – and possibly also a massage oil for your partner to use to on you when you're laboring.

Unassisted childbirth/Free-birth

Unassisted childbirth (UC) or 'free-birth' is a difficult topic to discuss because there is no research into it and it's a bit of a taboo in North America. This involves intentionally giving birth without the assistance of a professional birth attendant, as free-birthers believe that birth works best without interference. Unassisted birth is legal in some states in the US, and some people choose them because midwife-attended homebirths are illegal.

Childbirth workers, also called doulas, promote homebirth for low-risk women, and they tend to support birth choices for women in most circumstances. However, they generally do not advocate free-birthing without the attendance of a trained medical professional. It is, after all, a situation which many women in developing countries are forced to endure, with associated high mortality and morbidity – organizations such as UNICEF want all births to be assisted by a midwife or nurse so as to reduce maternal and neonatal mortality.[27] Giving birth in your preferred environment is a great idea, but if you want science on your side, take a midwife with you!

We don't know how many births are UCs because they may be recorded as births that took place before the arrival of the midwife, so it's difficult to know whether they were planned free-births or not. One researcher estimates that 'the maximum possible number of UCs per year in the United States is around 8,000, but it is likely lower than that.'[28]

Birth in a natural setting or 'land-based birth'

Some women speak of giving birth in a natural setting or remote green location as their ideal choice, but they avoid it because of birth fear or worries about causing trouble. If this is your chosen path, focus on things that increase your confidence about giving birth: look up positive birth stories and read them every day, connect with women who have given birth in natural settings without pain relief, and find other women who support your goal. Otherwise it's worth looking at birth options that increase your exposure to nature instead – you can, for example, make plans to spend the first stage of labor walking around the garden or the local park.

It's impossible to weigh up all the variables involved with a natural birth as locations and experiences differ so greatly. A planned natural birth in the woods near your home may not have much of an environmental impact, but having to drive for miles to an isolated location will of course use more resources than choosing a different birth setting. In terms of items to take with you, these will not differ greatly from those required for a homebirth, so you can still obtain most things second hand, which will reduce your carbon footprint further.

Waterbirth

Women who labor in water report feeling more relaxed,[29] and a thorough study that used a control group concluded that laboring in water is safe, although it found no significant difference in terms of reduced intervention rates.[30] However, there is research that suggests that water immersion during the first stage of labor reduces the need for an epidural or other anesthesia by almost 10 per cent.[31]

Unfortunately the jury is out on the safety of actually giving birth into water, with some experts recommending it and others arguing against it. One study recognized potential risks to the baby (such as water aspiration or snapped umbilical cord) but did not actually argue against waterbirth for low-risk women.[32]

Therefore, ACOG and the AAP state that waterbirth should be considered an experimental practice that should only occur in the context of a clinical research study. They incorrectly argue that waterbirth does not have any benefits and may pose dangers for the newborn.[33] However, the American College of Nurse Midwives (ACNM)[34] and the Royal College of Midwives (RCM)[35] have released statements that fully support the woman's choice to have a waterbirth.

In eco-terms it's a juggle – is a large pool of water to labor environmentally friendly? There is the cost of supplying and disposing of the water, the energy used to heat the water, and the plastic used to create the pool. But if using a pool helps you to avoid pain-relief drugs, it might be the greener option for you.

Does the place and manner of birth impact on your baby?

There is a lot of supposition about there being a lifelong negative impact of a birth experience on a baby, causing psychological harm that supposedly lasts well into adulthood. Many people cite these 'birth memories' as reasons to have natural homebirths, yet there's no evidence to support this claim, and plenty that indicates that babies can withstand the stress of being born. There is preliminary research that suggests that a natural birth may have better health benefits for a baby than a cesarean birth,[36] however a medically necessary C-section will still be better for a baby than risking its life. Likewise, there are increasingly more things that can be done to provide the benefits of a natural birth to a baby that doesn't enter the world that way as scientists begin to understand the complex way that birth works, for example the way that microbes can be transferred using vaginal 'seeding'.[37]

There is a lot of pressure in the alternative birth community for a woman to have a natural homebirth in order to protect her baby. This is sad because it leads to parental guilt and feelings of failure in new mothers when their births don't go to plan, and it's unhelpful because a homebirth environment does not suit every woman. And even if there *were* proof that babies were being traumatized by medical interventions during hospital births, most of those are necessary procedures and therefore in the baby's interests already. So listen to yourself and your own needs, take into account the science of birth, and ignore the negative voices. Choose the birth that is best for you.

Birth trauma

It is not known how much birth trauma impacts instances of post-natal depression (PND) and post-traumatic stress disorder (PTSD) in the US, but some parenting experts argue that there is a connection between a negative birth experience and postnatal mental health issues.[38] I would put emotional wellbeing of the mother and baby high up on the list of factors to assess when it comes to childbirth options.

With postnatal depression on the rise in the US, and many more cases under-reported and under-treated, it's a pressing issue. The 4Children report *Suffering in Silence* recognizes the role that birth can have on mental health: 'Other reasons why postnatal depression might occur include... Stressful life event during the pregnancy or after childbirth (including early or difficult birth),'[39] but research into the area is limited. It is clear, however, that there are risk factors for PND and PTSD which include a very complicated mix of objective factors (such as the type of delivery) and subjective ones (such as feeling a loss of control).

A study investigating traumatic stress after childbirth found that: 'Traumatic stress symptoms and having a PTSD symptom profile were both significantly related to the experience of an emergency Cesarean section or an instrumental vaginal delivery.'[40] The study also found that birth trauma was not related to the method of birth, as women who had given birth vaginally were just as impacted as those who had delivered by C-section. It was the level of intervention *combined with the lack of control* that made a significant difference to the mental health of the women involved. Hence, a 2004 study titled 'Birth trauma is in the eye of the beholder' found the following four themes that described the essence of women's experiences of birth trauma: 'To care for me: was that too much to ask? To communicate with me: why was this neglected? To provide safe care: you betrayed my trust and I felt powerless. The end justifies the means: at whose expense? at what price?'[41]

So it's not so much about getting your way during childbirth, but about having a say in what happens where possible, having your voice heard and respected, and feeling empowered by the process.

Avoiding birth trauma

Knowledge is power and informing yourself is one good way to prepare for your birth experience. Another is to accept that some situations are out of your control, but that you can still feel empowered during them. For example, you may do everything you can to ensure that you don't have a C-section, but may end up needing one anyway. Instead of letting this ruin your birth experience, liaise with your doctor to make the C-section as comfortable for you as possible. Good healthcare professionals want you to have a positive birth experience, but they may need you to tell them what they can do to help you to feel empowered through a medical procedure.

Ina May Gaskin, co-founder of US-based birthing center The Farm, is an outspoken advocate of a woman-empowering, evidence-based childbirth approach. The statistics of The Farm speak for themselves: the C-section rate is less than 2 per cent, compared to the US national average of 32.8 per cent in 2012.[42]

The Farm focuses heavily on the emotional wellbeing of the laboring woman, with an emphasis on supporting her through the pain of childbirth. As Gaskin states in her book *Ina May's Guide to Childbirth*: 'When avoidance of pain becomes the major emphasis of childbirth care, the paradoxical effect is that more women have to deal with pain after their babies are born.'[43] However, as flying to this specialist center is not an option for most readers, especially pregnant women, we can instead take heart from The Farm's approach and follow its lead. To begin with, prepare your body for the birth. Join a pregnancy yoga class, attend antenatal sessions, read positive birth stories, and arm yourself with the science. Look after yourself. Your emotional wellbeing matters.

Induction

Induction is used to bring on labor, usually when the woman has gone over her estimated due date by several days (the exact number of days allowed varies depending on her local health services). This is because there is evidence that it's safer for baby not to be born too 'late'.[44] However, due dates can be inaccurate and even wrong by several weeks depending on variables relating to the pregnant woman.[45]

According to the Childbirth Connection report, women's bodies should be trusted to begin laboring without the need for medical intervention.[46] You have the right to say no to induction, but equally you should always discuss your options with a doctor who takes your concerns on board. It may be that you can compromise and have an induction while having your needs met as well.

Other reasons for induction include:

A big baby?

ACOG guidelines do not recommend induction for macrosomia (a big baby), stating that 'Results from recent reports indicate that induction of labor at least doubles the risk of cesarean delivery without reducing the risk of shoulder dystocia or newborn morbidity'.[47] However discussions with mothers show both that medical professionals may err on the side of caution with supposed large babies and unnecessarily induce pregnant women on this basis, and that some women insist on induction because they think the baby will be too big for them to deliver naturally.[48] One study concludes that: 'Due to the inaccuracies, among uncomplicated pregnancies suspicion of macrosomia **is not an indication for induction or for primary Cesarean delivery**'[49] [my emphasis.] In addition, a 2009 Cochrane review[50] found that, in most cases, induction for suspected big babies does not improve the health of the mother of the baby either.[51]

Rupturing of the membranes

Rupture of the membranes is a general term which refers to the waters breaking. It can be spontaneous (happen naturally) or artificial (carried out as an intervention to induce or speed up labor). In the latter case, a doctor or midwife uses a small tool called an amniohook to pierce and break the woman's bag of waters.

Sometimes membranes rupture naturally or artificially and labor fails to progress, which means the clock starts ticking and panic begins to set in, especially in a busy hospital ward where midwives are taking care of several laboring women and know they need to change shifts. This can put pressure on a woman to have an unnecessary intervention. Remember, you can discuss your options as events unfold, but for low-risk mothers and babies, reducing unnecessary interventions and reliance on medical aid will generally give you the safest, greenest birth possible. So now let's look at things you can do to avoid medical induction.

What are the safe non-medical ways to induce labor?

- **Blue and black cohosh** are herbal remedies that are not recommended for bringing on labor. In one US survey, approximately 64 per cent of midwives reported using blue cohosh as a labor-inducing aid. There is, however, some controversy surrounding the use of blue cohosh for induction due to three serious cases where it harmed the baby when used near the delivery. [52] Black cohosh is sometimes used with blue cohosh to stimulate labor, but this therapy has been found to have adverse effects in newborn babies, which appear to be primarily due to the use of blue cohosh.[53] If you want to avoid medical drugs due to potential risks to your health and your baby, it makes no sense to use this herbal remedy either.
- **Castor oil** is deemed to be safe for bringing on labor, as a small study of 103

women found that a single oral 60 ml dose of castor oil increased the likelihood of labor starting within 24 hours.[54] However, the small sample size means that this data is not very reliable and, unsurprisingly, all the women studied reported feeling nauseated. If you can stomach it, go for it!

- **Drinking tonic water** is probably best avoided. It is often recommended by natural health practitioners to induce labor naturally, but in one case, a newborn baby was born with health disorders, perhaps because the mother drank more than a liter of tonic water a day at the end of her pregnancy.[55] The German Federal Institute for Risk Assessment advises pregnant women against drinking beverages like tonic water that contain quinine. If you do drink it, do so in moderation.
- **Eating dates** is a harmless and healthy natural option. According to one study, when consumed during the last four weeks of pregnancy, eating dates reduced the length of labor and the need for induction.[56]
- **Exercise** is often recommended to kick-start labor but there is little evidence to support this. There's no harm in keeping moving while in the first stages of labor, though.
- **Nipple or breast stimulation** may be beneficial in terms of a reduction in the number of women who are not in labor after 72 hours, and a reduction in postpartum hemorrhage, according to a review of the available research, although it is not recommended for women who are considered to be high-risk.[57]
- **Sexual intercourse** falls under the same research as exercise.[58] Female orgasms have been shown to increase uterine contractions, but only one study of 28 women resulted in useful data,[59] so the role of sexual intercourse as a method of promoting labor initiation remains uncertain.

See also the section below on 'Pregnancy yoga'. In addition, an *American Family Physician* Journal lists some other non-medical options that may be worth using in place of medical induction.[60]

There is no adequate scientific research to support the following methods to bring on labor: drinking raspberry leaf tea (safe from 32 weeks of pregnancy only[61]), taking evening primrose oil, acupuncture,[62] homeopathy, taking hot baths, eating spicy curries, eating pineapples, or having enemas, but, equally, no harm has been found from trying these methods. Keep yourself busy and active and, remember, your baby will arrive when s/he is ready to!

Write a birth plan

One of the main things you can do to have a low-impact, empowered birth is to write a thorough but concise birth plan. You should also keep your midwife informed about your birth choices during your pregnancy. Don't treat your plan like a sacred document, because it might go out of the window no matter how well you prepare for the birth. The important thing is to know your choices, and to have discussed them with your birthing partner and your midwife, especially if you have to make important decisions during labor, as that is not a good time to think rationally. You wouldn't go into most intense experiences unarmed, and birth is certainly an intense experience. Note that I said intense, not overly painful.

Although your birthing partner will be there to help carry your voice, for inexperienced partners it can be a daunting experience (especially if your partner cannot stand to see you in pain). For this reason it is worth doing two things. One, watch positive videos of women giving birth online together. Two, speak to a female childbirth worker or doula (the word comes from the Greek word for handmaiden) to help draft your birth plan; that way you can talk through your options with someone who knows how the medical industry works. You can also hire a doula for the duration of your pregnancy and for the birth if that is an option for you. As mentioned previously, having a known woman present during childbirth has been shown to significantly reduce the need for medical interventions, and we look at this again in the section below on 'Female birthing partners'.[63]

These are the main points to include in your birth plan.

Electronic fetal monitoring

When you enter hospital to give birth, a risk assessment will be carried out, and your birth plan will be discussed. If you are low-risk, you will be encouraged to be mobile and active, and the fetal heart rate will be checked every 15 minutes, using a hand-held Doppler or electronic fetal monitoring. If you are high-risk, you will be continuously monitored, but should still also be encouraged to be active.

You can request that your caregiver uses a Doppler instead of electronic fetal monitoring but some caregivers may still wish to use a fetal monitor. This device has to be strapped around your abdomen, which does not make it the most comfortable experience when you're having contractions. It also means that you have to stop moving around to be assessed, which is the last thing you want to do in the first stage of labor. Although some fetal monitors allow you to move around the room with them, this is still not ideal for you as it interrupts the birthing process.[64] You need to be able to move freely during labor, not just as a method of pain relief but so that you can zone out of your surroundings and into a space where you feel safe and tuned-in to giving birth to your baby.

I'm not being anti-science here – as ever, everything I share with you has scientific research as its starting point. According to a Cochrane review of this: 'Continuous monitoring was associated with a significant increase in Cesarean section and instrumental vaginal births. Both procedures are known to carry risks for mothers although the specific adverse outcomes were not assessed in the included studies.'[65]

So my advice here is, unless you have had a high-risk pregnancy, or your baby has actually been found to be under stress, or has an irregular heartbeat, you do not need this monitor to be strapped to you. You can choose to have your baby's heartbeat checked when you are ready, and you can insist that it is checked with a Doppler, which is what a midwife would do in the case of a homebirth. The hospital electronic fetal monitor strap is only tied around you with simple Velcro. So long as you have full understanding of why it is being used, you can make an informed choice to remove it.

Internal vaginal examinations

An internal examination procedure is when two gloved fingers are inserted into the woman's vagina to check the woman's cervix and assess labor progression through dilation and the baby's position. However, a study published by BMC Pregnancy &

Childbirth indicated that **vaginal examinations** to determine cervix diameter and baby's position had an accuracy of only 48-56 per cent – about the same as flipping a coin.[66] Another study found that in a group of 508 women, two clinicians differed in dilation measurements by two centimeters or more in 11 per cent of instances.[67]

Given the chance to, you should be able to tell whether you are making progress or not. If you don't, there are things that can help listed in the section below on 'Positions for birth.' An alternative could be using **the purple line** indicator, which is described by researchers as: 'a line of red/purple discoloration seen to arise from the anal margin and extend between the buttocks, reaching the nape of the buttocks at the onset of the second stage of labor.' [68]

A thorough review of this topic concludes: 'The purple line does exist and there is a medium positive correlation between its length and both cervical dilation and station of the fetal head. Where the line is present, it may provide a useful guide for clinicians of labor progress alongside other measures.'[69] This quoted study found that a line appeared for 76 per cent of women, so it is a viable alternative to internal exams and is worth discussing with your midwife, doula and birthing partner before the birth.

Membrane sweeps

Your midwife or obstetrician might ask you whether she can sweep a finger around your cervix (the neck of your womb) during an internal examination to separate the membranes of the amniotic sac surrounding your baby from your cervix. Sweeps are invasive, uncomfortable and the research shows that they don't actually work. 'Whether or not women underwent membrane sweeping, overall rates of induction, postmaturity, and prelabor membrane rupture were similar.' [70] For a small minority of women they can also be dangerous.

Just say no to this one.

Directed pushing/coaching

In terms of science to support spontaneous mother-led pushing, there is plenty of research.

You know that image of the laboring woman on her back being told when to push? Prepare to have your mind blown. It's completely made up: a laboring woman's body pushes on its own, and she follows its lead. Directed pushing, where someone coaches the woman on when to start and stop pushing, is actually associated with an increased risk of bladder problems and pelvic floor damage.[71] Another study demonstrates that management of the woman's birth 'has adverse effects upon the mother and baby. The view that the second stage of labor is of high risk, and needs to be hastened... perpetuates the use of directed, sustained pushing. When midwives work with normal physiology, they work with, not against the woman during the second stage of labor. Midwives must empower women to trust their own instincts.'[72]

When I attended pregnancy yoga classes before the birth, the teacher told us that we should only push when we felt our bodies pushing already (which, unless you are medicated for the birth, is not hard to do). So I added to my birth plan: 'do not coach me during labor unless I specifically ask you to'. My midwife was lovely, but she ignored this part of my birth plan. She just didn't understand that my uterus was doing the work for me, and all I had to do was push along with it. This may be how women who are pregnant and in a coma give birth to their babies, since they are not consciously able to push.[73] This phenomenon is known as the fetus ejection reflex.[74]

In terms of helping with labor progression, some of the research is conflicting, as one study indicates that directed pushing is not associated with negative outcomes, and does shorten the duration of the second stage of labor,[75] but another study concludes that: 'Directed pushing might slightly shorten the duration of second-stage labor, but can also contribute to deoxygenation of the fetus; cause damage to urinary, pelvic, and perineal structures; and challenge a woman's confidence in her body.'[76] The same study found it to be usual that women following their own urge to push wait naturally for each contraction to build and then push for a few seconds, take a few short breaths, then push again. Yet another study found that: 'Delayed pushing was not associated with demonstrable adverse outcome, despite second-stage length of up to 4.9 hours. In select patients, such delay may be of benefit.'[77]

An excellent review of this topic can be read on the website of the Royal College of Midwives, which concludes that: 'directed pushing in second-stage labor... may undermine physiological birth.'[78]

The key point to take from this is to listen to your own body before you listen to anyone else during labor. If you don't take pain-relief drugs, it should be clear when you need to push and when not, as you'll have an undeniable urge to start and to stop. If you have to think about whether you need to start pushing, don't. If you do take pain-relief drugs and can't feel when to push, you may wish or need to be coached. Unless you are considered high-risk or encounter complications, you can ignore anyone who tells you to push or stop pushing, or ask them to do so, depending on how you feel during labor. Some women do find coached breathing helpful, at the very least.

Positions for birth

During the second stage of labor, upright positions have been found to be optimal for birth as they significantly reduce the number of assisted deliveries, episiotomies, and impact less on fetal heart rate patterns.[79] Positions that have been found to work best are squatting, sitting, kneeling, using birth stools, or lying on your side. Keep in mind that squatting can be hard work for a laboring woman as we are used to sitting on chairs rather than on our haunches. This is where attending a weekly active-birth pregnancy yoga class beforehand will help you to prepare, by getting you used to squatting and using the associated muscles.

Lying on your back may make labor pain worse, according to research based on feedback from laboring women,[80] but if you do end up needing to give birth lying down, try to lie on your side instead, as this has been found to assist the process.

A note on men

Michel Odent is a childbirth specialist who argues that the presence of men during childbirth has a negative impact on the mother's experience because men can bring fear into the birthing room.[81] However, although research regarding the presence

Positions for birth

Kneeling with birthing ball

On hands and knees

Rocking

Lying on your side

Squatting

Leaning forward

Squatting with partner

Supported by partner

43

of the father during childbirth is mixed, Odent appears to be wrong on this subject. According to a study of laboring women: 'In the group in which the husband was present, the labor was shorter, the number of threatening intrauterine asphyxia cases and Cesarean sections was smaller, but there were more induced deliveries... The results suggest the importance of husband's presence at childbirth.'[82] Another, a study of Turkish parents, found that the father's presence had little negative impact: 'fathers' support in birth helped mothers to have more positive experiences in all aspects of childbirth.'[83] Similarly, according to a Cochrane review of the topic, 'Benefits were independent of whether the patient's husband or partner was also present.'[84]

So, although there is some conflicting research, overall the evidence shows no reason for excluding the father or male birthing partner from the birthing room. If you're in doubt about this, you should discuss it with your partner and go with what makes you feel most comfortable, while helping your partner to prepare for the birth in the best way possible. Regardless of whether your partner is male or female, so long as he or she is on hand during the labor you can always ask for space or hand-holding when you feel that you need it (it's hard to know beforehand how you will feel during labor). It's also worth noting that few of these studies looked at how prepared the father felt before the birth, and whether he had worked with his partner to prepare for the birth. Some active-birth yoga teachers and doulas do special sessions for couples and birthing partners leading up the birth, and are also available for private sessions to discuss birth options and preparation. If nothing else, writing a birth plan together will help to prepare male partners for the birth experience.

Female birthing partners and continuity of care

Where you birth is not as important as who is with you to care for you during the experience. Historically, women were supported by a midwife throughout pregnancy and labor, but in hospitals today this consistent support has become the exception rather than the norm. Historically, 'continuous care' – having the same female caregiver throughout pregnancy and labor – is believed to have led to healthier mothers and babies.[85]

For this reason, you may want to consider hiring a doula (who is not trained in medical procedures) because the aim of the doula is primarily to support the woman. According to a Cochrane review, 'It was less likely that women would need pain medications or have an operative vaginal delivery, a Cesarean section, or a five-minute Apgar score of less than seven when they had an experienced female caregiver – either a professional (nurse, midwife, or childbirth educator) or a nonprofessional (friend or family member who had given birth before, or a doula) – with them continuously during labor and delivery.'[86]

Doula presence has also been shown to significantly lower the risks for middle-class women in labor[87] (as opposed to the low-income women studied). However, doulas can be expensive, and any woman you know well and trust – for example, your mother, sister, or close friend – is a good alternative for a low-cost birth.

Pain-relief options

When it comes to pain relief, finding what works for you can be tricky because you can't know how you will react to the medication you are given, how well it will work for your body or whether it will be sufficient for your needs. Some women have what they call 'orgasmic births' where they liken any supposed pain to the feeling of an orgasm, which is interesting because, in terms of pain perception, a study found that 'A comparison of mothers whose labor ended with or without epidural analgesia corroborated previous findings that the level of pain toward the end of an experience greatly influences the way the overall experience is remembered.'[88] I'm not saying that it's all in the mind, but that an informed birth may help to change the way you experience pain.

The cost of drugs

The fact that pharmaceutical products find their way into our sewer systems, groundwater, and marine systems[89] is a well-known problem, but there are also the manufacturing costs of drugs to consider, both financially and to the environment, where medical waste tops the list for waste production.

In addition to this waste, there is the energy embodied in the manufacture of drugs to consider, plus packaging, transport, management and administration of medications, including disposable items like syringes and incineration of used materials. Avoiding pharmaceutical pain relief and aiming for minimal medical intervention is certainly, therefore, the greenest way to give birth. However, keep in mind that avoiding pain relief is not the best option if it means that you don't have a comfortable and satisfying birth experience, so take the medications if you feel that you need them – that's what they're there for! We'll look at the science-supported options for pain relief next.

Natural alternatives that may work, according to science, are:

Acupuncture The little evidence available shows that acupuncture may reduce the pain of labor, although it is generally not available in an OU or MLU setting. If you don't mind the idea of having needles used on specific areas of your body during labor at home, this could be a good option for you.[90]

Birthing pool or water for pain relief British healthcare guidelines recommend laboring in water for pain relief during the first stage of labor, but not in the second stage as it can slow contractions down.[91] There is evidence that immersion in water also reduces the likelihood of needing an epidural.

Controlled breathing, relaxation and massage The little evidence available has found that breathing and relaxation techniques, or massage undertaken by the birth partner during the birth, may significantly reduce the laboring woman's experience of pain.[92] Relaxation and yoga have been found to reduce pain, increase satisfaction with pain relief and reduce the rate of assisted vaginal delivery.[93]

Gas and air (Entonox) is a 50:50 mixture of oxygen and nitrous-oxide gas that you breathe in through a hand-held mouthpiece. Gas and air won't remove the pain but it can make it more manageable and can be used alongside other measures of pain relief. It can make you feel light-headed or sick but this wears off very quickly and you can easily take a break from it because you are in control of how much you use. Again, we have to consider distribution, storage and management costs of gas and air as environmental expenses but, of all the medical pain-relief options, gas and air has the least impact as it dissipates into the air and is not harmful to the environment. It is safe for your baby.[94]

Hypnotherapy or hypnobirthing is the use of self-hypnosis during childbirth. A systematic review of hypnosis for labor pain found that it had positive effects, but also pointed out some major flaws in the research.[95] So the jury's out on whether it really works, but there's no harm in trying it by using a CD or attending classes.

Pregnancy yoga One study found that regular yoga practice in the last 10-12 weeks of pregnancy improved maternal comfort in labor and may have facilitated labor progress.[96] Another study found that 'Yoga was associated with reduced pain, increased satisfaction with pain relief, satisfaction with the childbirth experience, and reduced length of labor when compared to usual care and when compared with supine position.'[97]

Other research has found that yoga is beneficial for mental health: 'A single session of yoga reduced both subjective and physiological measures of state anxiety,'[98] and mindfulness yoga in particular has been found to help with maternal depression rates and help with mother-baby bonding after the birth.[99] Yoga also helps women with high-risk pregnancies by reducing hypertensive-related complications of pregnancy and improving fetal outcomes.[100] You might want to sign up for a class right now.

Also... A hot wet cloth massaged over the woman's vulva has been found to reduce perineal tearing.[101]

Things that do not work, according to science, are:

Birthing/gym balls They may, however, help women to find a comfortable position to ease contractions.[102]

Homeopathy has repeatedly been found to be no more effective than using a placebo, and a Swiss report that claimed otherwise was found to be rife with errors.[103] In 2014 the Australian National Health and Medical Research Council (NHMRC) released a paper concluding that 'there is no reliable evidence that homeopathy is effective.'[104] It's harmless if you want to use it, but your money may be better spent on things that have been shown to help, like pregnancy yoga classes.

Music has not been found to help with pain relief but midwives generally encourage women to take their own music to the OU/MLU to play during labor, as a potential aid to relaxation.[105]

Reflexology has been tested for the treatment of various illnesses and ailments and has not been found to be effective for any of them, according to a systematic review.[106]

TENS machine TENS stands for transcutaneous electrical nerve stimulation. Electrodes are taped onto your back and connected by wires to a small battery-powered stimulator. Holding this, you give yourself small, safe amounts of current through the electrodes. TENS is a popular pain-relief option for many women, and TENS machines are found in pharmacies all over North America. However, research has found that using it does not provide pain relief.[107] It may help with feeling that you are in control of your pain, however, or work as a distraction. If you want to use one, some hospitals have TENS machines available to borrow, so check this beforehand. A cheap and eco-friendly option is to rent, rather than buy, your own machine. You will need to learn to use it towards the end of your pregnancy.

The following options are standard pain relief options offered in a hospital obstetric unit, and probably the least eco-friendly options

An epidural block is a local anesthetic that numbs the nerves carrying the pain impulses from the birth canal to the brain. For most women, an epidural gives complete pain relief, but it's not always 100-per-cent effective in labor.[108] So even if you plan to have one, it's worth looking into other methods of pain relief as well. It has to be administered by an anesthetist, so it won't be an option if you give birth at home.

Epidurals can interfere with the process of labor and birth in several ways. An IV drip runs through a plastic cannula in the vein. Epidurals can slow down labor, and increase the chances of needing assisted delivery. Your contractions and the baby's heart rate will need to be continuously monitored or checked more often, which means having a belt around your abdomen. An epidural may make your legs feel heavy, which makes it hard to walk around during labor. Even with so-called 'mobile epidurals', it is unlikely to be safe to bear weight. Generally, 'low dose' epidurals are used, which allow some movement and change of position within the bed, and retain some sensation for effective pushing. Though, again, pushing tends to be less effective with an epidural.[109]

Epidurals can prolong the second stage of labor and if you can no longer feel your contractions because of the numbing effect, the midwife will have to tell you when to push. This means that forceps or a ventouse may be needed to help deliver the baby's head.[110] Even so, aim for an upright birthing position where possible.[111]

A spinal block is a type of regional analgesia that's typically used to provide pain relief shortly before delivery. A spinal block provides complete pain relief in the lower body for about an hour or two. You'll remain awake and alert. A spinal block usually has little or no effect on the baby. Because spinal anesthesia blocks the ability to empty your bladder, you'll likely need to use a catheter as well. *Opiates/narcotics*

Different opiates have different benefits and drawbacks. You may be offered Morphine, Stadol, Fentanyl, Nubain or Demerol and can find out beforehand so you can find the best option for you. Narcotics can be injected into a muscle or given through an intravenous (IV) catheter. If you have an IV, you might be able to control your dosage. The medication takes effect in minutes. Narcotics don't stop pain altogether but they decrease the perception of pain for two to six hours and promote rest. They might cause sleepiness and nausea, and temporarily depress breathing for you or the baby.

Things to keep in mind when selecting narcotics are:[112]

The timing. In the early stages of labor, narcotics can decrease the strength of contractions and slow dilatation of the cervix. The best time to administer narcotic pain medication during labor is when your labor is very active (6-8 centimeters), just before you enter transition, or if your contractions become so overwhelming that you are losing control.

The method of delivery. Getting the pain medication during labor intravenously gives you relief more quickly than an intramuscular injection. Intravenous (IV) pain medication during labor also wears off faster. After an intravenous injection a mother usually feels some relief within 5-10 minutes; this relief may last around an hour. Intramuscular injections, on the other hand, typically take half an hour to an hour to reach full effect, but the relief may last three to four hours. Request a Heparin-lock, which allows you to move from your bed and to adjust positions more easily, rather than being tethered to a bedside an intravenous bottle.

A note on pain

Most women use some kind of pain-relieving strategies during labor, and many will use several. What's important is that the people who attend you in labor and childbirth are able to communicate with you to ensure that, as far as possible, you feel in control, are coping with the pain, and that both of you are clear but remain flexible about what needs to happen.[113]

Unrelieved pain during labor and post-partum has been shown to:
- Cause stress responses that can reduce the baby's oxygen supply
- Increase the risk of post-partum depression and post-traumatic stress disorder (PTSD)
- Interfere with breastfeeding
- Increase the risk of development of chronic pain conditions.[114] Labor pains are experienced differently by different women and for many women they are more about the intensity and duration of the experience than the feeling of pain itself. Other women find the need for stamina most difficult because there's no way of knowing how long a labor will last. These are all things you can prepare for during your pregnancy (to some degree) and, as mentioned earlier, preparation is the key to a positive birth experience. Keep this in mind, because it means that you can prepare to manage your pain. Write a clear birth plan, work with your birthing partner to help him or her to be your voice during labor, and you're on the right track.

Other birth issues to consider

Cord clamping

When a baby is born, s/he is still attached to the mother via the umbilical cord, which is part of the placenta. The baby is usually separated from the placenta by a midwife immediately clamping the cord.

A 2013 Cochrane review of the timing of cord clamping in healthy term babies suggests clamping the cord between one and three minutes after birth, which is known as 'delayed cord clamping'.[115] Although early cord clamping has been thought to reduce the risk of bleeding after birth (postpartum hemorrhage), the review found no significant difference in postpartum hemorrhage rates when early and late cord clamping (generally between one and three minutes) were compared. There were, however, some potentially important advantages of delayed cord clamping in healthy term infants, such as higher birthweight, early hemoglobin concentration, and increased iron reserves up to six months after birth. These need to be balanced against a small additional risk of delayed clamping causing jaundice in newborn babies that requires phototherapy (light treatment). The review concludes that 'Delayed cord clamping is likely to be beneficial.'

Some parents now prefer to use handmade, wool or cloth umbilical cord ties instead of plastic medical cord clamps because they feel nicer against the baby's skin. There is no data available on this at present, as it's a fairly new trend. However, plastic clamps are used because they are sterile (although arguably a cloth tie could be boiled before use to make it sterile as well) and because they are reassuringly tight, whereas cotton or woolen ties are more likely to break or loosen, which could lead to blood loss and could be dangerous for the baby. Go with the medical clamp and give your baby lots of skin-to-skin time instead of a risky cloth tie.

A natural Cesarean section?

Some women need to have a Cesarean section and this operation can theoretically be done in an empowering way, which is also known as a 'natural cesarean', 'woman-centered cesarean', 'gentle cesarean' or 'family-centered cesarean'.[116] The idea underpinning this approach is to make the operation as close to a vaginal birth experience as possible, and to empower the parents through offering choices, including: 'a "natural" approach that mimics the situation at vaginal birth by allowing (i) the parents to watch the birth of their child as active participants (ii) slow delivery with physiological autoresuscitation and (iii) the baby to be transferred directly onto the mother's chest for early skin-to-skin.'

However, the research concludes that 'no outcomes or safety data are presented to justify widespread utilization of this technique', which is why it isn't widely available at present.

Delivering the placenta

The third stage of labor is the delivery of the placenta. Ergometrine is usually the drug used to help the new mother with this. If you are at low risk of hemorrhage you can ask to have a physiological third stage – in other words, without drugs. Alternatively, you can choose to have an active third stage using only an injection of synthetic oxytocin (syntocinon) which has fewer side-effects than the combined syntocinon/ergometrine drug (the trade name for which is syntometrine).

The most recent Cochrane review on placenta delivery found that 'Routine "active management" is superior to "expectant management" in terms of blood loss, post-partum hemorrhage and other serious complications of the third stage of labor', which is why the third stage of labor is often managed by a midwife. However, the same review also states that: 'Active management is, however, associated with an increased risk of unpleasant side effects (e.g. nausea and vomiting), and hypertension, where ergometrine is used.'[117] Recent research suggests that having the injection may also cause long-term difficulties with breastfeeding.[118]

If you are at high risk of hemorrhage you will be strongly advised to have active management, because the benefits (not having a postpartum hemorrhage) outweigh the risks (of nausea and hypertension).

As breastfeeding stimulates the postpartum contractions that shrink your uterus to a smaller size, putting your baby straight to the breast can help to deliver the placenta.

In some countries, like New Zealand/Aotearoa, hospital staff give the placenta to the mother to take home so that she can follow the country's cultural tradition of burying the placenta under a tree. In the US and Canada you can ask to take your placenta home and bury it in your garden. This is a much greener option than allowing it to be disposed of as hospital waste.To eat or not to eat?

If you research eating your placenta, you'll find a wide range of opinions on the issue and a lot of unverified claims. There is no medical evidence supporting placentophagy, as it's technically known, and because every woman's placenta is unique, and dosages vary, so reported benefits remain anecdotal.[119] However, a recent review of 10 published papers that looked at the health benefits of placentophagy and found no evidence to support claims that eating a placenta cooked, raw or encapsulated can prevent postpartum depression, reduce pain, boost energy levels or increase lactation.[120]

Nevertheless, women choosing to eat their placenta has become something of a trend. It's true that many mammals do this, although we're unsure as to whether they do it for the nutrients or as a way of getting rid of the evidence of a birth immediately so that predators don't spot it, or both.

Some women choose to freeze their placenta and eat raw chunks in smoothies, while others pay professional 'placenta encapsulators' who take the placenta away to dehydrate it and transfer it into capsules that can be swallowed. However, there is draft law in progress by the Food Standards Agency regarding regulation of placenta encapsulation because of potential health risks relating to possible bacteria in the placenta.[121]

Environmentally speaking, taking your placenta home to bury it is a great option, as it will quickly decompose and provide nutrients for anything you plant above it, but eating it is probably no less green.Don't forget... skin-to-skin and breastfeeding

Don't forget... skin-to-skin and breastfeeding

Early skin-to-skin contact has been found to increase the rate and duration of breastfeeding, reduce infant crying, and improve maternal affection and mother-baby bonding.[122] No matter where you choose to birth and who is present at the time, you can almost always have immediate skin-to-skin contact with your baby.

Breastfeeding initiation at birth has both short- and long-term benefits for your baby, even if you can only do it for a short period of time. These include reduced bleeding, colostrum, increased rates of continuation of breastfeeding. See Chapter 3 for a more detailed look at breastfeeding.

Final note

However your birth experience works out, it's important not to put too much pressure on yourself or feel guilty about it afterwards. While you can be empowered to make informed decisions during childbirth, sometimes things just don't go as you hoped or planned for.

A drug-free homebirth is the most desirable outcome for the reasons I've already given: cost, resources, and physical and emotional health of mother and baby.

However, a homebirth is not always achievable or what the pregnant woman wants, and hospitals will only improve their practices regarding childbirth if women demand that they do so. It's also important to talk about the negatives as well as the positives of your birth experience with your partner, your doctor and/or midwife, and with other women who have given birth.

It's important to carefully select the appropriate, most supportive birth partner and/or doula, to be prepared for birth plans to change, as labor is unpredictable, to ask questions, and to be armed with accurate, current information. But it is also vital for women to engage with the many available midwifery services to enable them to make informed choices, allay fears, gain trust and feel listened to. Part of the midwife's role is to be a woman's advocate. You can work with staff to reduce intervention and achieve a normal birth and rewarding experience. There are steps that can be taken if a woman is unhappy with her care.

It's important to rest and take time to heal after the birth. Don't be afraid to ask people for help. This might not be news to most parents of newborn babies, but Australian research found that more than half the women studied were still showing signs of 'excessive daytime sleepiness' 18 weeks after having given birth.[123] This may be another reason birth trauma occurs, so don't be afraid to get help if and when you need it.

Summary

In preparation

- Prepare for your birth by reading positive birth stories and attending pregnancy-yoga or active-birth classes
- Use different muscles to practice giving birth in upright positions – squatting, sitting, kneeling, using birth stools, or lying on your side
- Learn about the purple-line indicator with your partner/birthing partner
- Research pain relief beforehand, including relaxation techniques, and practice them throughout your pregnancy
- Write a birth plan with a doula or other childbirth worker and your partner
- Communicate with your midwife about the birth you want.

The birth

- Ensure that you have a voice to speak for you during labor – a doula or other female caregiver, or your birthing partner
- If you have a homebirth, collect items you may need beforehand to save buying them new
- Consider low-carbon options for a land-based birth
- If you have a hospital birth, avoid unnecessary interventions by knowing the science and communicating your needs clearly

- Say no to membrane sweeps
- Say no to unnecessary electronic fetal monitoring; ask them to use a Doppler instead
- Say no to directed pushing unless you can't tell when to push naturally
- If you know you need to have a Cesarean, look up and discuss gentle Cesarean practices with your doctor beforehand
- If you are considered low-risk you can aim to deliver the placenta naturally, without drugs
- Arrange to take the placenta home to bury it or otherwise
- Stock up on eco-pads or cloth pads for afterwards
- Discuss your birth with healthcare professionals, friends and family; don't be afraid to talk about feelings of post-natal depression or birth trauma
- Rest!

And remember: childbirth can be empowering for pregnant women and their partners, a source of strength upon entry to new motherhood, a rite of passage. It can be low-impact and eco-friendly, with minimal pain, if you want to make it that way.

1 *Annu Rev Psychol* 2007, nin.tl/moralemotions 2 According to 'Intrapartum Care', NICE clinical guidelines, nin.tl/intrapartumcare 3 *Journal of Advanced Nursing*, 2001, nin.tl/birthsatisfaction 4 Outlined in *Science-Based Medicine*, 10 Dec 2009, http://nin.tl/midwivesandevidence 5 *Transforming Maternity Care*, nin.tl/hormonalphysiology 6 *Telegraph*, 3 Dec 2014, nin.tl/homebirthsbest 7 *BMJ* 2012;344:e2292, nin.tl/lowriskhomebirth 8 http://www.cdc.gov/nchs/data/databriefs/db84.htm 9 http://www.cdc.gov/nchs/data/databriefs/db84.htm 10 *Qualitative Health Research*, May 2012, nin.tl/birthCanada 11 ITV News, 12 Nov 2014, nin.tl/underfundedcare 12 *BMJ* 2011;343:d7400, nin.tl/birthplacestudy 13 http://www.theatlantic.com/health/archive/2012/03/the-most-scientific-birth-is-often-the-least-technological-birth/254420/14 *BMJ* 2011;343:d7400, nin.tl/birthplacestudy 15 Watch the NHS video at: http://nin.tl/hospitalDVT 16 For a full account, read 'Safe, Healthy Birth: What Every Pregnant Woman Needs to Know', nin.tl/safehealthybirth 17 *Scientific American*, 28 Aug 2012, nin.tl/helplessbabies 18 *Transforming Maternity Care*, nin.tl/hormonalphys 19 *BMJ* 2011;343:d7400, nin.tl/birthplacestudy 20 *BMJ* 2013;346:f3263, nin.tl/Netherlandsstudy 21 *BMJ* 2011;343:d7400, nin.tl/birthplacestudy 22 Am J Public Health 1992, 82, ajph.aphapublications.org/doi/pdf/10.2105/AJPH.82.3.448 23 Am J Public Health, Mar 1992, nin.tl/homebirthsafety 24 http://www.cdc.gov/nchs/data/databriefs/db84.htm 25 http://mana.org/about-midwives/state-by-state 26 http://pediatrics.aappublications.org/content/131/5/1016 27 nin.tl/UNICEFstats 28 http://ir.uiowa.edu/cgi/viewcontent.cgi?article=1387&context=etd 29 See 1.6.2.5 in http://nin.tl/NICEinductionguide 30 Acta Obstet Gynecol Scand, Apr 2001 nin.tl/warmtublabor 31 Cochrane Database Syst Rev, Apr 2009, nin.tl/immersedbirth 32 *BMJ* 1999;319:483, nin.tl/waterbirthmortality 33 http://www.acog.org/Resources-And-Publications/Committee-Opinions/Committee-on-Obstetric-Practice/Immersion-in-Water-During-Labor-and-Delivery 34 http://www.midwife.org/acnm/files/ccLibraryFiles/Filename/000000004048/Hydrotherapy-During-Labor-and-Birth-April-2014.pdf 35 https://www.rcm.org.uk/sites/default/files/Response%20to%20ACOG%20AAP.docx 36 https://www.braindecoder.com/vaginal-birth-cesarean-brain-development-1458553654.html 37 http://www.theguardian.com/lifeandstyle/2015/aug/17/vaginal-seeding-c-section-babies-microbiome 38 For example, this article by Sarah Ockwell-Smith: nin.tl/Ockwell 39 4Children report, nin.tl/sufferingsilence 40 J Psychosom Obstet Gynaecol, Mar 2002, nin.tl/Traumaticstress 41 Nurs Res Jan-Feb 2004, nin.tl/birthtraumaeye 42 The Farm's statistics can be found at nin.tl/TheFarmstats The US figure comes from cesareanrates.com 43 *Ina May Gaskin's Guide to Childbirth*, Bantam Doubleday Dell, 2003. 44 Green Med Info, 8 Jun 2012, nin.tl/postdateinduction 45 Hum Reprod, Oct 2013, 28 (10), nin.tl/pregnancylength 46 National Partnership for Women and Families, nin.tl/needlessintervention 47 http://www.aafp.org/afp/2001/0701/p169.html 48 Momtastic babyandbump nin.tl/UKearlyinduction 49 Am J Obstet Gynecol, Aug 2005, 193(2), nin.tl/macrosomicfetus 50 Cochrane Reviews are systematic reviews of primary research in human healthcare and health policy, and are internationally recognized as the highest standard in evidence-based healthcare. 51 Cochrane Database Syst Rev 2000, nin.tl/fetalmacrosomia 52 Can J Clin Pharmacol, Winter 2008, nin.tl/bluecohosh 53 National Center for Complementary and Integrative Health, nin.tl/reblackcohosh 54 Altern

Ther Health Med, Jan 2000, nin.tl/castoroiluse **55** BfR, 17 Feb 2005, nin.tl/quinineproblems **56** J Obstet Gynaecol, 2011, nin.tl/eatingdates **57** Cochrane Database Syst Rev, 2001, nin.tl/breaststimulation **58** BJOG, 12 Nov 2012, nin.tl/coitusandlabor and this study: 'Sexual intercourse for cervical ripening and induction of labor': Cochrane Database Syst Rev, 2001, nin.tl/coituslabor2 **59** *Am Fam Physician,* 15 May 2003, nin.tl/cervixripening **60** *Am Fam Physician,* 15 May 2003, nin.tl/cervixripening **61** Babycentre, nin.tl/raspberryleafhelp **62** Clin Obstet Gynecol, Sep 2000, nin.tl/nonpharmainduction **63** A doula, for example, see: Acta Paediatrica, Oct 1997, nin.tl/doularediscovered **64** J Perinat Educ, Summer 2004,nin.tl/laborprivacy **65** Cochrane review, 8 Nov 2013, nin.tl/fetalmonitoring **66** *BMC Pregnancy and Childbirth* 2010, **10**:54, nin.tl/thepurpleline **67** Buchmann EJ, Libhaber E: 'Accuracy of cervical assessment in the active phase of labor' in *British Journal of Obstetrics and Gynaecology* 2007 **68** *BMC Pregnancy and Childbirth* 2010, **10**:54, http://nin.tl/thepurpleline **69** *BMC Pregnancy and Childbirth* 2010, **10**:54, nin.tl/thepurpleline **70** NEJM Journal Watch nin.tl/nosweeping **71** Am J Obstet Gynecol., May 2005, nin.tl/coachingorno **72** Aust Coll Midwives Inc J, Sep 1996, nin.tl/pushingfuture **73** For example, Am J Obstet Gynecol, Sep 2003, at nin.tl/pregnantcoma **74** Birth 14:2, June 1987, nin.tl/fetusejection **75** *International Journal of Nursing and Midwifery,* May 2011, nin.tl/2kindspushing **76** J Midwifery Womens Health, May-Jun 2007, nin.tl/laborcarebestpractice **77** Obstet Gynecol, Jan 2002, nin.tl/activeversuspassive **78** Royal College of Midwives, nin.tl/directedpushing **79** Cochrane Database Syst Rev, May 2012, nin.tl/noanaesthesia **80** J Psychosom Obstet Gynaecol, Mar 2004, nin.tl/supineetal **81** *Guardian,* 18 Oct 2009, nin.tl/menstayaway **82** Lijec Vjesn, Aug-Sep 1997, nin.tl/husbandpresent **83** *West J Nurs Res,* Mar 2007, nin.tl/fathersattending **84** *American Family Physician,* 1 Oct 2002, nin.tl/caregiverpresence **85** Cochrane summary 15 Jul 2013, http://nin.tl/Cochranesupport **86** *American Family Physician,* 1 Oct 2002, nin.tl/caregiverpresence **87** Birth 35:2 Jun 2008, nin.tl/laborsupportCsection **88** *Psychological Science,* nin.tl/laborpainrule **89** WHO Bulletin, nin.tl/pharmaenviro **90** 'Intrapartum Care', NICE clinical guidelines, nin.tl/intrapartumcare **91** Point 1.6.2.5 from ibid. **92** NICE, op cit, nin.tl/intrapartumcare **93** Cochrane Database Syst Rev, Dec 2011, nin.tl/relaxationtechs **94** NHS Choices, nin.tl/NHSChoicesonpainrelief **95** Clin Psychol Rev, Aug 2011, nin.tl/hypnosislabor **96** J Perinat Educ, Summer 2008, http://nin.tl/normalbirth **97** Cochrane Database Syst Rev, Dec 2011, nin.tl/relaxationtechs **98** *Depression and Anxiety,* Aug 2014, nin.tl/antenatalyoga **99** Complement Ther Clin Pract, Nov 2012, nin.tl/mindfulnessyoga **100** Prev Med, Oct 2012, nin.tl/yogaandcomplications **101** Cochrane Database Syst Rev, Dec 2011, nin.tl/perinealtechs **102** NICE, op cit, nin.tl/intrapartumcare **103** *Science-Based Medicine,* nin.tl/Swisshomeopathy **104** NHMRC, nin.tl/homeopathyreview **105** NICE, op cit, nin.tl/intrapartumcare **106** Med J Aust, Sep 2009,nin.tl/reflexologyreview **107** NICE, op cit, nin.tl/intrapartumcare **108** 'The Obstetric Anaesthetists Association estimates that one in eight women who have an epidural during labor need to use other methods of pain relief'– nin.tl/NHSChoicesonpainrelief **109** nin.tl/NHSChoicesonpainrelief **110** NICE guideline 1.9.2 from nin.tl/intrapartumadvice **111** NICE guideline 1.9.7 from nin.tl/intrapartumadvice **112** Taken from http://www.askdrsears.com/topics/pregnancy-childbirth/pregnancy-concerns/managing-pain-during-childbirth/narcotic-pain-relievers113 NICE, op cit, nin.tl/intrapartumcare **114** https://www.sciencebasedmedicine.org/childbirth-without-pain-are-epidurals-the-answer/ **115** Pub Med Health, 20 Mar 2013, *nin.tl/timingcordclamping* **116** BJOG, Jul 2008, nin.tl/naturalcaesarean **117** Cochrane Database Syst Rev, 2000, nin.tl/activevsexpectant **118** *Breastfeeding Medicine,* Dec 2014, nin.tl/reducedbreastfeeding **119** For more information see nin.tl/placentophagia **120** EurekAlert! 4 Jun 2015, nin.tl/eatingplacenta **121** *Independent,* 15 Jun 2014, nin.tl/placentapillsban **122** UNICEF, nin.tl/everychildsafe **123** *Mail,* 4 Aug 2014, nin.tl/norushforwork

3 Diet and nutrition, part one: the science of milk

Why is breast best for baby?... How is dairy formula milk made?... The financial costs of formula... The environmental cost of formula and how to reduce it... Plastic, glass and disposable baby bottles... Practical information for breastfeeding mothers... Other things that can impact infant feeding choices... Other milk alternatives... A note on growth charts.

Many of us have heard that breastfeeding is the best option for feeding a baby, and there is also a strong argument that breastfeeding is the most environmentally friendly option available to parents. However, there's a lot of misinformation out there about why this is the case and, in addition to this, some women struggle to breastfeed for various reasons. Although breastfeeding rates in the US are improving, they are still considered to be low, with 74 per cent of women breastfeeding their baby from birth, 43.5 per cent still doing so after six months and almost 23 per cent after a year.[1] This compares with rates of 71 per cent in Peru, 72 per cent in Malawi, 74 per cent in Cambodia, the Solomon Islands and Nepal, 76 per cent in Sri Lanka – and 90 per cent in Rwanda, where children are often breastfed for over a year.[2] The UNICEF website has a detailed chart showing breastfeeding rates around the world and the links between breastfeeding and child health.[3]

Bottle feeding is seen as the 'normal' way to feed babies in the US,[4] and a national survey found that only a quarter of the US public understood that feeding a baby with infant formula instead of breastmilk increases the chances the baby will get sick. There is also a public perception that breastfeeding is inconvenient, as 45 per cent of US adults believed a breastfeeding mother has to give up too many habits of her lifestyle. Add to this a general sense that breastfeeding and difficulties in establishing breastfeeding are seen as threats to mothers' freedom and independence,[5] and it's no surprise that the breastfeeding rates are low. A state-by-state demonstration of the difference in breastfeeding rates across America can be seen in Figure 4 overleaf.

With this in mind, although this chapter outlines that breastfeeding is the most

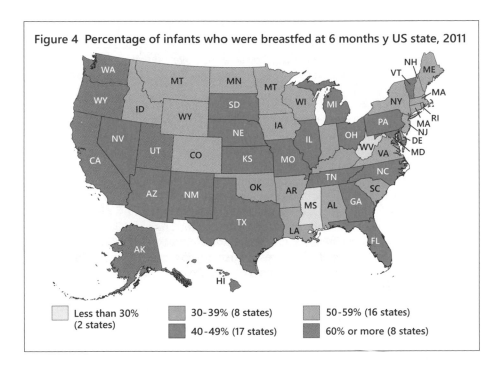

Figure 4 Percentage of infants who were breastfed at 6 months y US state, 2011

eco-friendly feeding option, we also look at how to formula feed in the greenest way possible, and the health and eco-credentials of various substitute milk options that are available for babies.

WHO says what?

The World Health Organization (WHO) states that:
'Breastfeeding is the normal way of providing young infants with the nutrients they need for healthy growth and development. Virtually all mothers can breastfeed, provided they have accurate information, and the support of their family, the healthcare system and society at large.

'Exclusive breastfeeding is recommended up to six months of age, with continued breastfeeding along with appropriate complementary foods up to two years of age or beyond.'[6]

Why is 'breast best' for baby?

In many countries breastfeeding has become a political statement due to formula-milk marketers pressurizing mothers to buy artificial milk. In China a very serious problem arose from formula-milk companies deliberately altering milks with melamine to mislead consumers into believing that the milk was rich in protein.[7] There are mistruths on both sides, however, so let's look here at the scientifically proven benefits of breastfeeding.

This is not all the research on breastfeeding that's out there, but it serves as a selection to give an idea of why breastfeeding is the best option for a baby's health and the mother's. For a much more detailed scientific overview of the benefits of breastfeeding, take a look at the scientific review *The Risks of Not Breastfeeding for Mothers and Infants.*[8]

The American Academy of Pediatrics states that: 'It has been calculated that more than 900 infant lives per year may be saved in the United States if 90 per cent of mothers exclusively breastfed for six months. In the 42 developing countries in which 90 per cent of the world's childhood deaths occur, exclusive breastfeeding for six months and weaning after one year is the most effective intervention, with the potential of preventing more than one million infant deaths per year, equal to preventing 13 per cent of the world's childhood mortality.'[9]

A report titled *Formula for Disaster: weighing the impact of formula feeding Vs breastfeeding on environment* was put together by the International Baby Food Action Network (IBFAN) and the Breastfeeding Promotion Network of India (BPNI).[10] It shows a correlation between higher rates of breastfeeding prevalence and lower rates of hospital admissions among infants under one year old for the following conditions:

- lower respiratory tract infections
- wheezing
- non-infective gastroenteritis
- otitis media (ear infection)
- lactose intolerance
- asthma
- infant feeding difficulties
- gastroenteritis
- eczema
- infant feed intolerance.

According to WHO: 'Breastfeeding lowers the risk of diarrheal disease by four- to fourteen-fold and the risk of respiratory illness by fivefold... Breastmilk also markedly improves nutritional status in infants... Breastfeeding has also been associated with lower rates of chronic diseases such as diabetes and inflammatory bowel disease and with improved neurocognitive development.'[11]

Research has found many other benefits to breastmilk besides nutrients.[12] For example: breastmilk contains natural stress hormone; the composition of breastmilk varies depending on the baby's gender and the wellbeing of the mother; and differences in milk can impact infant behavior as well as affecting growth and development.[13] One researcher observes that 'Formulas can copy mothers' milk food value, but not its hormonal content.'[14]

Scientists have also identified a molecule that is key to mothers' ability to pass along immunity to intestinal infections to their babies through breastmilk, as when a baby breastfeeds the antibodies go straight to his or her intestine and provide essential protection while building up immunity.[15] Antibodies provided by breastmilk are needed for healthy gut maturation, especially for preterm and low birthweight babies,[16] but the health benefits of these antibodies persist into adulthood.[17] A mother's breastmilk also contains special sugars that seem to selectively nourish the gut bacteria that infants need.[18]

Environmentally speaking...

Breastmilk is one of the few foods that is produced without pollution, packaging or waste, according to *Formula for Disaster,* which also gives a long list of reasons why breastfeeding is healthier for mothers, children and the planet. The report points out that breastmilk does not need to be 'skimmed, processed, pasteurized, homogenized, packaged, stored, transported, repackaged, dried, reconstituted, sterilized or wasted... It requires no fuel for heating, no refrigeration, and is always ready to serve at the right temperature.' Some of this report relies on supposition, and of course the parties behind it are pro-breastfeeding; however, they do make some very good arguments and refer to evidence where it is available.

And for mums...

An analysis of 47 studies in 30 countries found that the longer women breastfeed, the more they are protected against breast cancer.[19] The study concludes that: 'The lack of or short lifetime duration of breastfeeding typical of women in developed countries makes a major contribution to the high incidence of breast cancer in these countries.'

There is no formula that can mimic that.

How is dairy formula milk made?

Most artificial babymilk is heat-treated cows' milk that has been converted into a powder.[20] Unfortunately, rearing cattle has such a large carbon footprint that research indicates that giving up eating meat is even more eco-friendly than giving up driving[21] – and eating beef is particularly damaging.[22] This is because cattle need a lot of room for pasture, which often involves the clearing of wooded land, and this deforestation causes soil erosion, which leads to an increase in the significant greenhouse gases methane and nitrous oxide.[23] Cows also contribute to increased greenhouse gases directly through methane that they emit through belching and flatulence.[24]

In addition to this, cows are often fed grain that could go directly to hungry human mouths, and, although grass-fed cows are less carbon-heavy, their ecological footprints (hoofprints?) vary widely and are difficult to assess (we will look at this more closely in Chapter 4).

The financial cost of formula milk

The financial argument against formula feeding is fairly obvious because you have to buy formula milk and bottles and perhaps also a sterilizer, which mean you're spending more money than you would by breastfeeding. Breastfeeding has been found to be cheaper by a UNICEF-funded report,[25] which states that in the UK:

'If half those mothers who currently do not breastfeed were to do so for up to 18 months over their life, there would be [over the lifetime of each first-time mother]:
- **865 fewer cases of breast cancer**

- With cost savings to the National Health Service of over **£21** million ($33 million)
- Improved quality of life equating to more than **£10** million ($16 million).'

Some people argue that breastfeeding requires the mother to eat more because the baby is guzzling her calories. Certainly the mother may feel like eating more, but she doesn't actually *need* to – a very thorough review found that even breastmilk produced by poorly nourished mothers met their babies' needs.[26] Nor do breastfeeding mothers have to drink extra fluids.[27]

Food for thought

We've already looked at the research that shows that breastfed babies are healthier than formula-fed babies. However, let's briefly consider this in light of the WHO statement that breastfeeding is the *normal* starting-point. If we reverse the logic of the research here for a second, and take breastfeeding as the norm, then in fact formula milk *increases* specific health risks for your baby.[28] That's a pretty radical observation, I know. But it's worth thinking about.

The environmental cost of formula and how to reduce it

The publication *Formula for Disaster* gives a long list of reasons why formula feeding is detrimental to the global environment.[29] Amongst other things, it looks at:
- indirect water usage on dairy farms, such as milking system clean-up, milking parlor clean-up, milk bulk tank clean-up, prepping cows for milking, milk precooling, and staff facilities, as well as drinking-water supply for cows;
- energy used by the manufacturing process of turning liquid milk into a powder, and then adding water to turn it into a liquid again for consumption;
- energy and resources used for packaging the milk; and
- energy used to transport the finished product to supermarket shelves.

The report also states that: 'Globally, from every 100 kg raw milk produced and processed, only 20 kg (that is 20 per cent) is used for producing powdered milk, leading to production of 2.2 kg powdered milk. This means, for each 1 kg of powdered-milk production and processing, 21.8 kg CO_2-equivalent of greenhouse gas are emitted.'

Obtaining certified organic baby formula milk from manufacturers that feed their cattle grass, not grain, is one way to ensure that the milk you buy has a lower carbon footprint, as organic standards stipulate that cows are grass-fed.

Plastic baby bottles

At the risk of scaremongering, it's worth explaining the latest research on plastics here – that they may not be safe for your baby, despite now being BPA-free. BPA (Bisphenol A) was banned by the EU from baby bottles because it is an endocrine disrupter.[30] However, there is new evidence that the chemicals used to replace BPA in plastic products for children are in fact *just as dangerous as BPA*.[31] The good news is that not all BPA-free plastic products contain these harmful chemicals, but the bad news is that some of them do and there's no way of knowing which ones they are.

Typical infant feeding bottles are made of plastic, which is made of oil and thus carries a high environmental cost of its own. These bottles are also manufactured over-seas and transported to North America by ships or planes, covering many miles and using much energy to do so. However, some women need bottles for feeding expressed breastmilk as well, so it's not only formula feeders who use them. For the purposes of feeding expressed milk, one or two bottles should suffice for your needs. Baby bottles are not currently recyclable, but you can minimize their environmental impact by finding uses for them at home instead of throwing them away. Try using them to hold oil to grease creaky doors, to hold pens or paintbrushes, as painting tools in art projects, or as containers to hold craft supplies. Just don't send them to a landfill site.

Since formula milk has to be heated to be used safely, using a bottle sterilizer, energy from a microwave, or boiling water to sterilize bottles is a necessity. This uses resources, namely energy and water.

Glass baby bottles

A greener and safer option for feeding your baby is to use glass bottles instead of plastic ones. These are available at some children's goods retailers in the US.[32] One thing that makes glass bottles more green is that they aren't made with the aforementioned harmful chemicals used in plastic bottles, and another is that they are often easily recycled though ordinary glass recycling facilities. Glass also lasts longer than plastic, although since it can shatter it's worth cushioning bottles with cloth layers whenever you take them out of the house.[33]

Disposable baby bottles

You read that right. These are plastic baby bottles that are intended for single use. They are considered to be convenient because they are pre-sterilized, but they cost your pocket and the environment heavily. Sterilizing bottles is very simple and relatively cheap, but the main reason for using single-use disposable bottles appears to be shortage of organizational skills and time. These bottles are designed with 'on the go' parents in mind for use away from home, although the milk still requires heating, so you still need access to a microwave or sterilizer to use them. One way to make outings with formula milk easier is to find out beforehand which venues have heating and sterilizing facilities. Some children's stores offer these services for free and it can also be a nice way to meet other parents.

Since disposable baby bottles are designed for single use, you can't remove the lids and wash and reuse them. You can't recycle them either. There's still the issue of dangerous chemicals used in disposable baby bottles, and some parents have found these bottles have a faster flow than ordinary baby bottles, which can cause babies to gag on the milk and have colic, although this point is purely anecdotal rather than scientific (obtained from a Mumsnet discussion[34]).

Practical information for breastfeeding mothers

This topic is far too large to cover thoroughly in this book, so please see the Resources at the end of the book for more specific advice. It's essential, however, that we look at this topic at least briefly here because of the many myths people believe about breastfeeding.

Got milk?

Some people recommend herbal remedies, foods or medications for increasing milk supply (galactagogues). These pass into breastmilk. The effects of these remedies in large quantities on babies is not known, and there is no research to indicate that they actually do increase milk supply (fenugreek, for example, doesn't work[35]).

Keep in mind that anything found to be truly helpful probably won't be an alternative remedy, as it will have passed into medical use already. Most herbal remedies are fine to use in small quantities, for example as teas, but I mention this point because a survey found that many breastfeeding mothers use herbal remedies that have not been tested for safety in significant quantities.[36]

Front hold

The use of galactagogues and many products marketing themselves as milk producers to mothers shows a real lack of faith in women's bodies. In fact, at least 95 per cent of mothers have been found to be able to produce more than enough milk for their babies, especially when support and accurate information is obtained.[37] The majority of mothers who think that they have a low milk supply problem actually don't.

Get support

Remember the WHO statement that all women can breastfeed with accurate information and support? Women with friends who have breastfed successfully are more likely to choose to breastfeed, while negative attitudes of family and friends can pose a barrier to breastfeeding.[38] The AAP states that: 'As such, the pediatrician's role in advocating and supporting proper breastfeeding practices is essential and vital for the achievement of this preferred public health goal.'[39]

Cross cradle

Consider joining a group of breastfeeding mums who meet locally and regularly. There are many organizations that support breastfeeding in the US, including La Leche League USA and Breastfeeding USA. In addition, local sling meets, natural parenting groups, natural nappy groups and home birth groups can help, as there tends to be crossover with the people who attend them and breastfeeding parents.

Do it on demand

Some health visitors and parenting books recommend following milk feeding schedules, which means timing when you allow your baby to breastfeed. These don't work when your baby is crying and has to wait an hour to feed, since a baby has no concept of adult time or that the milk will be provided eventually.

Football hold

Some people argue that going by the clock 'trains' babies to sleep through the night sooner, but no link has been found between scheduled feeding and encouraging babies to sleep through the night. It's also not responsive to ignore a hungry, crying baby's needs.

Other pro-schedule feeders argue that controlling feeding creates hungrier babies who therefore drink more milk and supposedly obtain higher-fat milk. In fact, research shows that pre-feed fat levels are inversely related to the length of the inter-feed interval – in other words, the longer the time between feeding, the lower concentrations of fat in the milk, so feeding as regularly as possible will actually lead to chubbier babies.[40] La Leche League has a useful summary of the research behind this statement on its website.[41]

Other research has found that, when caregivers control their baby's feeding, they

Lying down

potentially override the child's internal hunger and satiety regulatory cues, and may interfere with the child's emerging independence and need for competence.[42]

In order to breastfeed successfully, a woman needs to be able to feed her baby as often as possible, as this increases and maintains her milk supply. A very thorough and readable survey advocates breastfeeding on demand and suggests that scheduled feeding may have negative repercussions for the baby.[43] Interestingly, there is also a study that suggests that babies who are fed to a schedule, whether by bottle or breast, do not perform as well at school academically as their demand-fed peers.[44]

Expressing milk and milk pumps

Women choose to express milk for a variety of reasons, including having to return to work, wanting to share night feeds with a partner, or obligations that take them away from their baby for a period of time.

For this purpose, there are two types of breast pump, the manual pump and the electronic pump. A manual breast pump is a small plastic apparatus that attaches to a bottle that collects the pumped milk. It's a simple device with a comparatively minimal environmental impact. If it means that you continue to breastfeed instead of buying formula milk, it's certainly a green option to invest in one. Manual pumps are available to buy from local pharmacies and *Which?* has a useful guide to choosing a manual breast pump on its website.[45] I'd recommend buying one new.[46]

An electronic pump will have a much larger environmental impact due to being mains-operated and made of several parts, so it requires more resources to construct it and requires energy to operate. However, electronic pumps may be more efficient at pumping milk than manual pumps, and they are available to hire from some groups and organizations. Alternatively you might be able to borrow one from a friend or buy one second-hand, which reduces the carbon footprint of using it to some degree.

The greenest way of expressing milk is the old-fashioned method of hand-expressing, which can be messy at first but works well for many women. The British charity National Childbirth Trust has a useful guide for hand-expressing breastmilk on its website.[47]

You'll need to store expressed breastmilk and there's no getting around the need to store it in plastic packets in the fridge or freezer at present.

A common breastfeeding myth is the idea that you need to 'pump and dump' milk – in other words, express milk and then spill it away, after having alcoholic drink. However, according to a review, 'occasional drinking while breastfeeding has not been convincingly shown to adversely affect nursing infants'.[48] So unless you're planning on drinking heavily, bottoms up!

Any breastmilk you can provide for your baby, whether your own or donated, even if you can only do it part-time or short-term, will have a positive impact on your baby's health and the environment.[49]

Other things that can impact infant feeding choices are:

- **Milk protein allergy** (MPA) is a recognized problem in infancy and might affect up to 15 per cent of infants.[50] The allergic reactions it provokes vary from child to child. Breastfeeding can be continued if allergens are avoided. For cow's milk protein allergy (CMPA), a breastfeeding mother must eliminate all cow's milk protein, then all bovine protein (milk and meat), and occasionally other protein sources such as soy from their diet.[51] For formula-fed babies, current options include specific allergen avoidance and special hydrolyzed protein formulas (EHFs), and amino acid–based formulas (AAFs), which are available through pediatricians who can help with MPA diagnosis and allergen avoidance.

- **Tongue-tie** is when a baby has a **tight piece of skin between the underside of their tongue and the floor of their mouth, whi**ch may impact breastfeeding. According to the UK National Health Service, only 3-10 per cent of newborn babies have tongue-tie, and it is more common in boys than girls.[52] It can be diagnosed by a lactation consultant and corrected with an operation called a frenotomy. Before going down this route, see a trained breastfeeding peer supporter to check your latch and to rule out other potential problems.

Other milk alternatives

Human milk banks are available across the US. If you have surplus milk supply and wish to donate breastmilk, milk banks exist for babies who are born too early and can't stomach any other kind of milk. The Human Milk Banking Association of North America will tell you all you need to know about the donating process (see Resources).

Thanks to the internet, an increasing number of women are able to turn to *individual milk donors*. A Facebook group called Human Milk 4 Human Babies matches donors to women in need. This is not the same as milk from official milk banks, as there is no testing involved, and untested donor milk is not government-approved on the basis that it might contain infectious diseases and carry a contamination risk. Some mothers choose to go down this route anyway, to reduce or eliminate the need to give their babies formula milk. Donated milk is typically expressed and offered for free to local parents, although there have been cases of women posting milk to those in need as well.

The *British Medical Journal (BMJ)* has published a report addressing the risks of buying unregulated breastmilk over the internet,[53] and La Leche League supports the *BMJ*'s argument but also supports mothers who choose to use unregulated milk.[54]

In traditional Mongolian society it is common for women to share breastfeeding roles by nursing each other's children,[55] and milk sharing used to be popular in the UK when aristocrats in particular relied on wet nurses to feed their babies. The idea of wet nurses may be having a resurgence in the US,[56] but nursing other people's babies is not a common practice in the US any more, and therefore not currently an easy option for most mothers.

Mixed or combination feeding is when mothers feed their babies with breastmilk and add formula to 'top up' the breastmilk feeds. This still gives your baby the benefits of breastmilk; however, topping up on formula can lead to a decrease in breastmilk supply because the baby becomes full and will suckle less. Remember, most women can and do produce enough milk for their babies. If you're worried that your baby is having trouble feeding or isn't gaining weight, other factors could be in play. Seek help from breastfeeding peer supporters and ask your doctor to refer you to a lactation consultant if problems are not resolved.

Soy-based formula milk is a complex topic. There is a lot of scaremongering about soy because, although there have been no specific health problems documented in human infants receiving soy formula, it is recognized that babies go through developmental stages that are sensitive to soy isoflavones, which are estrogens. Therefore, the theory is that babies are more likely than adults to be vulnerable to the estrogen-like effects of the phyto estrogens that are naturally found in soy.

However, soy milk that has been treated to make it suitable for infants does not have the same levels of estrogens in it. On this basis, the most recent Expert Panel evaluation expresses minimal concern about adverse developmental effects in babies who are fed soy infant formula.[57] Other research has found both benefits and potential problems with soy consumption for babies and young children, and advises caution overall.[58]

As with ordinary formula milk, soy formula milk comes with its own large environmental footprint, but the jury's out on whether soy or dairy milk is the greener option, because soy is also linked to deforestation and other environmental problems. However, human consumption of soy is actually not the main problem, as cows are also fed soy by many farmers, with a liter of dairy milk potentially using more soy in production than a liter of soya milk,[59] and Europe importing 39 million tonnes of soy a year, 90 per cent of which is for animal feed.[60]

Soy milks are not recommended for babies without consulting a health professional first.

Rice milk is not recommended as a main source of milk for babies or children under four-and-a-half because rice can contain high levels of arsenic, which is naturally present in soil.[61] High levels of arsenic are linked to an increased risk of certain cancers.[62] The same advice should perhaps apply to *baby rice*, although official guidelines do not reflect this because baby rice contains much lower levels of arsenic than rice milk. Baby rice has, however, been linked to bladder cancer in later life, and 'While the Food Standards Agency says that there is no danger to infants, the scientists would like regulations to be updated'.[63] See Chapter 4 for more information on this.

To be clear, rice milk is safe as an occasional drink for an older child, but not as a substitute for breastmilk or formula milk for babies under six months or as a main milk for young children.

Nut milks, nut-derived milks and oat milks are not recommended for babies under a year old because they do not contain the right quantity of nutrients or fat.[64]

A note on growth charts

Growth charts are used by health visitors to assess babies' weight gain. Most health visitors check that a baby is following a curve on the chart, although they can allow some leeway with this, as few babies put on weight in consistent patterns.

The American growth measurement system[65] was recently revamped. In 2006, the Centers for Disease Control and Prevention (CDC) concluded that clinicians in the US should use the 2006 WHO international growth charts[66] for children up to five years of age rather than the CDC growth charts.[67] These new charts describe the growth of healthy children in optimal conditions. The study concludes that:

'Clinicians should be aware that fewer US children will be identified as underweight using the WHO charts; slower growth among breastfed infants during ages 3-18 months is normal, and gaining weight more rapidly than is indicated on the WHO charts might signal early signs of overweight.'[68]

This is important news for breastfed babies in the US, as women who had children before the new charts were implemented may be used to thinking that their breastfed babies were underweight or growing too slowly, which helps to propagate the myth that women can't produce enough milk to breastfeed. In fact, under the new guidelines, slower weight gain and lower weight rates are seen as optimal health conditions, whereas fast weight gain is seen as likely to lead to obesity later in life. If you have a caregiver who worries you about your baby's weight gain, seek another opinion. Feeding your baby as often as possible will increase the fattiness of your milk, so don't give up and hit the bottle. You can do it!

Summary

- Breastfeeding is the best option for your baby's health, your health as a mother, and for the environment
- Babies should be given breastmilk exclusively until they are ready to wean onto solids (see the next chapter for more on this)
- Breastfeeding is cheaper and does not require the mother to eat more food
- Breastfeeding is better for the environment
- At least 95 per cent of mothers are able to produce more than enough milk for their babies, especially with support and accurate information
- Join a breastfeeding support group and don't be afraid to seek professional help or advice if you need it
- Human milk donors may be an option if you are struggling to breastfeed
- Breastfeed your baby on demand, not to a feeding schedule
- Choose organic formula milk for your baby
- Dairy formula milk has a high carbon footprint
- So does soy formula milk, although the footprint may be slightly smaller
- Rice, oat and nut milks are not recommended for babies
- Avoid buying plastic baby bottles, even if they are BPA-free plastics
- Choose glass baby bottles and reuse or recycle them when you're done
- Single-use disposable baby bottles are very environmentally damaging and should be avoided altogether

- Plan ahead when you need to feed your baby formula milk away from home, to make sterilizing bottles and heating milk easier
- If you need to express breastmilk, try hand expressing first
- If you produce plenty of breastmilk, consider donating some to a milk bank.

Finally... when should a baby be weaned onto solid foods?

Not yet! See the next chapter for details on why waiting for baby to reach specific milestones that typically appear around the six-month mark is the key to weaning a baby onto solids.

1 Figures from 2007 to 2009. http://www.cdc.gov/breastfeeding/policy/hp2010.htm–**2** Lorena Abano, The Richest, nin.tl/breastfeedingrates–**3** UNICEF, nin.tl/unicefnutrition–**4** http://www.ncbi.nlm.nih.gov/books/NBK52688/–**5** http://www.ncbi.nlm.nih.gov/books/NBK52688/–**6** WHO, nin.tl/whobreastfeeding–**7** *The Lancet*, nin.tl/breastmilkbrand–**8** Rev Obstet Gynecol. 2009 Fall; 2(4): 222-231, nin.tl/formularisks–**9** http://pediatrics.aappublications.org/content/129/3/e827–**10** BPNI/IBFAN, nin.tl/formulafordisaster–**11** 'Breastfeeding policy: a globally comparative analysis', WHO, nin.tl/globalanalysis–**12** Cochrane Database Syst Rev. 2007 Oct 17;(4):CD002972, nin.tl/lowbirthweight–**13** *Scientific American*, nin.tl/boys-girls-milk–**14** Katie Hinde of Harvard University's Department of Human Evolution, quoted in *Discovery News*: nin.tl/breastmilkvaries–**15** *Science Daily*, nin.tl/babies-immunity–**16** *National Geographic*, nin.tl/babysgut–**17** Eric W Rogier, 3074-3079, nin.tl/antibodies-regulate–**18** J Agric Food Chem. 2010 May 12; 58(9): 5334-5340, nin.tl/human-milk–**19** *Lancet*, 2002 Jul 20;360(9328):187-95, nin.tl/cancerandbreastfeeding–**20** Association of Breastfeeding Mothers (1991), nin.tl/ecologicalimpact–**21** As stated by Prof Tim Benton in the *Guardian*, nin.tl/giveupbeef–**22** Gidon Eshel, 11996-12001, PNAS, nin.tl/nitrogenburdens–**23** *Climatic Change* 2014, nin.tl/meatturnsupheat–**24** *News Discovery*, nin.tl/gassycows–**25** Article available at: NHS choices, nin.tl/breastsavings Research at *BMJ*, nin.tl/breastimpact–**26** Perspectives In Nutrition, nin.tl/poorlynourished–**27** According to '4 Water.' *Dietary Reference Intakes for Water, Potassium, Sodium, Chloride, and Sulfate*. Washington, DC: The National Academies Press, 2005, nin.tl/water-lactation–**28** *Scientific American*, op.cit, nin.tl/boys-girls-milk–**29** BPNI/IBFAN, nin.tl/formulafordisaster–**30** National Toxicology Program, Brief On Bisphenol A (BPA) report, nin.tl/briefonbpa–**31** Environ Health, 2014 May 28; 13(1):41, nin.tl/bpa-free-plastic oestrogen–**32** For example, Toys R Us http://www.toysrus.com/buy/8-31-12-tru-4-day-labor-day-sale/save-on-baby-/buy-1-get-1-50-off-dr.-brown-s-bottles/dr.-brown-s-glass-bottles-2-pack-4-oz-163h-p2-4239885–**33** *Los Angeles Times*, nin.tl/clear-advantage–**34** Mumsnet, nin.tl/mumsnetdiscussion–**35** Alamer M, Basiouni G, (2005), 'Feeding effects of fenugreek seeds (Trigonella foenum-graecum L.) on lactation performance, some plasma constituents and growth hormone level in goats', Pak J Biol Sci, 25:28-46. / Nice, FJ, (2011), 'Common Herbs and Foods Used as Galactogogues', ICAN: Infant, Child & Adolescent Nutrition, 3(3):129-132. / Swafford S, Berens P, (2000), 'Effect of fenugreek on breast milk volume', ABM News & Views, 6(3):21.–**36** BMC Complement Altern Med v.13; 2013, PMC3835544, nin.tl/australiasurvey–**37** Akre, J, (1989), 'Infant feeding. The physiological basis. Bulletin of the World Health Organization', 67 Supplement: 1-108.–**38** http://www.ncbi.nlm.nih.gov/books/NBK52688/–**39** http://pediatrics.aappublications.org/content/129/3/e827–**40** Woolridge, M 'Baby controlled breastfeeding: Biocultural implications. In Breastfeeding: Biocultural Perspectives', ed. P Stuart Macadam and KA Dettwyler. New York: De Gruyter, 1995.–**41** Breastfeeding Abstracts, May 1999, Volume 18, Number 4, pp. 28-29, nin.tl/cuefeeding–**42** HHS Author Manuscripts, PMC2530927 nin.tl/restrictivefeeding–**43** ICLS Occasional Paper 13.1, June 2014, nin.tl/maria-iacovou-survey–**44** *The European Journal of Public Health*, 2012, nin.tl/feedondemand–**45** Which?, nin.tl/whichbreastpumps–**46** For the reasons discussed in this blog post: nin.tl/buynewpump–**47** NCT, nin.tl/howtoexpress–**48** Basic & Clinical Pharmacology & Toxicology, 2014, nin.tl/alcoholandbreastfeeding–**49** BPNI/IBFAN, nin.tl/formulafordisaster–**50** Ann Allergy Asthma Immunol. 2002 Dec;89(6 Suppl 1):33-7, nin.tl/milkallergychildren–**51** J Pediatr. 1999 Oct;135(4):506-12, nin.tl/milkchallenge–**52** NHS, nin.tl/tongue-tie–**53** BMJ 2015;350:h1485, nin.tl/unregulatedmarket–**54** La Leche League GB, nin.tl/reportresponse–**55** According to Peaceful Parenting blog, nin.tl/mongolia-breastfeeding–**56** http://jobs.aol.com/articles/2012/01/20/the-return-of-wet-nursing/–**57** Composed of The National Toxicology Program (NTP) Center for the Evaluation of Risks to Human Reproduction (CERHR), nin.tl/panelevaluation–**58** Environ Health Perspect. 2006 Jun; 114(6): A352-A358, nin.tl/scienceofsoy–**59** *Guardian*, nin.tl/environmentalimpact–**60** *Guardian*, nin.tl/soyadamage–**61** UK Food Standards Agency, nin.tl/arsenicrisk–**62** NHS, nin.tl/arsenicwarning–**63** *Guardian*, nin.tl/cancer-risk–**64** NCT, nin.tl/choosingaformula–**65** MMWR Recomm Rep. 2010 Sep 10;59(RR-9):1-15, http://nin.tl/growth-charts–**66** BCMJ, Vol. 52, No. 3, April 2010, page(s)1521 Council on Health Promotion, nin.tl/who-charts–**67** CDC, nin.tl/chartsgrowth–**68** CDC, nin.tl/growthstandards

4 Diet and nutrition, part two: weaning

When should you wean your baby?... First foods... Other environmental costs... Encouraging healthy eating habits... Alternative weaning methods... Fussy eaters and neophobia... What should your baby be eating?... Is baby rice safe?... Should you eat meat?... What about milk?... Eat local... Organic versus non-organic foods... Soy and palm oil

This chapter is split into three sections. The first section looks at when to wean your baby onto solid foods (while continuing to give milk feeds); the second looks at the best approach for weaning your baby onto solid foods; and the third looks briefly at the environmental impacts of the food we eat.

Weaning: why is there confusion?

There are few areas where the information appears to be as confusing as over when to wean your baby. The American Academy of Pediatrics (AAP) recommends exclusive breastfeeding for about six months, followed by continued breastfeeding as complementary foods are introduced, with continuation of breastfeeding for one year or longer as mutually desired by mother and infant.[1]

You can be forgiven for thinking that the advice given to parents about weaning seems a little patronizing. Before 2001, the World Health Organization (WHO) recommended that infants be exclusively breastfed for 4-6 months with the introduction of complementary foods thereafter.[2] In 2001, this was changed and exclusive breastfeeding was recommended for the first six months of life. The AAP now agrees with these guidelines.[3]

However, there is some confusion over the WHO guidelines as well, because they could reflect the fact that in other countries risks of health problems from early weaning are greater,[4] and there is very little data available that looks at individual cases for weaning babies of different sub-groups. This has led to some persuasive and misleading articles written for and against early weaning, which again ignore the research that helps to distinguish early weaners from those who are not yet ready for solids.[5] Also, there is a myth that choosing to wean babies early onto baby rice will create night sleepers, but research has found that there is no link between sleep patterns and the early introduction of solids.[6]

Hence, the British Dietetic Association (BDA) states that: 'The introduction of solid food should commence at around six months of age' and 'Each infant should be managed individually, as they develop at different rates. Developmental signs of readiness for solid food, together with parental opinion, should be taken into consideration when advising on the ideal age to begin complementary feeding.[7] So one thing they agree on is that waiting longer than six months isn't good, as it's hard for exclusively breastfed babies to meet their nutrient and energy needs from breastmilk alone.[8]

When should you wean your baby?

To clarify, when I use the term 'weaning' here, I mean introducing complementary non-milk 'solid' foods to a baby, alongside milk feeds. I do *not* mean weaning off breastmilk or formula milk and onto solid foods completely.

Babies should never be weaned onto solid foods before 17 weeks (four months) of age,[9] although in the case of some health problems (cystic fibrosis, metabolic disorders, for example) this may be done under the guidance of a pediatrician. Few, if any, babies are ready for solid foods at 17 weeks, as their digestive systems are still developing and introducing solid foods too soon increases the risk of infections and allergies.[10]

Due to this, official guidelines recommend the six-month rule to be on the safe side. However, some babies *are* ready for solid foods before reaching the six-month milestone and there are *clear indicators* to distinguish them. These are developmental milestones that indicate the maturation of the baby's digestive tract.

Milestones that indicate readiness for weaning

- 'Self-sitting': your baby should be able to sit up unaided, without having to prop him or herself up with hands.[11]
- Your baby should show an interest in food.
- Your baby should be able to reach for an item and put it in his or her mouth independently.[12]

The AAP recommends weaning your baby at 'about' six months of age, and gives this as a guideline rather than a specific date.[13] It states that it is unlikely that the necessary milestones will appear before six months of age, and lists these as a baby being able to do the following.

- Stay in a sitting position and hold his/her head steady.
- Co-ordinate eyes, hands and mouth in order to look at food, pick it up and put it in his/her mouth.
- Swallow food: babies who are not ready for solids will push their food back out when they are fed solids.[14]

First foods: homemade vs commercial baby foods

Choosing what to wean your baby onto can also be confusing. Commercial babyfoods – foods found in packets and jars on supermarket shelves that are aimed at babies – have guidelines on them for feeding them to babies from four months old. This research concludes that: 'The... infant food market mainly supplies sweet, soft, spoonable foods targeted from age four months. The majority of products had energy content similar to breastmilk and would not serve the intended purpose of enhancing the nutrient density and diversity of taste and texture in infants' diets.'[15] This is not a recipe for creating healthy eaters.

Commercial babyfoods are also transported much farther than foods that are bought locally to make homemade meals, and require excess packaging (usually small jars or plastic pouches) and sterilizing.

Other environmental costs

We all know that packaging is a huge problem and that we need to reduce the amount we're sending to landfill, incineration or even to recycling plants which require energy to run. However, manufacturing and transport also play a large part in creating emissions and harming the environment, and the worst thing about this is that much of it is not even necessary – many foods are over-packaged. This is another issue that is resolved by cooking at home so long as fresh foods are bought directly from grocers, farmers' markets and butchers where minimal, if any, packaging is used.

The greenest option is to choose home-cooked meals over commercially produced babyfoods. Reducing the amount of packaging you use and supporting local businesses over supermarkets will also lower your environmental footprint.

Encouraging healthy eating habits

Weaning is not about rapidly transitioning your baby from milk feeds to three meals a day, but about widening food exposure, sensory experiences and helping to establish good eating habits. Offering the same foods repeatedly helps a baby to build a knowledge base of foods that are safe to eat. Hence, a study found that when, in the early weaning process, parents repeatedly exposed their seven-month old babies to a vegetable purée that their baby initially disliked (and that the parents would normally not offer again), this led to a significant increase in their babies eating those foods.[16] This appeared to be long-lasting because nine months later 63 per cent of the infants were still eating and liking the initially disliked vegetable purée. So it's always worth persisting in offering disliked foods to babies for at least eight more meals after the food is rejected.

In terms of creating healthy eating habits, parental eating habits are a strong influence, as mothers who struggle to control their own food intake have been found to have heavier children.[17] The good news is that these are life skills that can be relearned, and the same research found that both overeaters and undereaters responded to interventions to improve their ability to self-regulate their food intake. The research concludes that: 'Cues can be provided that help children to focus on internal signals and improve their ability to self-regulate energy intake.'

Studies show that the child-feeding strategies parents use can influence children's food preferences.[18] When children are given foods as rewards for approved behaviors, enhanced preference for those foods results. In contrast, when children are offered rewards for eating, that is, when rewards are dependent on their eating

('If you eat your vegetables, then you can watch TV'), the foods eaten to obtain rewards become less preferred. Although these practices can induce children to eat more vegetables in the short run, evidence suggests that, in the long run, parental control attempts may have negative effects on the quality of children's diets by reducing their preferences for those foods. Let's look at this in detail now.

A study found that, when children were pressured to eat by requests to finish their food at home, they weighed less.[19] Children who were not pressured at home consumed significantly more food when they were not pressured to eat and they made overwhelmingly fewer negative comments. The study concluded that 'pressure can have negative effects on children's affective responses to and intake of healthy foods'. Equally, encouraging a child to eat a specific food has been found to cause resistance to that food.[20]

Other research has found that 'infants have an innate ability to regulate energy intake' and recommends that 'Dietetics professionals should emphasize the potential adverse effects that coercive feeding behaviors can have on children's innate ability to regulate energy intake. This includes not only admonitions to "clean your plate," but over-restriction of intake that may be motivated by concerns that children are overeating.'[21]

This evidence that controlling the way your child eats and how much of it is eaten is unhealthy suggests that spoonfeeding creates unhealthy eating habits in babies and children.

Alternative weaning methods

Another approach to weaning is known as **baby-led weaning**. This approach was recently popularized by Gill Rapley's book *Baby-led Weaning* and it involves letting your child feed him or herself from the very beginning of the weaning process, without so much as guiding utensils to mouths. Rapley also argues against giving babies purées to eat, which she refers to as 'mush'.

A study on methods of weaning found that 'baby-led weaning promotes healthy food preferences in early childhood that could protect against obesity'.[22] However, the same research found that there was a higher incidence of underweight baby-led weaned babies compared to the spoonfed group. The researchers conclude that they don't know whether or not this is a cause for concern but that increasing healthy fats like nuts and avocados may help to counter the problem.

Baby-led weaning is a green option because it's less likely to create over-eaters and it involves home-cooked meals. You don't even have to use plates and bowls to engage in baby-led weaning, since most foods are not in purée form (and many bowls get flung across the room by excited babies). Instead of cooking separate meals for your baby you can portion off a chunk of whatever you're cooking, without the added salt or spices (many cultures do eat spices of course, but your baby probably won't like spicy foods unless you ate them throughout pregnancy and/or breastfeeding). Other foods adults eat can be cut down to size for babies to eat 'finger food' portions of them, or lightly steamed to make them easier to bite into.

Feeding this way may be messy (although any type of infant feeding is generally messy) as your baby squishes and experiments with the foods you offer, but it's worth it to create a healthy relationship with food and can actually (anecdotal advice alert) be quite fun!

A very thorough scientific review of baby-led weaning (BLW) concludes that: 'The primary focus of infant feeding needs to continue to be responsive feeding, in particular, responding to infant hunger and satiety cues; being patient and encouraging the child to eat, but never forcing them; and experimenting with different food combinations, tastes, textures. In many ways, BLW provides a framework for infant feeding that encourages responsive feeding... Baby-Led Weaning appears to be a feasible option for introducing complementary foods for many infants and could conceivably have beneficial effects on the infant's nutrition and development.'[23]

Criticisms of the baby-led weaning approach tend to center around the fact that Rapley doesn't like purées. However, BLW can include purées as part of the texture experience and the argument that human babies have never eaten food in mush-form is not necessarily true, as shown by use of pre-mastication (giving pre-chewed foods to an infant) practiced by some hunter-gatherer societies, for example when a mother has more than one infant and isn't producing enough milk.[24] (This was usually done with meat and nuts since hunter-gatherers weren't always able to cook them due to time and resource constraints.) Although I'm not arguing that anyone pre-chews their baby's food before giving it to them (and, in any case, the safety of this has not been ascertained due to problems, for example, arising from the health of the chewing parent's teeth[25]), it highlights that purées are not necessarily a modern mushy invention, but can add to the range of textures experienced by a child when made with nutritious ingredients at home.

Another positive thing about baby-led weaning is that it encourages parents to make healthy meals for themselves that baby can eat too. If you want your baby to grow up liking broccoli, you need to start eating it too – during or before conception, in fact.[26]

In terms of healthy diets for babies, nothing beats eating a range of fresh, unprocessed foods – ideally home-cooked meals. The important thing is to enjoy eating together as a family, as several studies have reported the benefits of eating *family meals* together, including healthier eating patterns and improved psychological wellbeing.[27]

A middle way?

One piece of research recommends combining self-feeding, solid finger food and spoonfeeding because they found a small number of infants (six per cent in their study) did not meet nutritional requirements through feeding themselves and controlling their own food intake.[28]

A note on choking

Parents sometimes confuse choking with gagging. All babies have a strong gag reflex to prevent them from choking. Choking clearly looks like food is lodged in the throat and the person cannot breathe, whereas gagging involves coughing, spluttering, spitting up food and even vomiting it up. Regardless of how you choose to wean your baby, make yourself familiar with the difference between gagging and choking. When your baby is gagging, it's okay to let them get on with it as it is a harmless process. Some babies retain this reflex for longer than others. It's worth learning the basic manoeuvre for helping a choking baby.[29]

Fussy eaters and neophobia

Neophobia is the fear of new things, which can include foods and may be a natural survival mechanism from cave-dwelliing times that leads babies to be suspicious of new foods or initially to refuse them. People tend to dislike Brussel sprouts more than potatoes. This is because sprouts, cabbages and broccoli have leaves with poisonous compounds that are difficult to digest.[30]

First aid: strong patting of baby's back to stop choking

Research has found that a new food needs to be offered between 5 and 10 times before it is liked by two- to five-year-olds.[31] When two-year-olds were given new fruits or cheeses, their preferences increased with frequency of exposure. This study concludes that, 'Neophobia is only reduced as we learn that the food is safe to eat and does not cause illness', as only one taste of a new food was sufficient to increase an infant's intake of that food dramatically, from an average of 30 grams at the first feeding to 60 grams at the second feeding. This reduction in neophobia impacts acceptance of similar foods, so that if an infant had experience with one vegetable, other vegetables (but not fruits) are more readily eaten.

Other research has found that children who were breastfed exclusively for six months were less likely to develop a preference for specific food-preparation methods by 78 per cent, food rejection by 81 per cent, and food neophobia by 75 per cent.[32] Breastfeeding and introduction of complementary foods after six months of age reduced the odds of picky eating during early childhood. The foods the mother eats during pregnancy also help to expose a baby to different tastes.[33]

If you're not breastfeeding, then changing the formula-milk brand you give your baby from time to time may help to expose him or her to slightly different flavors.

What should your baby be eating?

Research has found that eating an apple stops hunger more quickly than eating an apple purée or drinking apple juice,[34] so that's another strong argument for weaning onto home-cooked foods of varying textures rather than commercially bought purées.

It is unknown whether early weaning onto potential allergens or delayed introduction of these foods has any impact on allergies in children.[35] There is some evidence to suggest that introducing solid foods while breastfeeding between the ages of 4-7 months may have a protective effect against developing food allergies and coeliac disease.[36] There is no clear evidence that eating or not eating peanuts during pregnancy, breastfeeding or early childhood has any effect on the chances of a child developing a peanut allergy,[37] although children shouldn't be given whole nuts until they're over five years old because they are a choking hazard.[38]

Other foods you should avoid are:

- Sugar. This causes tooth decay. Try using mashed banana, breastmilk or formula milk to sweeten food instead.
- Salt. Too much is bad for baby kidneys. Avoid adding salt to baby food and avoid very salty foods like stock cubes and gravy.
- Shark, swordfish or marlin. The amount of mercury in these fish can affect a baby's growing nervous system.
- Raw shellfish. This can increase the risk of food poisoning.
- Raw and undercooked eggs. Eggs that have been cooked until both the white and yolk are solid can be given to babies over six months old.[39]

Is baby rice safe?

Some parents wean their babies onto baby rice and the AAP does suggest using baby rice as one of many first weaning foods.[40] However, there are some concerns that baby rice, particularly in high quantities, may not be safe for babies due to high levels of arsenic naturally found in the rice. There is a useful summary of the concerns and the research on the British National Health Service website which concludes that: 'These results may not be representative of other baby-rice brands than those tested, or other products containing rice, including adult rice. This study also does not investigate, or suggest there to be, increased levels of risk of any cancer from consuming these levels of inorganic arsenic. This research is likely to lead to further testing of food products and reconsideration of whether legislation needs to be introduced governing the inorganic arsenic content of foods.'[41]

The argument that arsenic is safe for babies because it doesn't cause cancer may well not be sufficient for you to take the risk of relying on baby rice, especially since there are plenty of alternative nutritious foods available for your baby. But keep in mind that feeding baby rice occasionally is considered to be harmless according to current guidelines and research.

To eat or not to eat?

Want to eat a more green diet but don't know where to start? You're not alone: the European Food Information Council (EUFIC) states that: 'While consumers are aware that food production has an impact on climate change, most research shows a clear lack of consumer knowledge of sustainable diets, as well as many misconceptions about them.'[42]

Should you eat meat?

Of the total annual greenhouse-gas emissions (GHGE) that contribute to climate change, about 20-30 per cent in the US originate from dietary intake, which is mainly due to high consumption of meat and dairy products (see Figure 3). However, if meat is replaced by fruits and vegetables while keeping the total dietary energy constant, the resulting diet can also have a high GHGE as increased quantities of carbon-heavy food are being consumed. Nevertheless, the UN has recommended that people move to a meat- and dairy-free diet.[43]

A study found that 5 per cent of US citizens follow a vegetarian diet or vegan diet[44], with many vegetarians and vegans now citing environmental or health concerns as reasons.[45] There is also a type of vegetarianism now called 'environmental vegetarianism'.[46] Many more people are flexitarians, who consciously reduce their meat consumption.

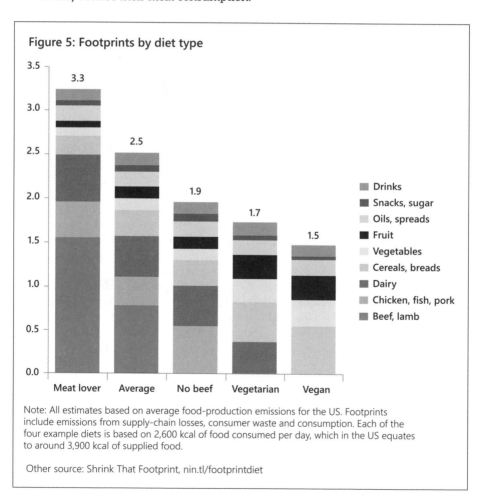

Figure 5: Footprints by diet type

Note: All estimates based on average food-production emissions for the US. Footprints include emissions from supply-chain losses, consumer waste and consumption. Each of the four example diets is based on 2,600 kcal of food consumed per day, which in the US equates to around 3,900 kcal of supplied food.

Other source: Shrink That Footprint, nin.tl/footprintdiet

Can you eat meat in an environmentally friendly way?

A very thorough review that compared assessments of the environmental impact of livestock products, including the production of pork, chicken, beef, milk, and eggs, concludes that the production of 1 kilogram of beef uses the most land and energy, and has highest global-warming potential, followed by the production of 1 kilogram of pork, chicken, eggs and milk.[47] Beef accounts for only 4 per cent of the retail food supply by weight, but represents 36 per cent of the diet-related GHG emissions.[48]

The impact of meat production is high compared with the milk and eggs because of the relatively high water content of milk and eggs. Among meats, producing beef protein has the highest environmental impact, followed by pork, with chicken protein having the lowest impact. To summarize then, the worst offenders are the methane-producing animals such as cows and sheep. Pigs and chickens, which generally eat a more mixed diet, are less environmentally destructive. Mussels are comparatively eco-friendly because they take relatively little energy to rear.[49]

Eating fish is, well, another kettle of fish. Oceanographer Sylvia Earle has been campaigning to save our seas for decades, and she argues the case so well for not eating fish that I'll simply reproduce her words here:

If people really understood the methods being used to capture wild fish, they might think about choosing whether to eat them at all, because the methods are so destructive and wasteful. It isn't just a matter of caring about the fish or the corals, but also about all the things that are destroyed in the process of capturing ocean wildlife. We have seen such a sharp decline in the fish that we consume in my lifetime that I personally choose not to eat any. In the end, it's a choice...

Our use of large-scale extraction of wildlife from the sea is profoundly detrimental to the environment... There's no question that a plant-based diet is better for you and better for the planet. If you ask me, the best thing is a plant-based diet – or a largely plant-based diet, with small amounts of meat coming from plant-eating animals.[50]

If you do eat meat, you can lower your carbon footprint by: buying only local grass-fed meat from local farmers, whose health and free-range credentials you can see for yourself; by reducing how often you eat it; and by switching from eating fish to mussels instead. If you're not prepared to change your diet, simply by taking part in Meatfree Mondays or Tofurky Tuesdays[51] or by limiting meat and dairy intake to a few times a week you will be doing the planet (and probably your body) a favor.

What about milk?

Cutting the greenhouse-gas emissions of conventional dairy milk is no mean feat. If you compare the ratios of global-warming potential to primary energy consumed, cattle-rearing is significantly more damaging than breeding pigs or chickens, as it also causes land and water degradation, deforestation, and the methane cows emit remains in the atmosphere 21-23 times more effectively than carbon dioxide (although the amount of methane a herd emits does vary to some degree depending on the breed and diet, as different diets can result in fewer methane emissions).[52] Conventional dairy farming also depletes nutrients in the ground and uses huge quantities of fertilizers which account for roughly one per cent of the world's total energy consumption – which is why some people argue that the greener option is to buy organic milk. Energy is also used to milk cows, as research in Ireland found that it takes 3.59 to 6.7 kWh of electricity per week to do so because of the milking, the cooling of the milk, and the heating of the water to wash the machines used.[53]

According to the scientific review *Environmental impacts of dairy processing and products,* 'dairy products are associated with large amounts of GHG and other environmental impacts when compared with most foods of similar nutritive content. It may be suggested that other sources of nutrients could replace milk-derived nutrients, based on our current knowledge of nutritional equivalency, and thus have significant environmental impact decreases from the lower dairy consumption rate.'[54]

What about packaging? Milk is often packaged in plastic HDPE bottles and, although about 35 per cent of them are now recycled into new bottles, this is still not enough to keep the rest out of landfill and it's not good enough to rely on recycling alone, which also uses energy and doesn't reduce use of resources. A 35-per-cent result is not 'efficient' for the planet. The greenest option is to reduce your dairy intake and buy local organic milk instead of factory-farmed supermarket milk.

In addition to this, there is the issue of phthalates, as research has found that infants with normal diets that are high in dairy products and poultry consume *double the amount of phthalates* than the Environmental Protection Agency considers safe.[55] Phthalates migrate into these foods in particular through plastic food packaging, gloves used in the preparation of food, conveyor belts during the packaging process and through the tubes used to milk cows.

A note on alternative milks

The relative impacts of non-dairy milk – such as hemp, soy, oats, rice and almond – are probably lower than the environmental footprints of dairy milk, but there is no conclusive evidence to back up this theory.[56] You can reduce problems of packaging by making your own milk at home, either using a tutorial (there are many available online) or using a milk maker. If you go with the latter option, try to buy it second-hand. People who make their own milks at home argue that this is healthier for children because it involves no added chemicals in the process, and that it saves money in the long run. However, keep in mind that certain milks should not be given to children as main milks – for example, rice, nut and oat milks – and that only breastmilk and certified formula milks are suitable for children under the age of two.

Eat local

A 'locavore' is a person who focuses on eating food that is locally produced rather than grown or manufactured overseas and transported long distances. Added to this are concerns of pollution and increase in greenhouse gases caused by the transport of food (including air miles), issues with manufacturing processes and excess packaging, and wanting to support organic, small and/or family farms over corporate agribusiness and monocrop culture. There is also the loss of nutrients during a week-long journey from soil to supermarket to consider, as an assessment by the Institute of Food Research compared nutrient levels in frozen vegetables to the nutrient levels in 'fresh' grocery-store vegetables and found that 'fresh' vegetables can lose up to 45 per cent of their nutritional value between being picked on the farm and arriving on a grocery shelf.[57] This is due to the length of time it takes for fresh vegetables to arrive at the supermarket.

Becoming a locavore involves the following:

- *Focusing on a local area*. This is usually a hundred-mile radius, but you can choose a smaller or larger area depending on where you live and your needs.
- *Starting small*. Instead of trying to source everything locally all at once, try swapping five regular food items in your kitchen for local foods, and go from there.
- *Supporting farmers' markets*. This means that your money goes directly to growers and travels a minimal distance. Find a market in your area at: localharvest.org
- *Joining the local community*. Signing up for a local vegetable box service or community-supported agriculture (CSA) scheme means that you can get to know the people who grow your food.
- *Addressing local stores*. Ask your supermarket manager where their meat and dairy is sourced from, and buy from retailers that sell food grown closer to home.
- *Taking control of consumption*. Visit a local farm to pick your own fruit and veg, stock up on local foods when they are available in abundance and preserve them for the winter as jams, pickles, and so on.
- *Buying from local vendors*. If you can't find locally grown food, you can focus on supporting local independent businesses instead. This helps to create a community and support individuals whose small businesses are likely to be more sustainable than large supermarket chains.[58]

The greenest options for improving your diet are to become a locavore, eliminate or limit the amount of meat, fish and dairy you consume, and change any animal products you do eat to ones that are locally reared and organic and therefore less environmentally damaging to produce..

A note on diets

Any diet that encourages you to reduce reliance on processed foods – for example, crisps, cereals, white breads, cakes and biscuits – is likely to lead to your feeling healthier as a result of eating more fresh foods in their stead. Examples include the 'Paleo Diet' and the gluten-free diet, both of which restrict these foods. However, eating high amounts of meat-based protein instead of processed foods is not recommended by health professionals and is linked to a range of health problems including high blood pressure and high cholesterol. Red meat in particular is problematic.[59]

The Academy of Nutrition and Dietetics does not recommend the paleo diet.[60] The low-carb diet, meanwhile, restricts carbohydrate consumption yet scientific research indicates that eating carbs are fine, and doing so in moderation can be achieved with any normal diet.[61] Although people on the low-carb diet were found to lose weight over a period of six months,[62] this did not last over the long term, and there are concerns that the diet could pose risks, including higher levels of bad cholesterol, bone loss and kidney stones.[63] The diet should not be followed for more than six months anyway.

Some people exclude gluten because in 2011 Dr Peter Gibson published a study that found gluten causes gastrointestinal distress in patients without celiac disease. However, a further study by Gibson, which took into account many other variables, led him to the *opposite* conclusion from his 2011 research.[64] Unfortunately it is the results of the former study that seem to have stuck in most people's minds.

There is no need to restrict any of these foods, and doing so for a baby's diet can have serious health consequences.

Organic versus non-organic foods

Is buying organic food better for the environment?

There is an ongoing discussion in the media about whether or not buying organic food is better for the environment. This is because they seldom look at the whole picture. Some organic practices are highly eco-friendly, but others are not – for example, organic farming doesn't use pesticides that impact local wildlife (including bees) but it does require more land use due to lower yields of crops.[65]

A life-cycle analysis of organic versus non-organic methods found that outcomes vary depending on the crops being grown; so many variables are involved that it is impossible to assess for every growing scenario.[66] However, there is no question that reducing pesticide and insecticide use on farms (as in the case of organic farming) is better for the birds and the bees. There is also no doubt that highly productive, non-organic farming systems are dependent on imported nutrients for their production through inorganic nitrogen fertilizer which damages the soil and is produced using energy from a non-renewable resource (fossil fuels). These points were not discussed in the life-cycle analysis.

Is organic food healthier?

A peer-reviewed study published in the *British Medical Journal* found that organic food is higher in antioxidants and contains lower levels of toxic metals and pesticides.[67]

Since organic farming reduces pesticide exposure,[68] each year the Environmental Working Group releases a 'dirty dozen list' of foods that you should always aim to buy organic. The group analyses Department of Agriculture data about pesticide residue and ranks foods based on how much or little pesticide residue they have been found to contain. Foods that are currently deemed to be highest in environmental contaminants and should always be purchased organically include: apples, strawberries, grapes, celery, peaches, spinach, sweet bell peppers, nectarines, cucumbers, cherry tomatoes, snap peas and potatoes, to name the worst 12.[69]

Foods that it's okay to buy non-organically include: avocados, sweetcorn, pineapple, cabbage, frozen peas, onions, asparagus, mangoes, papayas, kiwi, eggplant, grapefruit, cantaloupe, cauliflower and sweet potatoes.

Foods to avoid? Soy and palm oil

Soy gets a bad rap, but it's relatively easy to avoid, although perhaps harder for a vegan-on-the-go. However, there is evidence that if all the grain currently fed to livestock in the United States were consumed directly by people, it could feed almost 800 million people[70], so on that basis consuming meat is still more environmentally damaging than consuming soy as a vegan.

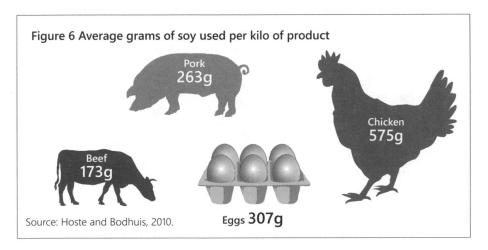

Figure 6 Average grams of soy used per kilo of product

Pork **263g**

Chicken **575g**

Beef **173g**

Eggs **307g**

Source: Hoste and Bodhuis, 2010.

The main issue with some of the soy intended for human consumption is the use of chemicals in its production,[71] as the US Cornucopia Institute's research *Behind the Bean* found that even so-called 'natural' soy products are often processed using hexane, a neurotoxin petrochemical solvent.[72] So, in the interests of health, buy organic soy. The other problem is deforestation linked to growing soy crops, so look for organic soy that is not sourced from rainforest regions and is grown as part of a crop-rotation system.

One food that is worth avoiding as much as possible to reduce your carbon footprint is palm oil. Palm oil is in everything from biscuits and spreads to shampoos and soaps, but palm-oil plantations are causing deforestation of the world's rainforests (primarily Borneo's), clearance of essential peat swamps (which store carbon), damage to biodiversity (including serious extinction risks to some species), and human rights issues, according to a report by the United Nations Environment Programme.[73]

Some companies are already ousting palm oil from their products but others have fallen for greenwashing in the form of palm oil that has been certified as deforestation-free by the new Roundtable on Sustainable Palm Oil (RSPO). Unfortunately RSPO-certified palm oil has been traced back to deforested areas as there is no easy way to be certain of where the palm oil is grown. Greenpeace has found that some of the corporate members of the RSPO are some of the most active companies involved in deforestation.[74] So avoid palm oil when you can and ask the manufacturers of your favorite products to stop using it altogether.

Summary

- There is no need to introduce solid foods to your baby before four months of age
- Most babies become ready for solids between 4-6 months of age but developmental milestones are better indicators than age
- Cook food from scratch and avoid commercial babyfoods altogether
- Go easy on the salt and sugar: babies don't need any added to their diets
- Wean using baby-led principles but don't be afraid to introduce purées too
- Never force a baby to eat; if you have genuine concerns about weight gain see a medical professional
- Learn the difference between choking and gagging and what to do in a choking incident
- Eat meals together as a family
- Offer 'disliked' foods repeatedly and in different forms
- Avoid baby rice altogether
- Reduce the amount of meat and dairy you consume as a family
- If you eat animal products, avoid the most environmentally damaging meats (cows, sheep); mussels are one of the best options
- Replace dairy milk with an alternative milk
- Become a locavore
- Support farmers' markets and sign up to a regular veg-box scheme from a local farm
- Buy organic food wherever possible, avoiding 'the dirty dozen' altogether
- Buy only organic, rainforest-friendly soy products
- Reduce the number of products you buy with palm oil in them.

1 http://pediatrics.aappublications.org/content/129/3/e827 2 *Am J Clin Nutr* February 2007 vol. 85 no. 2 635S-638S, nin.tl/optimalduration 3 http://pediatrics.aappublications.org/content/129/3/e827 4 *Am J Clin Nutr*, op cit, nin.tl/optimalduration 5 Including: BBC, nin.tl/bbc-breastfeeding and *The Telegraph*: nin.tl/telegraphweaning 6 Am J Dis Child. 1989 Sep;143(9):1066-8, nin.tl/infant-sleep 7 Association of UK Dieticians, nin.tl/bdacomplementary 8 *Am J Clin Nutr*, op cit, nin.tl/optimalduration 9 NHS choices, nin.tl/firstsolidfoods 10 NHS/Unicef, nin.tl/unicefweaning 11 Bayley N. The California Infant Scale of Motor Development. University of California Press; Berkeley, CA, USA: 1936 12 *Nutrients*. 2012 Nov; 4(11): 1575–1609, nin.tl/weaning-babyled 13 NHS, nin.tl/nhs-solids 14 '*Weaning and the weaning diet*' Report, op cit. 15 *Arch Dis Child* doi:10.1136/archdischild-2012-303386, nin.tl/nutritionalcontent 16 *Food Quality and Preference* Volume 18, Issue 8, December 2007, Pages 1023-1032, nin.tl/repeatedexposure 17 Pediatrics. 2000 Dec;106(6):1429-35, nin.tl/preschoolers-intake 18 Annu. Rev. Nutr. 1999. 19:41-62, nin.tl/foodpreferences 19 Appetite. 2006 May;46(3):318-23, nin.tl/finishyoursoup 20 Pediatrics. 1998 Mar;101(3 Pt 2):539-49, nin.tl/eatingbehaviour 21 J Am Diet Assoc. 2006 Jan;106(1 Suppl 1):S77-83, nin.tl/portions-energy 22 BMJ Open 2012;2:e000298, nin.tl/weaningstyle 23 *Nutrients*, op cit, nin.tl/weaning-babyled 24 According to Matern Child Nutr. 2010 Jan;6(1):4-18 (nin.tl/premastication) and Jared Diamond's book *The World Until Yesterday*. 25 As explained by Jared Diamond, op cit. 26 University of Colorado, nin.tl/pregnantmothers 27 Arch Pediatr Adolesc Med. 2004 Aug;158(8):792-6, nin.tl/mealsandwellbeing 28 *Maternal & Child Nutrition*, 2011; 7 (1): 27, nin.tl/nutritionalproblems 29 NCT, nin.tl/chokingguide 30 Yearbook Of Physical Anthropology 25:L-18 (1982), nin.tl/primatefeeding 31 Annu. Rev. Nutr, op cit, nin.tl/foodpreferences 32 J Am Diet Assoc. 2011 Sep;111(9):1363-8, nin.tl/picky-eating-behaviour 33 *Pediatrics*. 2001 Jun;107(6):E88, nin.tl/flavourlearning 34 *Appetite*, 2009

Apr;52(2):416-22, nin.tl/effectoffruit **35** Allergy UK, nin.tl/weaningbaby **36** NHS/Unicef, nin.tl/unicefweaning **37** Allergy UK, nin.tl/weaningyourbaby **38** NHS, nin.tl/avoidfoods **39** NHS, ibid **40** NHS, op cit, nin.tl/nhs-solids **41** NHS, nin.tl/arsenicwarning **42** European Food Information Council, nin.tl/healthysustainable **43** *Guardian*, nin.tl/meatdairyfree **44** http://www.vrg.org/blog/2011/12/05/how-many-adults-are-vegan-in-the-u-s/ **45** Mintel, nin.tl/veggienumbers **46** Wikipedia, nin.tl/enviro-veg **47** *Livestock Science*, Volume 128, Issues 1-3, March 2010, Pages 1-11, nin.tl/livestockproducts **48** http://onlinelibrary.wiley.com/doi/10.1111/jiec.12174/abstract **49** Bäljväxtakademin, nin.tl/proteinchoices **50** Ideas.Ted, nin.tl/stopfish **51** Sign up for a care package: http://www.tofurky.com/whyeatveg/tofurky_tuesdays_signup.asp **52** UN news centre, 29 Nov 2006, nin.tl/cattlegas **53** Agriculture and Food Development Authority, nin.tl/cowfootprint **54** *Journal of Dairy Science*, nin.tl/dairyscience **55** *Environmental Health* 2014, 13:43, nin.tl/food-monitor **56** *Guardian*, nin.tl/environmentalimpact **57** Gov.uk, nin.tl/fruitnutrition **58** PBS,nin.tl/bealocavore **59** NHS, nin.tl/redmeatcancer **60** http://www.eatright.org/resource/health/weight-loss/fad-diets/should-we-eat-like-our-caveman-ancestors **61** *Washington Post*, nin.tl/breadpastacarbs **62** *New Scientist*, nin.tl/studybacksdiet **63** EWG, nin.tl/pesticide-data **64** 2011 research: Forbes, nin.tl/noglutenintolerance; 2013 research: Gastroenterology, Aug 2013, nin.tl/nogluteneffects **65** Sense About Science, nin.tl/impactdebate **66** *NJAS – Wageningen Journal of Life Sciences*, Volume 58, Issues 3-4, December 2011, Pages 185-192, nin.tl/life-cycle-analysis **67** Newcastle University, nin.tl/organicvsnon **68** Boise State University, nin.tl/reduce-exposure **69** EWG, op cit, nin.tl/pesticide-data **70** http://www.news.cornell.edu/stories/1997/08/us-could-feed-800-million-people-grain-livestock-eat **71** *Guardian*, nin.tl/soyadamage **72** Cornucopia Institute, nin.tl/behind-the-bean **73** UNEP, Dec 2011, nin.tl/palmplantations **74** Greenpeace, nin.tl/forestclearance

5 Vaccines

Why we need vaccines... How vaccines work... What is herd immunity?... Eliminating disease... Are vaccines safe?... The cost of not vaccinating... Seven myths about vaccines... Why do people believe debunked and retracted theories?... What chemicals are anti-vaccinators against?... Vaccine options in the US and Canada... A note on autism

Are vaccines a green issue? In 2008 the celebrity couple Jenny McCarthy and Jim Carrey led an anti-vaccine rally in Washington DC.[1] One of the slogans they used was 'Green Our Vaccines', and supporters wore green t-shirts emblazoned with those words. Their argument: that vaccines contain toxic chemicals and need to be made green, and that they are not anti-vaccine but pro-'safe' vaccines. These statements may seem reasonable, except that vaccines are already safe according to an overwhelming majority of scientists and medical professionals, which means that McCarthy wants them to be safe by her own standards, despite telling Oprah that: 'The University of Google is where I got my degree from.'[2] Aside from lacking expertise in the areas of science, immunity, vaccines or in fact any medical topics, McCarthy's argument against vaccines has garnered support from parents in the US and abroad.

In terms of being safe and effective, vaccines are already green. For many people the definition of 'green' includes social justice, fairness, equality and quality of life. Children with measles in developing countries suffer needlessly. Losing a family member from a preventable disease or illness is a tragedy and reduces quality of life for other family members. In addition, acclaimed statistician Hans Rosling argues that, as people are lifted out of poverty, they attain better quality of life and vaccines play an important role in this.

As a green or 'alternative' parent, vaccines will be a discussion point with other parents and the purpose of this book is to give you the scientific facts and confidence to understand and discuss hot topics. Your own beliefs may be undermined if you lack knowledge on this issue that has become a major polarizing debate. So read on!

Do we need vaccines?

Thanks to a combination of vaccinations for lethal diseases (such as polio) and improved living standards (as with the widespread introduction of soap), we are no longer impacted by diseases in a way that makes them something that we fear. A similar example of their power in the past is the current spread of Ebola, which is prevalent in some countries, has created a lot of scaremongering in the media, and cannot yet be prevented with a vaccine. Some people fear that Ebola will become airborne and lead to a worldwide pandemic, despite reassurance from the scientific community that this is highly unlikely.[3] Now imagine if something like Ebola did spread across the US, so that many of us were impacted by people, particularly children, contracting it and becoming very ill or dying. This is how it used to be with the diseases that we vaccinate against today.

Let's take measles as a more relevant example to the US. If the measles vaccine had not been created then we would expect to see periodic epidemics of measles every decade or so, just like we did in the 1940s, 1950s and 1960s, with peaks of a few hundred deaths per year during epidemics.[4] During the large measles outbreaks in Europe in 2011, there were over 30,000 cases, which led to 8 deaths, 27 cases of measles encephalitis (a critical condition that causes brain swelling) and 1,482 cases of pneumonia. Not surprisingly, most of these cases occurred in unvaccinated children (82 per cent), or incompletely vaccinated people (13 per cent).[5] These are preventable tragedies. When Roald Dahl's daughter Olivia contracted measles at the age of seven in 1962, she seemed to be recovering fine at home in bed until she suddenly became very ill and died within a matter of hours. This experience prompted Dahl to appeal to other parents through a personal letter to vaccinate their children.[6]

The reduction of people being vaccinated has led to recent outbreaks around the world of diseases that had previously been wiped out, including measles in Europe, with the UK reporting more than 2,000 measles cases in 2012, the largest number in almost a decade, and in 2011 France reported a massive measles outbreak with nearly 15,000 cases.[7] Only the Democratic Republic of Congo, India, Indonesia, Nigeria and Somalia suffered larger measles outbreaks that year.[8] In the US, the prevalence of whooping cough shot up in 2012 to nearly 50,000 cases. Last year cases declined to about 24,000 through use of the vaccine.[9]

Today, measles kills about 122,000 people each year around the world.[10] Some of the people who die are healthy individuals, others have weak immune systems or are infants who are too young to have the boosters required for maximum immunity from the disease. Medical intervention prevents outbreaks to a large degree, but highly infectious diseases can still spread easily in pockets of unvaccinated groups, as is occurring presently with children across the US contracting measles. Some do get better alone at home, but they have to be quarantined and kept under close watch. Others have to go into hospital quarantine, and they need medical treatment – with chemicals – all for the sake of avoiding the chemicals that are in vaccines in the first place. The blunt truth here is that no-one cares about side effects from treating mumps or rubella when the alternative is that the child may die. Three million children's lives are saved every year by vaccination,[11] and three million still die every year from preventable illnesses around the world because they do not have access to immunizations.[12] Scientists and health professionals want this number to be zero. At the time of writing, an unvaccinated six-year-old boy in Spain is critically ill in hospital with the first case of diphtheria in the country in 28 years.[13] His mother has now reportedly had his younger sister vaccinated. It's not only better for the environment to have your children vaccinated, it's the ethical option too.

How vaccines work

If you've forgotten your high-school biology lessons, here's a quick refresher. Vaccines work by triggering the immune system to produce its own antibodies, as though the body has been infected with a disease, and this is called 'active immunity'.[14] If the vaccinated person then comes into contact with the disease itself, their immune system will recognize it and immediately produce the antibodies they need to fight it.

In many cases, vaccination provides lifelong protection against a disease, but how long a vaccination lasts depends on various factors. Some vaccines provide very high levels of protection – for example, MMR provides 90-per-cent protection against measles and rubella after one dose. Others are not as effective – the typhoid vaccine, for example, provides around 70-per-cent protection over three years. Flu vaccines are prepared to immunize people against the virus that epidemiologists expect will rear its head in the next flu season.

Newborn babies are naturally protected against several diseases, including measles, mumps and rubella, because antibodies have passed into them from their mothers via the placenta.[15] This is called 'passive immunity', and it lasts for a few weeks or months, except in the case of measles, mumps and rubella, where it may last up to one year, which is why the MMR jab is given to children just after their first birthday.

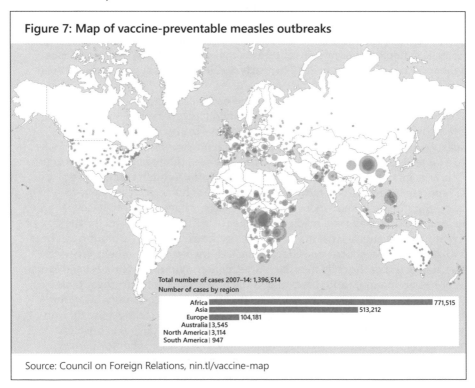

Figure 7: Map of vaccine-preventable measles outbreaks

Total number of cases 2007–14: 1,396,514
Number of cases by region

Region	Cases
Africa	771,515
Asia	513,212
Europe	104,181
Australia	3,545
North America	3,114
South America	947

Source: Council on Foreign Relations, nin.tl/vaccine-map

In the journal *Nature,* Yale University researchers explain how a common ingredient in many vaccines stimulates and interacts with the immune system to help provide protection against infectious diseases.[16]

Figure 7 is shocking when you consider that the global outbreaks of measles from 2008-2014, (along with mumps, rubella, polio, and whooping cough) could have been mostly, if not entirely, prevented by vaccines that are available in the US. The Centers for Disease Control and Prevention (CDC – the US vaccine regulatory body) estimates that 164,000 people around the world die from measles each year,[17] yet the US has recently seen a drastic increase in whooping cough, which causes around 195,000 deaths per year.[18] Outbreaks also become more likely because anti-vaccinators tend to 'cluster'.[19]

The majority of the global deaths from these diseases occur in impoverished regions with no or little access to vaccines, and a child in the developing world is 10 times more likely to die of a vaccine-preventable disease than a child in an industrialized nation.[20] In the case of developed countries like the US and Canada, they shouldn't exist at all.

What is herd immunity?

Put simply, some people cannot be vaccinated due to certain medical conditions, allergies or a compromised immune system. A compromised immune system means that they have a higher risk of complications from contracting preventable diseases than completely healthy individuals, and may not be able to fight off any disease alone. So if there's an outbreak, your child might recover fine with medical help, but an immuno-compromised child or adult is likely to suffer. So having your child vaccinated means that you are reducing the likelihood of an outbreak, which creates a 'herd immunity' for the most vulnerable members of society.

Nowadays, thanks to herd immunity, the risks of not vaccinating are different. For a disease like polio they're practically non-existent: to catch it in the US a person would have to be in contact with someone from parts of the world where polio is still endemic. On the other hand, polio is part of the regular childhood vaccination program in the US because if no American children were immunized then it would be easy for one traveler to bring an infection from abroad to start a devastating nationwide polio epidemic. Sadly, polio recently returned to Europe due to lack of vaccination.[21]

Eliminating disease[22]

As more members of a population are vaccinated, a disease can be eliminated completely and end the vaccination program as the number of potential victims is reduced. The more infectious the disease is, the greater the number of people who have to be vaccinated to keep the disease under control. Measles is highly infectious, which is why there have been recent outbreaks of the disease. At least 90 per cent of children have to be immune in order to stop the disease from spreading.[23]

Vaccines aren't always 100-per-cent effective, so it's still possible for a vaccinated child to become infected by a disease. This is why the vaccine debate is so polarizing: because, while the 'anti-vaccinators' argue that they don't want chemicals in

Figure 8: Measles cases pre- and post-vaccine in the US, 1950-2007

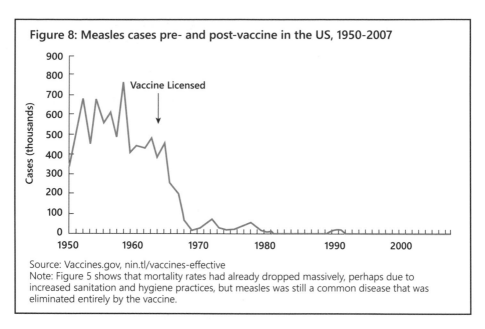

Source: Vaccines.gov, nin.tl/vaccines-effective
Note: Figure 5 shows that mortality rates had already dropped massively, perhaps due to increased sanitation and hygiene practices, but measles was still a common disease that was eliminated entirely by the vaccine.

Figure 9: Vaccines work: India from 1975 to 2012

VACCINES WORK:
INDIA

DISEASE	BEFORE VACCINES # of cases		AFTER VACCINES # of cases		% DECREASE	
Smallpox	·1975	23,546	·1976	0	100%	eradicated
Polio	·1980	18,975	··2012	0	100%	no wild polio virus case since 2011
Tentanus Neonatal	·1988	11,849	·2012	588	95%	
Total	·1980	45,948	·2012	2,404	95%	
Diphtheria	·1980	39,231	·2012	2,525	94%	
Pertussis (whooping cough)	·1980	320,109	·2012	44,164	86%	
Measles	·1980	114,036	·2012	18,868	84%	

💉 = 10,000 reported cases
🔔 = 0 reported cases

drastically reduced

References

• Rabindra Nath Basu, R.N., Ježek, Z. & Ward, N.A. "The Eradication of smallpox from india." World Health Organization, South-East Asia Regional Office. 1979.

• WHO VPD Monitoring System. Last Updated 20 Oct 2013. Accessed 20 Oct 2013: http:apps.who.int/immunization_monitoring/globalsummary/incidences?c=IND

• Polio refers to all polio cases (indigenous or imported), including polio cases caused by vaccine derived polio viruses (VDPV); it does not include cases of vaccine-associated paralytic polio (VAPP) and cases of non polio acute flaccid paralysis (AFP).

Source: Johns Hopkins IVAC, nin.tl/polioprogress

their children, the pro-vaccinators can see the huge implications of this choice for society and global health. People who choose not to vaccinate their children against infectious diseases are putting not only their own children at risk, but also other people's children.

The GAVI Alliance (formerly The Global Alliance for Vaccines and Immunization) was formed in 1999 to ensure that every child in the world is protected against vaccine-preventable diseases. Thirty years ago, one in four children died before the age of five. Today, that number is one in ten. Almost 75 per cent of the world's children are now vaccinated against the six main killers (measles, polio, diphtheria, whooping cough, tuberculosis and tetanus), and the number of deaths from these illnesses and diseases has more than halved since 1980. Vaccination has been so successful that we now rarely see the worst killers like diphtheria, polio and preventable types of meningitis – see Figures 8 and 9.

A note on boosters

Some vaccinations require boosters to provide maximum immunity, but they vary depending on the vaccine. In the case of chicken pox (varicella), one dose of the vaccine is 85-per-cent effective at preventing any form of varicella, and almost 100-per-cent effective against severe varicella. Studies have found that the two doses of vaccine are 88- to 98-per-cent effective at preventing all varicella.[25]

What are the risks of vaccinating vs not vaccinating?

If you are weighing up the relative dangers of highly infectious or lethal illnesses and vaccines that carry small risks of side effects, then the least risky option is to vaccinate your children.[26] In terms of both serious and mild side effects from vaccines, anti-vaccinators often argue that these are kept hidden from parents, but in fact they are available to read both online and in package inserts for vaccines, just as you can for any medication, which all carry risks of side effects. On the other hand, measles, polio and other such diseases carry high risks of complications and can result in death. Having measles has also been found to predispose children to other infectious diseases for a number of years afterwards.[27]

Also, allergic reactions are listed as side effects but a child can be allergic to any ingredient – for example, soy, nuts, eggs – that has been used in the vaccine, so this is not to do with supposed 'hidden chemicals' in vaccines but to do with allergic history that runs in families. It does not apply to all children, but to specific risk groups, which scientists are getting better at identifying. Children who are identified as allergic beforehand are told not to get specific vaccinations.

Statistics show that you are more likely to die or become injured in a car crash than from a vaccine – any vaccine. In the list of the 25 most likely causes of death the top four are heart disease, cancer, stroke and land vehicle accidents, but are you going to stop driving? Is it worth the risk? If only the anti-vaccinators put their energy into building safer roads, the world would be a safer place for our children than it currently is.

Are vaccines safe?

Parenting is always about weighing up risks versus benefits, as nothing is completely safe. Children are at risk whenever they climb trees, whenever they travel anywhere by car, or ride a bike. A very, very small number of children are injured by vaccines.[28]

Vaccines do contain chemicals, but your entire body is also made up of chemicals.[29] Everything we eat is made of chemicals. Vaccines contain very small, safe amounts of chemicals that are naturally occurring in our environment, and also some that aren't found naturally. They have been tested rigorously for their safety.

The cost of not vaccinating

At the end of the 2012–13 measles epidemic in the UK, there was a total of 1,455 measles notifications for the whole of Wales, 664 of which were in Swansea.[30] A total of 88 people were hospitalized for measles infection during the epidemic. One death was reported: a 25-year-old man suffering from pneumonia brought on by measles infection died in April 2013.

The cost associated with treating the infected people and controlling the outbreak exceeded £470,000. Meanwhile, research that looked at the impact of outbreaks in Sydney, Australia, concludes that: 'the estimated total cost… of containing this particular case of measles was A\$2,433, with staff time comprising the major cost component. Considerable effort and resources are required to manage measles outbreaks. The total cost of this outbreak to the PHU alone is likely to have exceeded A\$48,000.'[31]

This time, money and resources could be used in so many other vital areas of medicine – as demonstrated in Chapter 2 on birth.

Seven myths about vaccines

WHO summarizes the main myths behind the fear of vaccinations on its website,[32] but here is a summary of the most discussed aspects.

Myth 1: Vaccines cause autism

In 1998, Andrew Wakefield and a dozen associates released a research paper in The Lancet claiming to have linked the measles, mumps, and rubella (MMR) vaccine to the onset of autism through studying 12 anonymous children.[33] This was big news and it hit the headlines. However, other scientists who tried to replicate Wakefield's findings couldn't find a MMR-autism link.[34] It was later discovered that Wakefield had made the results up, and that he had a conflict of interest,[35] but not before creating a decade-long health crisis in the UK related to fear of the MMR vaccine.[36] Prior to this, the MMR vaccine had been given to all children at a year old since the late 1980s in the UK, and had almost eradicated measles and rubella from the country. It had not caused a correlating increase in autism – see Figure 10.

What was the conflict of interest? Investigative reporter Brian Deer, who won awards for his work on the Wakefield case, found that Wakefield had been secretly funded to create evidence against the vaccine two years before the Lancet

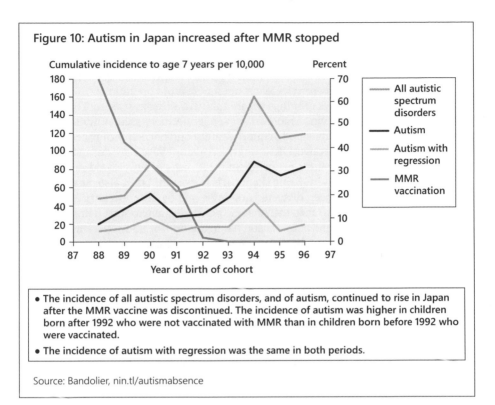

Figure 10: Autism in Japan increased after MMR stopped

Cumulative incidence to age 7 years per 10,000 — Percent

- All autistic spectrum disorders
- Autism
- Autism with regression
- MMR vaccination

Year of birth of cohort

• The incidence of all autistic spectrum disorders, and of autism, continued to rise in Japan after the MMR vaccine was discontinued. The incidence of autism was higher in children born after 1992 who were not vaccinated with MMR than in children born before 1992 who were vaccinated.

• The incidence of autism with regression was the same in both periods.

Source: Bandolier, nin.tl/autismabsence

paper was published.[37] Wakefield had been hired to attack the MMR vaccine by a lawyer, Richard Barr, who hoped to raise a lawsuit against drug companies that manufactured the vaccine. Wakefield and Barr were successful in this regard, as they made a lot of money out of the scandal they created. Brian Deer also found that in 1997, almost nine months before the press conference at which Wakefield called for single vaccines, he had filed a patent on his own supposedly 'safer' single measles vaccine, which only stood any prospect of commercial success if parental confidence in MMR was damaged.[38]

In 2010 an ethics review board concluded that Wakefield had falsified the data in his report.[39] This led to an immediate retraction of the original paper and he was struck off as a doctor. The board branded Wakefield as 'dishonest', 'unethical' and 'callous'. They found him guilty of three dozen charges, including the abuse of developmentally challenged children. Does this sound to you like someone who speaks for children's rights?

However, like lethal diseases, fear is contagious and it spreads quickly. Whereas people in underdeveloped countries are crying out for vaccines,[40] some people in the developed world now see all vaccines as dangerous and as issues of personal choice – even though the original scandal only involved the MMR vaccine in the first place. Other public figures, such as Bob Sears, Jenny McCarthy and Joe Mercola, have taken up the anti-vaccination fight, keeping the scaremongering and lies very much alive.

Myth 2: 'Big Pharma' profits from you vaccinating your children

Proponents of alternative medicine such as Dr Joe Mercola regard the pharmaceutical industry – 'Big Pharma' – as conspiring to promote entirely worthless products purely for profit. Yet Mercola himself runs a business selling alternative health products at staggering prices: clearly not a non-profit operation.[41]

It's essential to be skeptical of things we are told, including in science. Thanks to that skepticism about vaccines, more trials were done, more studies undertaken, more questions asked and answered about the safety and necessity of vaccines. Even so, the results still point overwhelmingly in favor of vaccinations, and it's easy to look up the relevant information about this (from peer-reviewed sources, not people's blogs) to learn why. Being skeptical is important but it also means that when the information has been dissected and reviewed by different parties, all the evidence has to be taken into account. At some point we have to start being skeptical about being skeptical! At some point reason has to abound, or else superstitions and conspiracy theories have free rein. This is how science works.

In fact, pharmaceutical companies do not significantly profit from vaccines, and from 2013 to 2014 not a single vaccine made it into the top 50 profitable drugs. The number-one-selling vaccine only made it to number 76.[42]

Myth 3: Non-vaccinated children are healthier

There has been a lot of noise about supposed 'studies' that claim to have found unvaccinated children to be healthier than vaccinated ones.[43] All of this noise is about the same study, which wasn't a study at all, as it had no basis in science. It was actually an **online survey** in which a homeopathic doctor in Germany, Andreas Bachmair, asked parents of unvaccinated children to complete an **anonymous form**. He then compared the rates of illnesses from these forms to those that are published for all children (by the German Health Interview and Examination Survey for Children and Adolescents or Kinderund Jugendgesundheitssurvey, KiGGS) and concluded that unvaccinated children are healthier. Does that sound thorough to you?

In contrast, a real scientific study in Germany looked at medical records from KiGGS to determine 'whether unvaccinated children and adolescents differ from those vaccinated in terms of health'.[44] Among the diseases they looked were allergies, eczema, obstructive bronchitis, pneumonia and otitis media, heart disease, anaemia, epilepsy, and attention deficit hyperactivity disorder (ADHD). Unsurprisingly, this second study found that unvaccinated children were more likely to get vaccine-preventable diseases. However, it also concluded that 'the prevalence of allergic diseases and non-specific infections in children and adolescents was not found to depend on vaccination status'.

Finally, a study of vaccinated and unvaccinated children found that children who received immunizations against diphtheria, pertussis, tetanus, Hib and polio within the first three months of life had fewer infections with vaccine-related and unrelated pathogens than the unvaccinated group.[45]

So, since these unvaccinated and vaccinated children had the same incidence of allergies, pneumonia and other conditions, plus unvaccinated children were also more likely to have vaccine-preventable diseases like measles and mumps, vaccinated children are actually healthier than unvaccinated children.

Myth 4: Vaccines overload and weaken a child's immune system

Some anti-vaccinators worry that that the normal vaccine schedule is too difficult for a child's immune system to cope with,[46] but multiple studies have shown that vaccines do not weaken a child's immune system.[47] As soon as a baby is born, he or she comes into contact with a large number of different bacteria and viruses every day. In fact, research has found that if a child was given 11 vaccines at the same time, it would only use a thousandth of their immune system.[48]

A very detailed review by a team led by Dr Paul Offit in 2002 clearly explains the science behind immunity and vaccines in detail and concludes that: 'Current studies do not support the hypothesis that multiple vaccines overwhelm, weaken, or "use up" the immune system. On the contrary, young infants have an enormous capacity to respond to multiple vaccines, as well as to the many other challenges present in the environment. By providing protection against a number of bacterial and viral pathogens, vaccines prevent the "weakening" of the immune system and consequent secondary bacterial infections occasionally caused by natural infection.'[49]

So again, the opposite of the myth is actually true here.

Myth 5: Natural immunity is a viable alternative to vaccines

Measles is so infectious that, in the days before vaccines, practically everybody without immunity caught it, so it spread through the population until everyone who had recovered from it had gained immunity and then there would be a few years of respite until enough new children had been born without immunity to sustain another epidemic.[50] Many people refer to this as 'natural immunity', but natural immunity from measles only works when everyone in a population contracts measles. When this happened in the past, the people who could not recover died. That's why the vaccine was created, to reduce death rates, and it has done so. So yes, we could allow diseases such as measles, polio and whooping cough to resurface, and allow the 'weakest' or unluckiest people to die. But we don't condone this as a society, thankfully.

Some anti-vaccinators argue that building natural immunity through breastfeeding can stave off things like polio. Unfortunately, before formula milk was invented and breastfeeding was the only way to feed babies, diseases like polio were still rife. There is no evidence that eating a good diet will prevent disease either. As one unvaccinated, frequently ill adult writer says: 'If you think your child's immune system is strong enough to fight off vaccine-preventable diseases, then it's strong enough to fight off the tiny amounts of dead or weakened pathogens present in any of the vaccines.'[51]

Myth 6: Vaccines are linked to higher infant mortality rates

Anti-vaccinators often try to link infant mortality rates (the number of deaths per 1,000 live births) together with the number of vaccines that a country gives its children. If vaccines weren't dangerous, they argue, then why would the infant mortality rate in the US be higher than the infant mortality rate in some countries that don't protect their children from as many vaccine-preventable diseases? Many experts have pointed out that simply comparing infant mortality rates between different countries isn't reliable because they don't all count live births in the same way.[52] CDC states that premature births, which affect as many as one in nine babies, are behind the higher infant mortality rates in the US.[53]

In any case, infant mortality rates have decreased by at least 12 per cent in the US since 2005, which shows that any supposed mortality-vaccine link cannot exist.

Myth 7: Vaccine shedding spreads viruses

Vaccine shedding is not an issue with most vaccines, including live vaccines,[54] but a few vaccines, including those for rotavirus and oral polio, can shed the vaccine strain of virus after it is given to a child.[55] The oral polio virus is no longer used in the UK. However, you can shed the virus without actually contracting rotavirus or polio infection, or giving it to anyone else, and this is really only a problem if you're in contact with someone who is immuno-compromised.

On the other hand, Flumist is a nasal-spray flu vaccine that can shed, but it is rare for this actually to cause flu symptoms in someone, even a person with a weakened immune system (unless they are severely sick).[56]

The Medical Advisory Committee of the Immune Deficiency Foundation is not worried about vaccine shedding from vaccinated children overall, but they talk about creating 'a "protective cocoon" of immunized persons surrounding patients with primary immunodeficiency diseases', and state that except in the case of the (no longer administered) oral polio vaccine, close contacts of patients with compromised immunity 'can receive other standard vaccines because viral shedding is unlikely and these pose little risk of infection to a subject with compromised immunity.'[57]

It is also possible for a person to catch chicken pox from the vaccine but this happens extremely rarely: between three times in 21 million vaccinations[58] and five times in 55 million vaccinations.[59]

Strangely, there are anti-vaccinators who argue that vaccines are bad because of the supposed infections spread by vaccine shedding, but they then take their children to chicken-pox parties in order that they will catch the disease.[60]

Why do people believe debunked and retracted theories?

This question is beyond the scope of this book but one reason is that many people simply don't understand the way that science works. This led, for example, to an Italian court ruling that MMR vaccination caused autism in a child in 2012,[61] based on the retracted *Lancet*/Wakefield paper,[62] and also to convicting six scientists of manslaughter for failing to correctly predict the magnitude of the 2009 earthquake![63] These examples are known as the 'Dunning-Kruger effect' in science: a case of individuals who are unaware of how poor their grasp of the topic is but think that they know best.[64]

There's a lot of unkindness between pro- and anti-vaccinators, and mean words further no cause. Some parents are scared into not vaccinating by supposed experts like McCarthy and Mercola, while others distrust the medical industry based on negative past experiences. People do change their minds: earlier this year a mother of seven became pro-vaccination after her unvaccinated children all caught whooping cough.[65] Whoop.

What chemicals are anti-vaccinators against?

Aluminum is added to most vaccines to make them more effective. Aluminum is also found naturally in drinking water and infant formula milk.[66] It has not been found to be harmful to children in the quantities used in vaccines, and children consume more aluminum in natural human breast milk[67] than they get from vaccines.[68]

Antifreeze, or ethylene glycol, is not an ingredient in any vaccine, but has been confused with polyethylene glycol, a completely different chemical, by anti-vaccination campaigners like Jenny McCarthy.[69]

Formaldehyde is a residual ingredient (meaning that most of it is removed) that is used to inactivate toxins, viruses and bacteria that might contaminate the vaccine during production. Our bodies naturally make formaldehyde and there is 50 times more formaldehyde in a pear than in any vaccine.[70] It is only harmful in high quantities (as with many other things, including water[71]).

Monosodium glutamate (MSG) is used as a stabilizer in a few vaccines. MSG is found naturally in seaweed and has been found to be safe for human consumption except for a few very select individuals with specific health problems.[72] MSG is safe according to the Food and Drug Administration, the World Health Organization and the Food and Agriculture Organization of the United Nations.

Thiomersal is a mercury-containing preservative that is added to some vaccines. Anti-vaccinators claim that mercury causes autism but research[73] shows that it doesn't and the WHO and the US Food and Drug Administration (FDA) agree that thiomersal is safe. However, thiomersal has not been used in most vaccines since 2001 with the exception of some flu vaccines.[74]

What are the vaccine options?

The 5-in-1-vaccine, also known as the DTaP/IPV/Hib vaccine, is one of the first vaccines a baby is given. It's a single injection which protects your baby against five serious childhood diseases: diphtheria, tetanus, whooping cough (pertussis), polio and Hib (Haemophilus influenzae type b).

The chicken pox (varicella) vaccine is used to prevent varicella-zoster virus, the herpes virus that causes flu-like symptoms and itchy blisters that can last for weeks, lead to permanent scarring, and in some cases lead to bacterial infection of the blisters which has to be treated with antibiotics and can result in swelling of the brain.[75]

Worryingly, chicken pox has become a childhood 'rite of passage' in anti-vaccination circles in some parts of the US, where people throw 'chicken pox parties' to help spread this potentially lethal disease. In Belgium, where children aren't routinely immunized against the disease a young girl died in April 2012 from severe complication of chicken pox, leading her mother to set up an association to inform parents of the dangers of chicken pox and to encourage them to seek vaccination for their children.[76]

Chicken pox is much more serious when caught by babies, pregnant women, immuno-compromised people, and previously unexposed adults (approximately 5-14 per cent of adults with chicken pox develop lung problems like pneumonia).[77] Like all herpes viruses, varicella never truly goes away, but can be reactivated at any time as shingles, which carries the risk of some very serious complications.[78]

There has been a safe and effective vaccine against varicella since 1988, and it has been part of routine childhood vaccinations in the US since 1995, now included in the routine MMR course (known as MMRV[79]). The World Health Organization includes the varicella vaccine on its list of essential medicines.[80]

For a detailed, science-based overview of the topic of chicken pox and vaccination visit the Nature Nurture Parenting blog.[81]

The seasonal influenza, or flu, vaccine is used to prevent a very serious group of illnesses that can result in hospitalization or death.[82] For those worried by rare but potential convulsions occurring in children following seasonal flu vaccination,[83] these convulsions are not dangerous, as nearly all children who have a febrile seizure recover quickly and are healthy afterwards.[84]

Febrile seizures can happen with any condition that causes a fever, and up to five per cent of young children will have at least one febrile seizure, usually when they're ill.[85] The most common age range to have a febrile seizure is 14-18 months and the recommended age for the first doses of MMRV, MMR, and varicella vaccines is 12-14 months old, which is why it's important not to delay recommended vaccine schedules.

The Hib/Men C vaccine is given as a single injection to boost a baby's protection against two different diseases: Haemophilus influenzae type b (Hib) and meningitis C, which are potentially fatal and can both cause meningitis and septicemia (blood poisoning).

The HPV (Human papillomavirus) vaccine is an immunization program to prevent cervical cancer. Launched in 2008, the HPV vaccine is offered routinely to girls aged 12-13, and those under the age of 18 are also able to access the vaccine free of charge. Currently there are two vaccines on offer – one covering two strains of cancer-causing HPV, the other also including protection against genital warts. The theory is that vaccinating girls will also indirectly protect boys.

This vaccine is not routinely offered to adults because it doesn't treat HPV, but can prevent it, so the aim is to give it to girls before they are likely to have an infection, in other words before they become sexually active. Statistics show that the infection of college and university-aged women within 24 months of becoming sexually active increases to 40 per cent.[86] That's a lot.

Again, the HPV vaccine has been blamed for causing all kinds of illnesses, but rigorous testing has not found any of the accusations to be true.[87]

Men B vaccine is not used to prevent meningitis B which is a serious illness.[88] One family whose daughter suffered serious disabilities after contracting Men B in the

UK is helping to lead the fight for a free Men B vaccine there.[89] It's important for parents to be aware of the symptoms of meningitis.[90]

The Men C vaccine protects against infection by meningococcal group C bacteria, which can cause two very serious illnesses: meningitis and septicemia. Babies have their first Men C vaccination when they are three months old, and a second dose of Men C at 12 months, which is combined with the Hib (Haemophilus influenzae type b) vaccine and is called the Hib/Men C booster.

The MMR (measles, mumps and rubella) vaccine requires two doses to complete the course.

Measles, mumps and rubella are highly infectious and can have serious, potentially fatal complications, including meningitis, swelling of the brain (encephalitis) and deafness.[91] Mumps can cause excruciating pain and sterility for adolescent boys and young men. Tetanus can cause agonizing spasms and take up to a year to recover from.[92]

Outbreaks of measles have been rising in recent years in unvaccinated pockets of population. There is a lot of useful amount of information on the CDC website regarding the many scaremongering claims that the MMR vaccine is not safe, so take a look if you're worried and want to know the science and truth behind the safety of the vaccine.[93]

The single mumps vaccine that was once available in the UK was removed after it was found[94] to be ineffective.

The Pneumococcal vaccine (pneumonia vaccine) protects against pneumococcal infections which, at their worst, can cause permanent severe brain damage, or even kill.[95]

The Rotavirus vaccine has been recently introduced in the UK because rotavirus is the leading cause of severe diarrhea in infants and children worldwide, leading to more than half a million deaths each year in children under the age of five.[96] A small risk of intestinal problems caused by the vaccine was found but nevertheless the benefits of the vaccine outweigh this small risk. An oral vaccine against rotavirus infection is given as two doses for babies aged two months and three months alongside their other routine childhood vaccinations.

The Whooping cough (pertussis) vaccine is essential because pertussis is quite common and babies who are too young to receive vaccinations are at greatest risk. Young babies with whooping cough often become seriously unwell and are admitted to hospital because of their illness. In 2010, 10 children died in California in the worst whooping-cough outbreak to sweep the state since 1947.[97]

Pregnant women can protect their babies from whooping cough by getting the vaccination, ideally between 28 and 32 weeks of pregnancy, although they may be given the vaccine up to 38 weeks.

Ironically (considering the MMR-Autism scare) the Rubella vaccine (part of MMR) has actually been found to *prevent* ASD.[98]

Delayed vaccination

Some people delay giving the MMR vaccine because they think their child isn't physically ready for it. However, if you delay it past 15 months, research has shown that the likelihood of side effects for some vaccines is actually doubled.[99] So parents who worry about potential side effects actually increase the likelihood of them happening. This is why it's essential to follow official guidelines regarding when vaccines should be administered.

The CDC immunization schedule lists the recommended timings for all of the listed vaccinations on its website.[100]

A note on autism

One reason people cling to Wakefield's original argument is because they say that autism rates are increasing around the world. However, rates aren't believed to be actually increasing, it's simply that improved diagnosis is leading to more people being assessed as autistic. In fact, it's not just improved diagnosis, but changed diagnosis – in other words, what is considered autistic today was not necessarily called autistic when we were children.

Also, symptoms of autism often appear around the age that the MMR jab is given, which propagates the myth. This research concludes that 'Evidence that early signs of autism are present during infancy, before obvious symptoms are noticed, indicates that the onset of autism occurs well before vaccination.'[101]

Japan stopped giving the MMR vaccine between 1988 and 1992 but a study of 30,000 children found that, in the city of Yokohama, the number of children with autism *continued to rise* after the MMR vaccine was replaced with single vaccines.[102]

In fact, the biggest link to autism has been found to be air pollution.[103] If only people were up in arms about that instead of a supposed autism-vaccine link.

One last thing. Autism is not a deadly condition. It's a set of character traits that some people have and some people don't, and it's offensive to say that there is something 'wrong' with children if they are autistic (supposedly because of a vaccine). Nevertheless, this is what many anti-vaccinators argue, and organizations like Talk About Curing Autism are offensive to autistic people. Take the time to read the powerful article at nin.tl/betterthanmeasles written by an autistic person who finds it upsetting and unfair that people would prefer their children to contract measles than to risk being autistic.

Conclusion

While this chapter is a very comprehensive summary of why you should vaccinate your child, t's also important that you don't just take my word for it. All the studies I have mentioned are referenced. I have come across many anti-vaccination articles that claim science is on their side, yet when you look up the 'studies' they cite, they are actually just blog posts on other anti-vaccination websites, or results from very biased surveys on their own website. They call this science. But it's not the same as scientific research by people who have no conflict of interest regarding their reasons for doing the research. If you appreciate the value of science, you will already be pro-vaccination.

It's important that we learn from history too. Read about Andrew Wakefield. Read about the diseases we vaccinate against, about their symptoms and the complications and death rates. We are lucky to live in a country where we have access to these life-saving vaccinations, which reduce unnecessary suffering for our children, their parents and families. But we have to defend them or they won't continue to work.

Summary

- Vaccines are safe, they work – and they are green.
- The risks of not vaccinating are far greater than the very small risks associated with vaccinating
- Vaccinated children are generally healthier than non-vaccinated children
- Vaccines do not overload children's immune systems
- Vaccines should not be delayed by alternative vaccination schedules
- Vaccinations do not cause autism.

1 Science-Based Medicine, nin.tl/toomanytoosoon 2 *The Nation*, nin.tl/false-equivalence 3 Scientific American, nin.tl/airborne-ebola 4 Based on previous government figures: nin.tl/measlesdeaths 5 About Health, nin.tl/anti-vaccine-myths 6 Roald Dahl website, nin.tl/oliviasdeath 7 NPR health blog, nin.tl/vaccinefears 8 Centres for Disease Control, nin.tl/measlescontrol 9 CDC, nin.tl/incidencegraph 10 About Health, nin.tl/avoidingmeasles 11 Vaccine, 1999 Oct 29;17 Suppl 3:S120-5,nin.tl/vaccinationimpact 12 NHS, nin.tl/global-vaccination 13 IFLScience, nin.tl/diptheriaSpain 14 NHS, nin.tl/vaccines-work 15 See 67 16 NIH/National Institute of Allergy and Infectious Diseases, nin.tl/vaccine-booster 17 CDC, nin.tl/aboutmeasles 18 CDC: nin.tl/pertussis-cases 19 NPR, nin.tl/clusterrisk 20 NHS, op cit, nin.tl/global-vaccination 21 http://qz.com/493730/polio-is-back-in-europe-because-people-arent-vaccinating-their-children/ 22 NHS, op cit, nin.tl/global-vaccination 23 NHS, op cit, nin.tl/vaccines-work 24 CDC, nin.tl/vaccines-faqs 25 CDC, nin.tl/varicellaprotection 26 NHS, nin.tl/vaccine-benefits 27 National Public Radio, 7 May 2015, nin.tl/measlesmystery 28 More information on these few but specific cases available at the data sheet for the MMR vaccines: nin.tl/merckdata and nin.tl/oxford-journals 29 For an excellent explanation of the chemicals found in vaccines, see The Nib: nin.tl/nibcartoon 30 Wikipedia, nin.tl/swanseaepidemic and nin.tl/swanseanote 31 Commun Dis Intell Q Rep. 2013 Sep 30;37(3):E240-5, nin.tl/sydneymeasles. 32 WHO, nin.tl/myths-facts 33 *The Lancet* (retracted), nin.tl/mmr-autism, 34 Lancet. 1999 Jun 12;353(9169):2026-9, nin.tl/noevidence 35 Brian Deer, nin.tl/lancetsummary 36 Brian Deer, nin.tl/uptakestats 37 Brian Deer, op cit, nin.tl/lancetsummary 38 Brian Deer, nin.tl/lancetscandal 39 *BMJ* 2011;342:c5347, nin.tl/mmrcase 40 *Vaccine*, op cit, nin.tl/vaccinationimpact 41 Dr Mercola online store, nin.tl/mercolashop 42 Skeptical Raptor, nin.tl/profitsconspiracy 43 Science blogs, nin.tl/respectfulinsolence 44 Neurologica, nin.tl/vaccinehealth 45 J Infect. 2000 Sep;41(2):172-5, nin.tl/morbidityreduced 46 The Pediatric Insider, nin.tl/alternativevaccine 47 *Pediatrics*. 2002 Jan;109(1):124-9, nin.tl/parentsconcerns and Immunol Rev. 1990 Jun;115:11-147, nin.tl/protectionunit 48 NHS, nin.tl/vaccinevideo 49 *Pediatrics*, nin.tl/scienceimmunity 50 Useful herd immunity demonstration available op12no2.me: nin.tl/immunityherd 51 *Slate*, nin.tl/unvaccinated 52 Science-Based Medicine, nin.tl/falserelationship 53 CDC, nin.tl/maternal-infanthealth 54 About Health, nin.tl/vaccineshedding 55 Polio Global Eradication Initiative, nin.tl/oralvaccine and Immunization Action Coalition, nin.tl/rotavirusvaccines 56 NHS, nin.tl/childrensflu and About Health, nin.tl/recognizeflu 57 Immune Deficiency Foundation, primaryimmune.org 58 MedTV, nin.tl/chickenpox-after-vaccine 59 Immunization Action Coalition, nin.tl/varicella-qanda 60 Seattle Children's Hospital, nin.tl/chickenpoxparties 61 *Daily Mail*, nin.tl/mothersvictory 62 Read an overview on Forbes, nin.tl/courtrulings 63 Forbes, nin.tl/earthquakecase 64 Forbes, op cit, nin.tl/courtrulings 65 *Independent*, nin.tl/motheropinion 66 About Parenting, nin.tl/formulasecond 67 *Science of the Total Environment*, Volume 170, Issue 3, 29 September 1995, Pages 165-170, nin.tl/harmfulcontents 68 *Pediatrics* December 1, 2003 vol. 112 no. 6 1394-1397, nin.tl/harmfulcontents 69 She states: 'People don't realize that there is aluminum, ether, antifreeze, still mercury, in the shots.' Science-Based Medicine, nin.tl/antivaccinevoice 70 Quote: 'The human body produces and uses formaldehyde as part of the process of metabolism. The amount of natural formaldehyde in a 2-month-old infant's blood (around 1.1 milligrams in total) is ten times greater than the amount

found in any vaccine (less than 0.1 milligrams). A pear contains around 50 times more formaldehyde than is found in any vaccine.' University of Oxford's Vaccine Group, nin.tl/vaccine-ingredients **71** *Scientific American*, nin.tl/watercankill **72** Smithsonian, nin.tl/msgtruth **73** *Pediatrics* January 2009; 123:1 e164-e169, nin.tl/bobsalternative **74** CDC, nin.tl/thimerosal **75** NHS, nin.tl/chickenpox-complications **76** ESTW, estwvzw.be **77** NHS, op cit, nin.tl/chickenpox-complications **78** NHS, nin.tl/shingles-complications **79** CDC, nin.tl/mmrv-information **80** WHO, nin.tl/essentialmedicines **81** Nature Nurture Parenting, nin.tl/varicellaguide **82** CDC, nin.tl/flubasics **83** MHRA, nin.tl/fluvaccinesafety **84** CDC, nin.tl/febrile-seizures **85** *Guardian*, op cit, nin.tl/vaccinedenied **86** Quote: 'Studies of newly acquired HPV infection demonstrate that infection occurs soon after onset of sexual activity. In a prospective study of college women, the cumulative incidence of infection was 40% by 24 months after first sexual intercourse. HPV 16 accounted for 10.4% of infections.' CDC, nin.tl/ **87** http://www.nhs.uk/conditions/vaccinations/pages/hpv-vaccine-cervarix-gardasil-safety.aspx **88** Meningitis Research Foundation, nin.tl/menbvaccine **89** BBC, As this family found: nin.tl/bbc-menbreport **90** NHS, nin.tl/meningitis-symptoms **91** NHS, nin.tl/mmrvaccine **92** *NZ Herald*, nin.tl/tetanusagony **93** http://www.cdc.gov/vaccinesafety/vaccines/mmr/mmr-studies.html **94** BBC, nin.tl/bbc-health **95** NHS, nin.tl/pneumococcal **96** CDC, nin.tl/cdc-rotavirus **97** *Scientific American*, nin.tl/vaccination-talk **98** BMC Public Health. 2011 May 19;11:340, nin.tl/rubella-autism **99** *Scientific American*, nin.tl/delayrisk **100** http://www.cdc.gov/vaccines/schedules/ **101** *Paediatr Child Health*. 2002 Nov; 7(9): 623-632, nin.tl/autism-risk **102** *New Scientist*, nin.tl/japanautismrises and *Journal of Child Psychology and Psychiatry*, Vol 46, Issue 6, pp 572-579, Jun 2005, nin.tl/autismincidence **103** IFL Science, nin.tl/airpollutionautism

6 Diaper science: getting to the bottom of it all

Why it's confusing... Disposable diapers: what they're made of; potential concerns; what to buy... Eco-diapers: how disposable are they really?... Types of reusable or cloth diapers... Try before you buy... Join a community... Drying diapers... Elimination communication, or going diaper-free... Wet wipes... A note on 'potty training'

If someone had told me, before I became a parent, how hard it would be to get my head around choosing the greenest option for clothing my baby's bottom, I would have laughed at them. In fact, working out what the greenest diaper option is for your baby is not so funny. For the parent who wants to be environmentally friendly, there is a lot of information to sort through on the topic, some of which is inaccurate. A lot of it is just a major pain in the butt. However, there *are* clear, green, achievable options available for the aspiring green parent, so bear with me while we go through the options here.

Why it's confusing

Much of the confusion in the diaper debate comes from a misunderstanding of the environmental cost involved with producing reusable cotton diapers versus the eco cost of not using them, as discussed in a popular *Washington Post* article[1]. This can be likened to the results of a report that was published by the UK Environment Agency (EA) in 2005.[2] This report, titled 'Life Cycle Assessment of Disposable and Reusable Diapers in the UK' was designed to calculate and compare the environmental impacts of reusable diapers and disposable diapers.

However, the report was not very thorough in some key areas and it incorrectly concluded that 'there was no significant difference between any of the environmental impacts'. First, much of the research used in the report comes from the Environment Agency's own surveys which use small samples of the UK population and have been poorly conducted. To quote the journalist Leo Hickman: 'Why did the Environment Agency survey 2,000 parents using disposable nappies [the British word for diapers] compared with just 117 using washables, meaning that (taking into account the weighting towards those using older-style nappies which use more cloth), many of the assumptions are based on the habits of just 32 people?... [The Report] can't help but leave me suspecting the influence of the mighty nappy manufacturers in all this somewhere.'[3]

Aside from this data bias, there are other reasons to mistrust the results of the UK Environment Agency report. [If this British-sourced information doesn't interest you, skip to the end of Figure 11.] The report argues that the production of disposable diapers is a more significant environmental factor than the waste factor – in other words, the fact that disposables end up in landfill sites or are incinerated.[4] The report does not assess the many problems associated with landfill sites besides releasing methane, and it assumes that there is a positive benefit to landfill waste which is energy captured for electricity. That's a bit like saying it's okay to waste food so long as you're composting it: the logic doesn't quite stand up.

- The report only looks at the environmental impacts of two types of reusable diapers: flat diapers used at home, and commercially laundered prefold diapers. Other types of reusable diaper exist but were not assessed.

- The report looks at the environmental impact of having diapers commercially laundered, which means having them washed and delivered to your doorstep by an outside laundry agency. The EA surveyed 22 laundry service providers, but did not assess how much of the reusable diaper community uses this cleaning service and uses it regularly. I surveyed 205 cloth diaper users from all over the UK through two sources: a popular cloth diaper organization[5] and a parenting magazine,[6] and of the 205 people only 6 had ever used a commercial laundering service for cloth diapers – and even those not for every diaper wash and not necessarily with every child.[7] Most people were unaware that such a service existed.

- The report takes into account the mainstream varieties of washing detergent that damage the environment and calculates their impact, including that of softeners. It fails to consider eco-friendly detergent and softener options for washing cloth diapers. In fact, many reusable diaper companies state that softeners should not be used as they can damage reusable diapers.[8]

- The report assumes that all cloth diapers are purchased new, which significantly increases the report's assessment of the environmental impact of making reusable diapers overseas, shipping them to the UK and sourcing cotton crops for their manufacture (see Figure 11).[9] Of the 205 people I surveyed from all over the UK, 164 said they bought some of their diapers second hand.

- The report does not take into account the end of the life of cloth diapers because 'Assumed nappies are sold for reuse and wraps/pants are disposed of in domestic waste. No burden has been allocated for final disposal of nappies.' This is confusing because cloth diapers can't all be both purchased new and reused at the same time.

- The report assumes that the cotton used to make cloth diapers is non-organic, therefore it takes into account all the related pesticide use and water toxicity created by the production of non-organic reusable diapers. However there are many different brands of organic reusable diaper available to buy in the UK and the US.

- The report works on the assumption that parents wash cloth diapers at 60-degree temperatures and above (see Figure 11) using inefficient washing machines, and concludes that the highest impact of cloth diapers is from electricity usage from washing and drying them, while assuming the use of the highest-energy methods possible for both these things.[10] Many cloth diapers cannot actually be washed at 60 degrees and manufacturers recommend 40-degree washes only.

- The report assumes that diapers are often tumble dried,[11] even though tumble dryers are possibly the most high-energy kitchen appliances available in the home and many cloth-diaper users choose to avoid them in order to be as green as possible.[12]

Due to these and other criticisms, the UK Environment Agency reviewed and slightly updated its report,[13] but it did not address all the listed factors, and failed to do so before the media ship had sailed into reporting that reusable diapers are just as bad for the environment as disposable diapers.

In addition to this, there are many myths about reusable diapers out there because research into them is limited and manufacturer claims vary widely.

Now that we know why people are confused about the eco-credentials of reusable diapers, let's look at how different types of diapers tally up in the environmental arena.

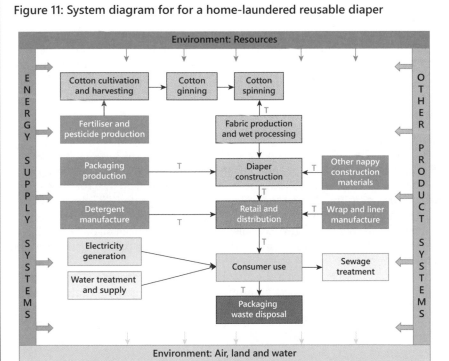

Figure 11: System diagram for for a home-laundered reusable diaper

Note: The main transport steps (marked with a T) between processes and life-cycle stages have been included in the assessment. Waste management associated with production and the supply chain has also been included.

Disposable diapers

Disposable diapers create millions of tons of waste each year,[14] and every child is reliant on them for two-and-a-half to three years (or more) from birth, which is a huge cost to the environment and to your purse. Disposable diapers are sent to landfill sites or for incineration for disposal, neither of which is an environmentally friendly option.

What they're made of

Manufacturing disposable diapers is a high-energy process. Each diaper contains a number of components, including:

- A shaped pad enclosed in a waterproof casing
- A liner made of the plastic polymer polypropylene, which protects the baby's skin from wetness
- A pulp-based tissue layer of wood fluff pulp
- A super absorbent polymer (SAP) that draws in and contain the baby's urine and feces
- A plastic bottom layer
- Non-woven fabric, derived from non-renewable petroleum
- Elastic strands and adhesives.[15]

According to research undertaken by the University of Vermont, wood fluff pulp is created 'from long-fiber softwoods, which are conifers such as pines, cypresses and spruces. Many conventional diaper brands purchase their fluff pulp from companies that use a whitening process that is elemental chlorine free (ECF), where chlorine gas is not used, but the chemical chlorine dioxide is used in bleaching.'[16]

Potential concerns

When Greenpeace Germany discovered that there was a toxic chemical called tributyl tin (TBT) in many items on sale in Germany, including disposable diapers, Scientific Analysis Laboratories Ltd confirmed their findings.[17] As a result of this, the Women's Environmental Network undertook chemical analysis of disposable newborn diapers in the UK and also found that they contained TBT, an endocrine-disrupter that is also known as the 'gender bender hormone'. TBT is known to disrupt sex hormones in shellfish, and WEN called for its removal from all diapers in 2000 when the studies were undertaken. I contacted WEN for an update on this issue but received no response.

There are also concerns that using disposable diapers increases a baby's scrotal temperature, which may impact on future fertility and the general health of the baby. While evidence in this area is lacking, it's worth noting that diapers are not subject to government controls or independent testing and disposable diaper manufacturers do not need to disclose the contents.[18]

I'll stop there.

Whether you're looking at health impacts or environmental impacts, disposable diapers are undoubtedly damaging, and anything you can do to reduce your reliance on them will certainly impact the planet, and will potentially impact your child's health as well. However, I appreciate that disposable diapers are the easiest option for most parents, and this information is not intended as a condemnation. Please use it as an invitation instead to attempt forming new habits surrounding diaper usage. Even if you can only commit to using one or two less disposable diapers a day than usual, you will still significantly reduce the environmental and health impact of clothing your baby's bottom.

What to buy

If you choose to use disposable diapers, look for the greener brands. There are more natural options available that are kinder to the environment and are made from biodegradable materials, and these will be looked at in the next section. If you can only buy mainstream brands of disposable diapers, then buying disposable diapers that are as efficient as possible will mean that your baby gets through less of them.

Eco-diapers? Compostable, biodegradable or eco-disposable diapers

'Eco-diapers' are considered to be disposable diapers that biodegrade much faster than conventional disposable diapers, or diapers that break down into harmless matter when composted.

Why it's confusing

There's no doubt that biodegradable diapers are more environmentally friendly than disposable diapers in terms of what they contain and how they are sourced, but critics say that they can be *worse for the environment than conventional disposables in terms of disposing of them. This is because when organic matter rots in an oxygen-free environment like a landfill site, it produces methane, and methane is actually a more harmful greenhouse gas than carbon dioxide.*[19] According to Chris Goodall, author of *How to Live a Low Carbon Life*, this production of methane from biodegradable waste makes it much worse for the climate than non-biodegradable waste.[20] A study also found that biodegradable products are not necessarily more environmentally friendly when disposed of in landfills because a *slower* rate of biodegradation is actually more environmentally friendly. [21]

In its assessment the Environment Agency report takes into account the fact that landfill methane in the UK is captured in a process called energy recovery, and used as an energy source for heating and electricity.[22] This captured gas is the UK's largest source of green energy,[23] with high efficiency.[24] However, not every landfill site in the world is eligible for energy recovery, as there are strict requirements that have to be adhered to on a landfill site before it is eligible, and only *some* of the methane released can be captured from any site, so it's not a sustainable solution to keep creating more on the basis of energy capture.

How eco are they really?

All matter can be composted and will eventually break down over time given the right conditions, so the term 'biodegradable' diapers is a little misleading. As mentioned previously, sending compostable matter to landfill sites isn't green, as it can't break down due to a lack of oxygen in landfill conditions.[25] Anything that gets sent to landfill, whether it is described as degradable or not, will take a very, very long time to break down, releasing methane as a by-product. Otherwise it is sent for incineration, which is just as bad for the environment and releases toxic chemicals and pollution into the atmosphere.[26] Landfill sites are deliberately managed to minimize degradation because of the problems of excess methane production.

Composting diapers on the other hand, when done properly, does break them down quickly due to the presence of oxygen, but this does not pose an environmental problem as the composting process releases significantly fewer greenhouse gases than would occur in a landfill site.[27]

Can you home-compost eco-diapers?

Some eco-diapers do specifically break down into plastic-free harmless matter, but there is no thorough analysis available to tell us which brands actually deliver this. In order for diapers to truly become nutrient-rich compost, you need to compost them yourself at home so that there is good moisture content in the decaying matter and enough access to oxygen.[28] In order to do this you'll need a lot of space in your back garden, as babies get through a lot of diapers, wear them for years, and the diapers need to be left alone for years to break down. A single compost bin in the garden will get full quickly, but with several larger compost bins used on a rotating basis you may be able to compost many of them yourself.

Compostable diapers need to spend years decomposing because of potential pathogens in them. According to Joe Jenkins' book on composting human waste products titled *The Humanure Handbook*, fecal matter needs to be heated to a certain temperature through a hot-composting process in order to destroy all potential pathogens.[29] If you're not prepared to commit to this long-term project, it's best to leave the diapers to break down in the compost bin for as long as possible (Jenkins recommends a minimum of two years[30]) and then avoid using the finished compost for growing edible plants.

Recommended eco-disposable brands

According to various websites, the best eco-disposable diaper brands are: Nature Babycare diapers, Moltex diapers, and Bambo Nature diapers. These diapers are considered to be the greenest because they are free from bleaching agents, TBT and perfumes.

Which disposable diapers should you choose?

If you're mostly concerned with the *potential* impacts of standard disposable diapers on your child's health, then you'll want to opt for the eco-diapers with the highest ratings.

If you're 100-per-cent sure that you're never going to stop using disposable diapers on your children, the *greener* option for you may be to buy the most efficient (most absorbent) mainstream brand diapers available. I say 'greener' here because although disposable diapers cannot be considered to be green, eco-diapers do get points for containing sustainable wood pulp and other environmentally friendly materials, and they usually haven't been bleached.

In terms of disposal, the jury's out. If you want to be as green as possible while using disposable diapers, buy compostable brands and opt for a home-composting system as far as possible. Anything else will harm the environment. Sorry.

Reusable or cloth diapers

There is now a large range of reusable diapers available in the US and these come under the banner of 'reusable', 'washable' or 'cloth' diapers but they include all manner of contraptions designed to suit your baby's needs. Entering the cloth diaper world can leave any parent drowning in a quagmire of information, so let's look at the basics of what's on offer.

A word on terry diapers. These were used by our great-grandparents back when disposables weren't an option and they were basically cloth towels that were folded around the baby's bottom half and sealed with a large safety pin. They needed to be soaked in sterilizing solution between uses. Doing so is no longer necessary today.

Types of reusable diaper

All-in-ones. These are shaped, fitted diapers made of a waterproof outer layer and an absorbent inner layer. They are fastened with Velcro or popper fastenings. All-in-one diapers are generally considered to be as easy to use as disposable diapers as no folding or pinning is required and they go straight from use to the washing bucket.

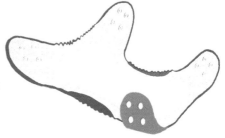

All-in-one

These might be the easier diapers to start out with to get a feel for using reusable diapers. My firstborn didn't get on with them because her legs were too chubby for shaped diapers to fit around, but they did give us a nice introduction to reusable diapers.

Shaped or fitted diapers. These are similar to all-in-ones, as they do not require folding and are very easy to use. The diaper is shaped to fit your baby, just like a disposable but a little more versatile as it fastens with poppers or Velcro. However, these diapers are designed to hold urine, so they still require an outer waterproof cover. The cover will not need to be replaced every time the inner layer is changed, but will if it gets wet.

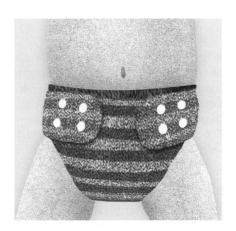

Shaped or fitted

The shaped diaper is very convenient but can sometimes have a longer drying time due to the thickness of the material. Choose diapers made from a quick-drying fabric like cotton.

Flat diapers. These come in two types, terry diapers and prefold or 'wrap-around' diapers. They require folding around the baby's bottom, which in my experience is easy to do, but you also need to use a separate outer waterproof cover as liquid will soak through the flat diaper. Some flat diapers come with Y-shaped fasteners as well.

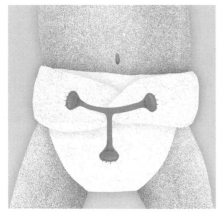

Terry

Terry squares are old-school diapers that are basically cotton towels to be folded around your baby's bottom and fastened with a large safety pin or plastic grip. They are still a popular choice for some parents today. Terry diapers no longer require pre-soaking to be sanitized like they used to, as the efficiency of modern washing machines and detergents means that this stage can be left out. You have to learn how to fold terry towels but once you've mastered that it's really easy to do, and there are various tutorials for different folding techniques available online for free. It may be easier to ask someone who uses cloth diapers to walk you through a few different folding techniques. A waterproof diaper cover goes over the folded terry square.

Prefold diapers are rectangular diapers that fold into a pad without the use of a separate fastening, and slot into a waterproof cover. The prefold diaper does not need to be folded around the hips as it is designed to be slim fitting.

Prefold

For this reason, my chubby daughter did not get on with prefolds at all, but they suited my skinnier second-born perfectly.

Flat diapers are generally the cheapest reusable diapers on offer.

Keep it simple

There is a wide range of reusable diapers available and it can be tempting to try many different types. Some boast that they are made of bamboo or hemp that has been grown in a more eco-friendly manner than cotton diapers; others claim to hold more fluids because they are made of microfiber, and so on. I suggest avoiding these until you're sure of the type of diaper you want to proceed with first, as you risk getting bogged down with all the choices otherwise. Also, there are many variables involved with these different kinds of diaper that are difficult to assess in terms of eco-impact, so don't fall for manufacturer claims.

For example, hemp and bamboo may be grown more sustainably but both materials take a longer time to dry than cotton, which is a significant point here in parts of the US where the weather does not allow year-round line drying, which means that we may have to use energy to dry our clothes. Fleece may be super soft against your baby's skin and quicker to dry but it doesn't allow your baby's skin to breathe. I'm not saying that these diapers have greenwashed claims, but it's difficult to see the bigger picture with any of them, so rest assured that using ordinary cloth diapers will already reduce your impact on the environment in a significant, positive way compared with disposable diapers, and anything else should be taken with a pinch of salt.

Are they safe?

Modern cloth diapers do not require soaking in bleach; in fact this can ruin most diapers. There doesn't appear to be a scientific consensus on the temperature that cloth diapers need to be washed at to kill pathogens, but many people use 40-degree washes without reporting any problems and since liners are designed to catch any fecal matter it should be sufficient to wash the actual diapers at 40 degrees. One report suggests that short 55-degree washes kill any pathogens[31], but high-temperature washes can damage modern diapers and since your baby won't be putting cloth diapers in his/her mouth, blitzing diapers is not something to worry about.

Things to consider: cost

- What can you afford? The cheapest option is to use flat cotton terry towels that you fold yourself and fasten using safety pins or plastic diaper grips. You'll need to buy a large number of these, but you'll only need a few separate waterproof covers to put over the top, as they won't need changing each time.
- Prefold diapers are a little more expensive, but they may suit some babies over terry diapers because of their shape.
- Shaped fabric diapers cost more and you'll need to buy separate waterproof covers to put over the top, but these won't need replacing with every diaper change.
- All-in-one diapers are the most expensive type on offer, as they require washing every time they are dirtied. Because they are made of an absorbent material and several layers, they can take longer to dry than other reusable diapers, so you'll need to invest in a large quantity of them as well.

Choosing sizes

- Reusable diaper sizes are based on the weight of your baby. These are similar to disposable diaper sizes, which are small (7-20 lb), medium (20-30 lb) and large (35 lb+).
- Most reusable diapers are available in two sizing options: birth-to-potty and sized.
- Birth-to-potty diapers are one size but are adjustable so they are designed to fit all babies at any stage from small to large, 7-35 lb.

Try before you buy

As babies vary so much in chubbiness and length, you may want to try out a few types and brands of reusable diapers to see what best suits your baby before investing in a batch of chosen diapers. I recommend doing a trial run first. You can do this by buying a few basic diapers second hand or contacting local reusable diaper users and asking to try a few different diapers out. In my experience, the cloth-diaper community can be very generous and will happily lend or give away diapers to new cloth-diaper converts. If that's not an option where you live, some local authorities are actively promoting cloth diapers as part of their waste-reduction strategies, so it's worth doing some research.

Once you've decided which diapers to go with, you can easily pick them up online in bulk through websites like eBay or second hand through local diaper initiatives and groups. Don't be deterred by the different choices on offer – the chances are, the colourful fancy-looking cloth diapers were coloured using dyes that you want to avoid anyway. Simple plain cotton ones will do, and will allow your baby's skin to 'breathe', which helps to prevent diaper rash and won't cost the Earth.

If you must buy new reusable diapers, invest in organic diapers and locally made diapers where possible, or have a go at making your own, to keep the environmental cost down. Alternatively, *Ethical Consumer* has an excellent breakdown of reusable diapers with the least environmental impact, which rates the top brands of organic cloth diapers as: Bummis, Cottontail, Imse Vimse, Itti Bitti D'lish, Mother-ease, Poplini, Swaddlebees, and Totsbots, which all score 19/20.[32] *EC* also has a thorough guide on reusable diapers available through its website for a small fee.

As with disposable diapers, another factor to take into consideration is how absorbent, comfortable and well-fitting the reusable diapers you invest in are. To assess this for yourself, take a look at the *Which?* guide that was compiled from survey results from experienced cloth-diaper users, which lists the best reusable diaper brands as FuzziBunz (67 per cent score), Bumgenius (62 per cent), Blueberry (62 per cent), Bright Bots (60 per cent), and FLIP Diaper (60 per cent).[33]

Join a community

Other parents can be very helpful in advising on diaper use, so look for a local reusable diaper community. They tend to come under the umbrella of 'natural parents' or 'babywearers' who attend sling meets. Otherwise your midwife or health visitor may be able to put you in touch with other green parents. Popular online forums like Mumsnet and Netmums are useful resources to help gauge opinions of other parents who are already using different types of diapers.

You will also need: liners

Invest in biodegradable liners to reduce the number of soiled diapers you need to wash and decrease your eco-impact even further. The way they work is simple – you put a liner in the cloth diaper, so that the diaper itself escapes contact with feces and saves the need to do a high-temperature laundry wash. Most liners can also be flushed straight down the toilet, which makes them no different than using toilet paper on your baby's bottom. Look for perfume-free, unbleached liner brands where possible.

You will also need: boosters or inserts

Once you have chosen your diapers, you may want to buy or make some 'boosters' or 'inserts' to pad them out. These are simply wads of shaped cloth that are inserted into reusable diapers to soak up more urine and to stop the actual diaper from getting wet. Although some kinds of diapers are sold as not needing boosters, I suggest investing in them anyway because they will significantly reduce how many diapers your baby gets through, and they can be handy for overnight use or when you're out and about, as they are easy to change without having to change the entire diaper. Alternatively, you can make your own, as they're really only wads of absorbent cloth.

Washing diapers

Of course, washing reusable diapers uses water, and this cannot be avoided. Luckily, most new washing machines are now fairly energy efficient, but if you can invest in an A-grade energy-efficient washing machine, even better. Much of the environmental impact here depends on the temperature at which you wash your diapers. Diapers soaked with urine will be fine at 30 degrees and, as mentioned earlier, a high-temperature wash (55 degrees) is only needed to destroy potential pathogens in diapers that have come into contact with actual feces.

Keep it simple

Cloth diapers do not require soaking in chemical solutions, and the Go Real diaper information service says that doing so with treatment powders can damage modern fabrics and stop Velcro from working.[34] What you will need instead is a few buckets with tight lids for storing diapers in between washes. An easy way to adapt to this process is to keep a bucket for soiled diapers that require hot washes next to the changing mat, with a clear label on it to distinguish it from the bucket for wet diapers that can be washed at a normal temperature. Keep this one on the other side of your changing mat. You can also line the bin with a drawstring mesh material or mesh bag so that the diapers can easily be transferred to the washing machine with ease and without dirtying the bin. Wash them when you have a full load and you'll significantly reduce your baby's carbon footprint (check your washing machine manual to see how much a load can weigh – many machines take up to 11 lb/5 kg[35]). If you want to wash diapers before collecting a full load, wash it on a half-load instead.

Drying diapers

Line-drying is the greenest option for drying cloth diapers, but as this is weather-dependent it is not always possible in North America, so...

The next low-impact option is to invest in a simple *heated indoor drying rack* placed in a room where a window can be left open to keep the humidity down, or used alongside a dehumidifier. It works by emitting a very low amount of heat, enough to dry your clothes overnight but not enough to significantly increase your energy bill. Buy a foldable drying rack so that it can easily be packed away when not in use.

If you don't have room for a drying rack and you are using cloth diapers in winter, you may have to resort to the old method of drying them on *indoor radiators* when they are on anyway, using a purpose-made drying rack that sits on the radiator. Another option is to use a rack or fire guard in front of an indoor fire if you have one.

Tumble dryers are the ultimate environmentally damaging option, as they use vast amounts of energy and will significantly increase your electricity bill because of this.[36] It's worth checking how much energy your machine uses by investing in or borrowing an electricity usage monitor which attaches to the machine and tells you how much energy it uses. Gas tumble dryers are the most energy-efficient types of driers, although few people in the US invest in them. Don't bother buying a new A-grade drier, though, as the carbon cost of its manufacturer will cancel out what you save by using the more energy-efficient model.[37] Your clothes will last longer if you avoid tumble drying them too.

If you have to use a tumble dryer, you can do a few things to lower the environmental impact. These are:

- Use the maximum spin cycle for your laundry, or the rinse option at the end, to ensure that the diapers are as dry as possible before putting them in the dryer.
- Remove the diapers from the dryer when they're still slightly damp and let them dry naturally, as the final part of tumble drying is the most energy-intensive.
- Clean the lint filter after every use, as a blocked filter stops the air from circulating freely, which means that clothes take longer to dry.
- Keep your tumble drier in good condition by seeing to repairs when they are needed, as this should extend its lifetime and improve efficiency as well.

Aim for fuller washing loads, wear clothes more than once before washing them, and check forecasts so you can line-dry whenever they're clear.

That's all you need to cloth diaper a baby. Remember, our ancestors probably used strips of material such as animal hides, and many people in the world still do. In the same vein, some parents make their own cloth diapers at home out of recycled materials like strips of cotton, which are then folded and safety-pinned together like they used to do in the olden days. So don't get caught up in buying lots of new cloth diapers and spending a fortune on them. Sewing is not one of my key skills, so rest assured that if you're able to go down this route, you're greener than me!

The financial cost of diapers

Choosing reusable diapers over disposables can halve the amount of cash the average parent spends on diapers according to Waste & Resources Action Programme (WRAP).[38] You can make even more savings if you hold onto the diapers and use them for a second baby, sell them when you're done with them, or swap them with other parents for larger sizes.

Elimination communication, or going diaper-free

The term 'elimination communication' was coined by Ingrid Bauer, who argues that many cultures in the world do not use diapers at all, and claims that these diaper-free babies do not have 'accidents' like they do here in the western hemisphere.

Elimination communication, also called 'diaperless technique' is considered to be one of the more 'radical' parenting options a parent can choose. Basically it means that your baby is diaper-free for some or most of the time, that mum and dad learn to spot when baby drops hints that s/he wants to urinate or defecate, and that a routine is formed where the parent gets the baby to the toilet or potty on time following these signals.

Why they do it

There's no question that this option is radically better for the environment than using diapers. Although it may require more clothes (and carpet) washing due to diaper-free accidents, and of course toilet flushes mean water usage, elimination communication still requires much less water and energy usage than is involved in the process of creating disposable and reusable diapers, since the need for any purpose-made diapers is – excuse me – *eliminated* by the technique.

Parents who practice elimination communication report that it increases their bond and communication with their baby, helps baby to get used to and control his/ her bowels and bladder through getting used to the feeling of needing to urinate and defecate, and that it is the cheapest option for dealing with baby bottoms. Elimination communication is certainly kinder to a parent's wallet than having to buy diapers, but unfortunately there is no research available to support the former claims.

Many proponents of elimination communication also argue that children used to be out of diapers before the age of two, while the average age is now between the ages of three and four,[39] and that the diaperless technique allows children to toilet train earlier than the current average age. Again, there is no research to support this, but it remains a widely held belief in the diaper-free parenting community.

How does it work?

Practically speaking, parents who practice elimination communication lie or sit their babies on washable sheets or old towels with waterproof layers underneath. An old shower curtain will suffice for the transition period, with a cloth layer on top. The cloth will soak up any urine or feces, while the plastic layer will protect the floor underneath. By the time baby is mobile, a parent who has been using elimination communication should be able to tell when baby is ready to 'go' and get him or her to the toilet or potty, which should prevent accidents from occurring.

This may sound tricky, but consider it to be no different than knowing your baby's cues for hunger – you probably work your day around feeding your baby without even thinking about it consciously or realizing that you do it. Parents who use elimination communication simply extend this to do the same with their babies' toilet habits as well.

Is it for you?

A professional document on the topic of elimination communication titled *Discussion: Toilet Training in Early Childhood* looks at different cultural and social practices that impact toilet-training habits.[40] It offers insight into a topic that is under-discussed in North America and provides a more holistic view of the factors involved with teaching children to use the toilet.

Just as babies learn new habits through diaper-to-potty-to-toilet practices, parents can learn new habits for the way they care for their babies. If this option is appealing to you, dive straight in and see if going diaper-free is for you. Read Bauer's book on the subject, *Diaper Free: The Gentle Wisdom of Natural Infant Hygiene*, and join a diaperless community. There are many online forums to help you get started and for support. Any reduction in the number of diapers you use will certainly reduce your family's impact on the environment, so even if you only go diaper-free for a few hours a day, this will help the environment. What have you got to lose?

Wet wipes

Single-use wet wipes are certainly popular and convenient. Unfortunately, most wet wipes contain **parabens**, a group of preservatives including Methylparaben, Ethylparaben, Propylparaben, Isopropylparaben, Butylparaben, Isobutylparaben and Benzylparaben. Parabens have been found in human breast tumors, although there is no solid evidence that they cause cancer.[41] Another study found that propylparaben affects male reproductive functions, including sperm production.[42]

Wet wipes are also very damaging to the environment. A baby might be wiped 12 or more times as day before being toilet trained, and these wipes end up in landfill sites.[43] For manufacture, wipes require resources including wood pulp, plastics, energy, water and chemicals, and in some cases they are perfumed with questionable chemicals as well. Wet wipes do not do your purse strings any favors either, but we have come to rely on them because they are easy to use and convenient. For the green parent, there are other options.

Can they be composted?

As with compostable diapers, unless you have a hot-compost system at home, you can only compost used wipes in the garden if you're sure you won't use the compost for a few years. This will give any potential pathogens time to break down, and wipes will need to be composted amongst a good range of organic matter in order to break down properly. However, this may be a more achievable goal than composting actual diapers as wipes take up little space in a compost bin.

Reusable wipes

A low-impact alternative to commercial wet wipes is to make your own reusable wipes at home, out of recycled materials like old towels and clothes. Cut them into strips of baby-sized and regular-sized washcloths and keep them in a small cloth wipe bucket next to the changing station. Natural soap and essential oils may seem like nice additions but they are not necessary and some essential oils like lavender and tea tree are actually endocrine-disrupters ('gender benders') and should not be applied to children.[44]

Keep a bottle of water next to the changing table, and a bowl. Add fresh water to the bowl and use the home-made wipes to clean baby up every time s/he does a poo. For urine, you don't need to wet wipe at all, or you can use the edge of a cloth diaper if you're using reusables.

If you're using cloth diapers, these home-made reusable wipes can be washed as part of your usual routine. To keep environmental impact low, the same rules apply here as they do with cloth diapers – avoid small washes, don't iron your wipes, and so on. The only potential issue here is that wipes used on feces may require a high-temperature wash, although arguably washing reusable wipes at higher temperatures is still more green than buying commercially made wet wipes.

Choose the best brands

If you simply can't give up wet wipes altogether, you can instead opt for the greener alternative of unscented, biodegradable and compostable wipes with organic ingredients. According to Shop Ethical! the most eco-friendly, bottom-friendly baby wipe brands are: Nature Babycare by Naty, Gaia by Gaia Skin Naturals, Swisspers, Wotnot by ECOdirect, and Sorbies.[45]

A note on 'potty training'

Modern disposable diapers contain a highly absorbent material called polyacrylate, which is used to absorb many times its own weight in liquid and essentially works by drawing moisture away from the baby's bottom. For this reason, some parents argue that babies who do not predominantly wear disposable diapers tend to potty train earlier and with ease as they learn when they need to go from the wetness felt in the non-disposable diaper. There is no evidence to support this claim, but it's worth keeping in mind if you're keeping your baby in diapers and s/he is ready to stop wearing them.

On the other hand, while it's true that the sooner you 'potty train' your baby you can swap diapers for toilet flushes which are, arguably, more eco-friendly, putting pressure on a child to potty train when he or she is not ready has been shown to make the transition more difficult and actually take longer.[46] The best way to proceed is to watch for cues that your child is ready to transition, then follow his or her lead. Most children are ready to begin the process between 24 to 27 months, but some children become ready earlier or later than that.

Some parents prefer to avoid the term 'training' altogether since it implies that the parent is teaching the child to use the potty. They prefer the term 'child-led' instead as the child learns to communicate his or her need for the potty to the parent. If you think your child is ready to give up diapers but s/he doesn't grasp using the toilet after a few attempts, go back to using diapers and try it again in a few days or weeks. An average time frame for success in toilet training is three to six months, so it's a slow process and many children continue to wet the bed occasionally at night until they are five years old.[47] Make sure you have a waterproof mattress, or waterproof cover to protect the mattress.

Once you're free of diapers, you're out of the 'environmentally red zone', because no more diapers equals lots of green.

Signs that your child is ready to use the toilet include the following.

- S/he is able to communicate his or her needs to you
- S/he can follow simple verbal instructions
- S/he responds positively to praise
- S/he shows signs of independence, of wanting to do more things for him/herself
- S/he copies your behavior or the behavior of older children

- S/he shows signs of knowing when s/he needs to go to the toilet
- S/he gets upset as soon as her/his diaper is dirty
- S/he has longer periods with a dry diaper, which means that her/his bladder is able to store more urine.

Since disposable diapers can *potentially* hinder the toilet transition because your child is used to feeling dry and doesn't always know that s/he has urinated, you can try switching to cloth training diapers for the transition period, or using elimination communication during it.

Potties and alternatives

Potties are made of plastic, they generally aren't obtained second hand or donated after use, and they usually aren't recycled. If you want to save the plastic, go without. My first daughter went from potty to toilet within a matter of days and I wish I'd avoided the potty stage altogether as it only made things more complicated for her – learning to use the potty first, then learning to use the toilet. Instead, there are toilet seats you can buy that affix onto toilet seats to make them usable for small children as well as for adults. I recommend investing in one of these: it's still a plastic contraption, but smaller than a potty and will be used for much longer.

Final word

No parent can do everything, so please take the advice here as it is intended and not as dogma or judgment on your own personal choices. There is no reason that you can't do a combination of the listed methods if that suits you best: for example, you could use elimination communication and cloth diapers in the day at home, biodegradable diapers when you are out and at night, compost when you can, and so on. It will take some trial and error to work out what's best for you and your child, and to work out what is realistically achievable for your family, but there is no question that reducing the environmental impact of diapers is achievable for you. Even if you only change the brand of diapers and wipes you buy, you will make a difference.

Summary

- Any reduction in use of disposable diapers is better for the planet
- If you only need to use a few disposable diapers, perhaps for nights, try biodegradable diapers and compost them at home in the garden
- Trial different reusable diaper types before you invest in them
- Buy them second hand and in bulk
- If you do buy new cloth diapers, go for certified organic cotton, locally made where possible, and unbleached
- Invest in an A-grade high-efficiency washing machine

- Wash diapers in full loads only and use high-temperature washes for soiled diapers only
- Buy liners to avoid high-temperature washes as much as possible
- Line-dry diapers when you can
- When line drying is impossible, dry them indoors on a drying rack next to an open window
- Never tumble dry your diapers
- Pass reusable diapers on. Resell them, trade them or gift them to friends and family
- Try elimination communication; if you can go completely diaper-free, you're an eco-queen/king and I salute you
- Try to avoid using conventional single-use wipes and buy eco-friendly wipes instead or make your own
- Wean your baby off diapers when s/he shows signs of being able to use the toilet
- Don't buy a potty

And in case it wasn't clear earlier, you don't need to iron your diapers. Really. Not ever.

1 https://www.washingtonpost.com/opinions/why-cloth-diapers-might-not-be-the-greener-choice-after-all/2015/05/08/32b2d8dc-f43a-11e4-bcc4-e8141e5eb0c9_story.html 2 Environment Agency, nin.tl/nappyassessment 3 *Guardian*, nin.tl/*itwontwash* 4 Quote: 'For the disposable nappy system, the main sources of environmental impact are raw material production and conversion of these materials into disposable nappy components, for example, fluff pulp and super absorbent polymer.' Environment Agency, op cit, nin.tl/nappyassessment 5 The Natural Nursery, naturalnursery.co.uk 6 *JUNO magazine* 7 This data is available upon request from the author. 8 Diaper Ever After, nin.tl/washingandcare 9 Quote: 'Most of the terry nappies that are sold in the UK are believed to be manufactured outside of the UK.' Environment Agency, op cit, nin.tl/nappyassessment (emphasis mine) 10 Quote: 'For the home laundered nappy system, the main source of environmental impact is the generation of the electricity used in washing and drying the nappies.' Environment Agency, op cit, nin.tl/nappyassessment 11 Quote: 'Due to limitations of the survey, no precise data were gained regarding percentage of washes that are tumble dried. Survey respondents made multiple choices regarding drying. 50 per cent of terry users in the Environment Agency surveys selected the tumble drying option. However, tumble drying selection totalled 19 per cent of all the Life Cycle Assessment of Disposable and Reusable Nappies in the UK 63 selections made. We have assumed that tumble driers are used to dry 19 per cent of nappy wash loads.' Environment Agency, op cit, nin.tl/nappyassessment 12 *Guardian*, nin.tl/*switchofftumble* 13 Updated report available at nin.tl/nappylifecycle 14 In the UK alone the figure is 400,000 tonnes per year, according to The Nappy Alliance, nin.tl/nappyreport 15 From research courtesy of The University of Vermont, nin.tl/sustainability-assess 16 Ibid. 17 Women's Environmental Network nin.tl/genderbendernappies 18 *Dumping the Diaper!* Reusable Diaper Report, Sustainable Wales, 2000. 19 BBC, nin.tl/methanefacts 20 Available to purchase from Amazon, nin.tl/amazon-lowcarbon 21 Environ Sci Technol, 2011, 45 (13) nin.tl/biodegradeproblems 22 'Once collected, the gas can be disposed of by flaring or recovered for its energy value – it is a valuable fuel which has added value due to its classification as a renewable energy source under the Renewables Obligation and so any electricity generated is eligible for ROCs. It is estimated that around 63% of landfill gas is currently flared or utilised – this is forecast to rise to 72% in 2005.' Oxford University, nin.tl/methaneukreport 23 Due to its classification as a renewable energy source under the Renewables Obligation, see previous footnote. 24 'One tonne of biodegradable waste is thought to produce between 200 and 500 cubic metres of landfill gas with a calorific value of up to 20 MJ per m3 (5.5 kWh/m3).' Oxford University, op cit, nin.tl/methaneukreport 25 According to The Nappy Alliance, 'Environmental claims made by manufacturers of disposable nappies with regards to the reduced weight of their products and the fact that some of their nappies are now 80% decomposable are irrelevant given that the vast

majority of disposable nappies will end up in landfill, where it will take approximately 500 years for them to decompose.' **26** 'Existing data shows that burning hazardous waste, even in "state-of-the-art" incinerators, will lead to the release of three types of dangerous pollutants into 'Even in "state-of-the-art" incinerators, will lead to the release of three types of dangerous pollutants into the environment: 1 - Heavy metals; 2 - Unburned toxic chemicals; and 3 - New pollutants - entirely new chemicals formed during the incineration process.' Greenpeace, nin.tl/greeenpeacedetox **27** Quote: 'Our analysis shows that recycling and composting can produce significant emissions reductions, and are thus compelling tools to include in climate plans.' EPA, nin.tl/reducingghgs **28** Ohio State University Bulletin, nin.tl/compostingprocess **29** *The Humanure Handbook*, humanurehandbook. com **30** According to Joe Jenkins in The Humanure Handbook, op cit. **31** Quote: 'Temperatures above 131°F (55°C) do kill pathogens in a short time'. Oikos, nin.tl/composting-pathogens **32** Ethical Consumer, nin.tl/reusablenappies **33** Which?, nin.tl/bestreusables **34** Go Real, nin.tl/washingguidelines **35** Wise Geek, nin.tl/machinecapacity **36** *Guardian, op cit, nin.tl/switchofftumble* **37** *Guardian, nin.tl/laundry-footprint* **38** Quote: 'The total cost of using real nappies can be half that of using disposables. A 2006 study* has estimated costs from birth to potty for real and disposable nappies as: • Buying real nappies and washing them at home costs from £182.50 to £359 • Buying disposable nappies costs from £615.16 to £922.74.' from 'A Guide to Using Real Nappies', nin.tl/realnappyguide **39** NHS, nin.tl/toilettrainingtips **40** Royal Society of Medicine, nin.tl/rsmtoilettraining **41** J Steroid Biochem Mol Biol. 2002 Jan;80(1):49-60, nin.tl/oestrogenicactivity **42** Int J Toxicol. 2008;27 Suppl 4:1-82, nin.tl/safetyassessment **43** Growing A Green Family, nin.tl/wipe-savings **44** National Institutes of Health, nin.tl/lavendercure **45** Shop Ethical, nin.tl/babywipeguide **46** Huffington Post, nin.tl/dontpottytrain **47** University of Michigan Health System, nin.tl/startingpotty

7 Baby essentials

What you really need and where can you buy it... Bedding and feeding items... Strollers and pushchairs... Wear your baby: types of sling... Car seats... Other essential items... Choose eco-friendly... Pass it on

We've looked at how reducing consumption that drives environmental degradation and climate change is essential for creating a healthy planet for our children to live in, so now let's look at addressing this consumerism.

According to estimates from a parenting website[1] that takes into account government figures, a typical new US mother may spend as much as $7,000 preparing for a baby. However, many of these products are unnecessary and sold as the result of clever marketing tactics, according to one marketing expert.[2] Since everything you buy new leaves a hole in the ground because it requires resources, creates greenhouse gases because it requires fossil fuels to make, plus has probably been transported to you using oil, and packaged in plastic (which is derived from oil) along the way, buying second-hand goods can significantly reduce your environmental impact. It's a much cheaper option, too, as so many parents sell baby items for low prices at fairs and garage sales or give them away for free.

Except perhaps in a couple of cases which will be outlined here, there is no good reason not to buy second-hand goods for your baby, as long as you give them a good clean first and check that they are not damaged. UK consumer product assessment website *Which?* has a useful guide of things to look for in essential items on its website.[3] Remember, even with new goods there can be product recalls and concerns for safety. The chances are that a used, tried-and-tested item is going to have a parent's stamp of approval, but if you're unsure of product safety you can look up brands and models online before committing to buy a product from a second-hand seller.

What do you really need?

Depending on where you live, what you read and who you know, the items you need to buy for a new baby can vary from just a few products to several pages' worth of goods. Most of these items aren't at all necessary and end up being used very little, and I would argue that all any baby really needs is its parents and immediate family. That said, there are plenty of things people buy and use to make the parenting journey easier for themselves, and with a little savviness you can get hold of these items at minimum cost to your wallet and the environment.

Where can you buy it?

Since you have several months of waiting to do before baby arrives, this is when you can write a list of things you think you will definitely need and things you may need, and reassess the list when baby arrives. You can search for the things you definitely need in the meantime.

Good places to look for second-hand baby goods are websites like Gumtree, eBay and Amazon sellers. Gumtree is often the cheapest option because there are no fees involved for sellers for listing products, although you are limited by what's for sale in your local area and there's no way to trace a seller or get a refund if anything goes wrong. For peace of mind you might prefer to buy second-hand goods using eBay or Amazon, because they guarantee refunds for damaged items and the seller has an obligation to make things right if you're not happy, although both take cuts from the sellers and require posting items. Therefore, the greenest option is to buy items locally, through parents' groups, local charity shops, spring/school fairs, fundraisers for children's groups and local garage sales. It's easy to find listings for events through social-media sites and checking local newspaper listings.

To try getting hold of items for free, ask in your local Freecycle and Freegle groups: the guidelines are clear once you have registered. Also check listings in local papers and local groups on social media, as there are always parents around who want to pass on used baby products when they've decided to stop having children. The less fussy you are, and the earlier you start looking for essential items, the more you will get for free or very cheap.

When all else fails and you resort to buying an item new, it's worth reading up on what different labels mean, such as fair trade and organic. A useful overview of green labels can be found on the UK environment ministry website.[4]

Bedding to begin with

Where will your baby sleep?

Most parents buy a crib for night-time sleeping and a Moses basket for transporting from room to room in the daytime, but when baby first arrives it is quite possible that s/he is not going to happily lie down and sleep for long anywhere except in mum or dad's arms. Some babies do quickly learn to stay asleep in cribs and Moses baskets, and some don't. Since all babies wake up every few hours to feed, day and night, some people find that cribs can be more of a cumbrance than a help.

An alternative to buying a new crib is to borrow one from someone who has kept theirs to have more children, but isn't having more yet. Remember as well that a stand-alone crib is not the only option out there: as discussed in Chapter 1, co-sleeping and bedsharing are also options. A side-crib or 'co-sleeper' is a type of crib with an adjustable side that can be lowered or removed to join the end of your bed. That way you can be next to your baby all night while having your own space, and won't have to get out of bed to feed her/him.

Plenty of parents around the world, and some in the US, choose not to use a crib at all if it means having to settle a baby several times a night, or makes breastfeeding harder to do. To do this safely you can buy a cheap and simple bed guard to create a barrier at the side of the bed so baby can't fall off. Some parents choose to pack away the bed frame and sleep with baby on a mattress on the floor to avoid worrying about accidents from falling out of bed. The only research available on this topic, however, found that most injuries resulting from children falling out of bed while asleep occur when they are older and in cribs or top bunk beds.[5]

Bed Guard

Whatever sleeping option you choose, you will still need to obtain cotton baby blankets, as a baby should never sleep under a duvet due to risks of suffocation and overheating It's worth picking these up second hand before baby is due, or asking for them as practical gift options when baby arrives. If you buy them new, then obtain organic blankets where possible.

If you do buy or borrow a second-hand crib, it's recommended that you buy a new mattress for it, because a used crib mattress can get soft in the middle and soft or older mattresses as well as fluffy bedding such as comforters, pillows, sheepskins and polystyrene-bean pillows have been associated with a higher risk of sudden infant death syndrome (SIDS).[6] A cot mattress that is firm, flat, fits the cot with no gaps and is clean and waterproof, is absolutely fine to use for your baby. If this is your first baby, you can take an experienced parent friend along with you to look at a second-hand crib mattress before you buy it, so that they can look it over and assure you that it's safe. If you're unsure and want to buy a new mattress, buy an organic one, because it will reduce chemical exposure.[7]

Also, tuck the bottoms of any baby blankets under the bottom of the mattress, so that it doesn't reach above baby's head, and can't be pulled higher in the night by active baby hands. Babies are meant to sleep on their backs to reduce SIDS risk.[8]

Bedding later on

Even if you're not co-sleeping at home, you may wish to plan to do so when you're away from home, which will also save you needing to buy and transport a carrycot for overnight journeys. Many parents end up co-sleeping when they haven't planned to anyway, so it's worth preparing for it, as a few basic safety precautions do need to be adhered to for co-sleeping parents (in the same way that cots require a basic knowledge of the risks and the precautions).[9]

The safe sleep seven

If a mother is:
1 A non-smoker
2 Sober
3 Breastfeeding
And her baby is:
4 Healthy
5 On his/her back
6 Lightly dressed and unswaddled
And they:
7 Share a safe surface
Then the baby's risk of SIDS is no greater than in a crib, and any breathing hazards have been hugely reduced.

Diapers to begin with

We covered the greenest option for diapers in Chapter 6, but it's worth repeating here that cloth is best, second-hand is ideal, and low heat washes are okay for urine-soaked diapers. Line-drying is essential where possible, and going diaper-free is for the committed!

Feeding to begin with

We covered the greenest ways of feeding babies in Chapter 3. However, for those who have to formula feed, or for breastfeeders who need bottles to express milk into, this information is for you.

Since even BPA-free plastic bottles have been found to contain chemicals that are just as dangerous as BPA,[10] glass bottles are the safest option for your baby. Glass baby bottles are available in large stores across Canada and the US.

If you want to use muslin cloths for cleaning up baby messes instead of buying new packaged ones, make your own by upcycling old fabrics, or knit a few squares out of some scrap yarn. It can be helpful to have a calming project like knitting to do while waiting for the baby to arrive, but obviously not everyone can knit or sew – in which case find a baby fan who'll be happy to do this for you!

For mothers who are breastfeeding and experience sore or cracked nipples, applying expressed breastmilk after every feed can helps to avoid this problem. Failing that, others prefer to apply lanolin or petroleum jelly after every feed, but the limited research available has found that applying nothing or expressed breast milk may be equally or more beneficial in the short-term experience of nipple pain than the application of an ointment such as lanolin.[11]

For nipple pain, it's always worth getting a breastfeeding peer supporter or lactation consultant to check your latch and make sure baby isn't feeding at a funny angle or in a way that makes your nipples sore. If nipple pain persists, some people turn to using a nipple shield, which is a cupped silicone shape with a hole it in that protects your nipple while feeding, but these have not been found to reduce nipple pain.[12]

Feeding later on

Tableware

Most children's plates, bowls and cutlery items are made of plastic. Since glass tableware products are likely to be easily broken by children, you may wish to buy second-hand steel cups and plates instead. Indian tiffin jars are round, metal food containers that are used across India for eating away from home, and they are available to buy new online, but they are not easy to come by second hand. Farlin tableware is made of bamboo plant cellulose, made of organic materials and has the best eco-credentials.

Also, you may not be able to ditch plastic from your home altogether, so keep in mind that the research shows the main issue is plastic products that are used to *heat* food in, so avoid buying plastics that are designed with this in mind, and say goodbye to pre-packaged microwave meals if you haven't already – they are not great for the environment anyway since they require vast amounts of packaging.

For tips on preparing plastic-free, low-carbon meals, and for a detailed overview of different methods of weaning babies onto solids, turn to Chapter 3.

Clothing to begin with

According to one survey, more than half of all parents admit to buying clothes that end up never being worn.[13] It's a worrying trend, and one that can be curbed by making conscious consumer choices.

What's in your baby's clothing?

A Greenpeace report titled 'A Little Story About the Monsters in Your Closet' investigates the levels of specific chemicals in children's clothing.[14] The accompanying technical report concludes that:

'The use of these and other hazardous chemicals during manufacture can be expected to result in releases from manufacturing facilities, including within wastewaters, in addition to the presence of chemical residues in the products themselves.'

The environmental case for avoiding these chemicals is clear, but what about your child's safety?

A critique of the report by the toxicology department of Public Health England addresses the key concerns posed by Greenpeace.[15] It states that:

'The presence of these chemicals in the articles does not mean that there will be an exposure of the person wearing the clothing. Exposure would depend on the degree of transfer from the clothing and the absorption of these chemicals across the skin. Skin is a limited route of exposure for these chemicals and exposure limits are based upon the major routes of exposure, namely ingestion and inhalation. From a human health perspective, therefore, there is very little in this report that should cause concern. The only caveat to this statement would be the case of antimony as data are limited and where data are available from occupational exposures these are complicated by co-exposures to arsenic.'

Antimony is a metalloid that is found in 70 per cent of polyester polymer production and may be present in clothes containing polyester. Avoiding polyester altogether is a good option for concerned parents.

The critique also gives a comprehensive breakdown of some of the chemicals listed in the Greenpeace report, outlining that endocrine disruptor Nonylphenol ethoxylates (NPEs) residues remain in the clothes at purchase but would be rapidly removed when the clothes are washed at home. It concludes that, while 'Monsters' gives the amounts of specific hazardous chemicals in the clothing items, which are undoubtedly bad for the environment, it offers no real data regarding the risk of likely exposures to our children's health, since these chemicals may not be absorbed through their skin.

While this is an important point, it doesn't actually assure us that no harm will come to our babies from wearing clothes with these chemicals in them. Just to be on the safe side, buying preloved, prewashed, second-hand clothing for your baby is a safer option than buying new, or certified organic, fair-trade clothing if you have to buy new items of clothing.

A note on fair trade

According to Treehugger.com, many mainstream brands like Gap, H&M and Abercrombie & Fitch source clothes from garment factories where workers face long hours for very little money, forced overtime and potentially deadly conditions.[16] Although I make the case for buying local goods when you do buy them new, so as to cut down on transport emissions, when you do buy from abroad it's always worth supporting fair trade where possible.

Is buying organic clothing better for the environment?

Typical baby clothing and bedding is cotton grown using synthetic pesticides and fertilizers – and bleached and dyed with yet more harsh chemicals. According to an article in *Scientific American*, 25 per cent of the world's pesticides and 10 per cent of insecticides are used on cotton crops every year.[17] In addition, petroleum scouring agents, softeners, brighteners, heavy metals, flame and soil retardants and ammonia are used in the processing of cotton once it is harvested.

Organic farming practices are better for the environment.[18] Conventional agricultural practices release nitrous oxide, a potent greenhouse gas, and soluble nitrates that leach into groundwater and suffocate marine life. According to the Soil Association, instead of chemical inputs, organic cotton farmers use a range of natural techniques to maintain healthy soils and restrict pests, weeds and diseases.[19] Central to this is the growth of a range of food crops alongside cotton – each contributing specific functions within the organic system while also promoting food security. Contrary to common belief, organic cotton production is economically competitive with its conventional counterpart. A long-term study in India recently revealed that, despite producing lower average yields, net profits of organic cotton systems are in fact similar, or sometimes better, than those of conventional systems due to the significantly reduced input costs and the higher price of organically produced cotton.

The United Nations recognizes the importance of organic farming for food security, as: '[Research] shows that organic agriculture is a good option for food security in Africa – equal or better than most conventional systems and more likely to be sustainable in the longer term. The study's analysis of 114 cases in Africa revealed that a conversion of farms to organic or near-organic production methods increased agricultural productivity of 116 per cent. Moreover, a shift towards organic production systems has enduring impact, as it builds up levels of natural, human, social, financial and physical capital in farming communities.'[20]

Human impact

As with non-fair-trade goods, workers pay the price when it comes to non-organic agriculture.

There are no reliable estimates regarding how many people suffer from pesticide-related health effects in developing countries because of many variables, which are explored in a World Health Organization bulletin.[21] However, acute pesticide poisoning does cause significant morbidity and mortality worldwide, especially in developing countries,[22] and studies have demonstrated the annual rates of acute pesticide poisoning to be as high as 18.2 per 100,000 full-time agricultural workers and 7.4 per million among schoolchildren.[23]

Is organic farming better for local wildlife?

Yes, almost certainly.[24] Organic farms use fewer chemicals, including insecticides and pesticides that can harm wildlife, and they are typically much more diverse than conventional farms because they do not use monocrop principles that destroy the biodiversity required by wildlife ecosystems. Numerous studies have found that organic farming increases the numbers of plants and animals in and around the land farmed and is better for species diversity overall.[25]

How much clothing do you need?

Although new and branded little baby outfits are alluring, they tend to be impractical when the baby has thrown up or has an exploded diaper at 3am in the morning. Stick to buying simple one-pieces or babygrows, which are designed to be removed easily and washed frequently, but don't stock up on huge amounts of them because your baby is likely to outgrow them fairly quickly.

In summer you may prefer sleeveless and legless babygrows, but in winter you'll find sleeved and legged ones better for keeping warm. Layers, rather than thick clothing, are best for dressing babies in as they can get too warm or too cold quite quickly (babies take a while to regulate their own temperatures). Cotton clothing is also best for this reason, as babies can overheat in thick materials like fleece, although merino wool has also been found to be safe for temperature control.[26] Baby's temperature control is aided by giving him or her plenty of skin-to-skin time on your chest.[27]

You may be tempted to buy new clothes for your newborn baby but second hand will do just as well and they are likely still to be soft, as in all likelihood the baby who wore them only had a few wears out of them before outgrowing them. As mentioned previously, they will also have been washed many times, which reduces the amount of chemicals on them. Wash them in a gentle eco-friendly powder.

If you do have to buy new clothing, organic is the way to go.

As a rough estimate, you'll probably need:

- Eight babygrows for both day and night, or four babygrows and two nightdresses for the night – use socks with the nightie if it's cold
- Two cardigans, wool or cotton, and light rather than heavy
- A couple of light cotton blankets to wrap your baby in
- A wool or cotton hat and mittens in colder temperatures
- Two pairs of scratch mittens to stop baby scratching itself. These are quite small and easily pulled off so they can be replaced with ordinary cotton children's socks if necessary
- A sun hat for going out if it's hot or bright in warmer months
- A snowsuit in winter.

Hats off!

It used to be routine practice in hospitals to put a hat on a newborn baby immediately after birth, and send him or her home in it. Recently this idea has been debunked by UNICEF, which states that: 'it is especially important that outdoor hats are not used indoors; the inability of young infants to easily control their own body temperature means that the head is an important area for heat regulation/dissipation and hats should be removed when the baby is sleeping indoors.'[28]

Babies that were born prematurely, of low birth weight or have difficulty maintaining their temperature, do need to wear a hat indoors until they reach a certain healthier weight or are able to maintain their body temperature.

Shoes or no shoes?

Your baby won't need shoes until he or she can walk, but maybe you'll see a pair that looks cute and want to buy them. Maybe you will and they'll change the way your baby's feet develop by restricting their growth unnecessarily (as some people argue). Certainly they will add to your carbon footprint (!). But it's best not to bother with baby shoes at all. To keep little toes warm in winter, add extra socks.

When your baby does start learning to walk, simple knitted or felt booties are fine for walking indoors, and some people choose to buy 'barefoot shoes' outdoors as well,[29] although there is no evidence that they are better for our feet than normal shoes.[30] It's perfectly fine to buy second-hand shoes: Tracy Byrne, a podiatrist and leading pediatric researcher who specializes in infant foot development states that: ' It is okay to buy second-hand [shoes] as long as you can see and feel that the shoes have not broken down, or don't have a very poor wear pattern on the soles and heels. When buying second-hand shoes you must ensure that they can be washed in the machine or the insole wiped with surgical spirit to kill off any residual verruca virus/athletes' foot or fungal nail infection.'[31]

The greenest options are to aim for second-hand clothing and shoes, and to go organic if you do buy new. If the materials used to make new items were sourced close to home, even better.

Clothing later on

Clothes swapping, or 'swishing' is becoming popular across the US, including for children's clothes, and these are excellent ways to pass on used clothes and obtain the sizes you need, all for free. If there aren't any in your local area, consider setting up your own with a group of friends or your local parenting group.

As older children's rate of growth is slower than a baby's, it's much easier to buy clothing in bulk, which is also a cheaper option: look for 'clothing bundles' for specific age groups on eBay and you'll find listings of large amounts of good-quality clothes of all ranges for sale as a single transaction. These bundles can be searched by seasons as well, as winter or summer clothing. Even with the small environmental cost of posting them to you, this is your greenest option for buying clothes for an older child, alongside local jumble sales and so on.

If you do buy clothes new – for example, if you need an outfit for a special occasion, or if there are family members on the scene who really want to buy new clothes as birthday presents.

Travel to begin with: strollers

Deciding which stroller to buy can be a difficult decision, thanks to the many different brands and models available to the American parent. A study involving over 2,000 children found that parent-facing strollers are better than outward-facing buggies and pushchairs, because children in front-facing varieties are significantly less likely to talk, laugh and interact with their parents than those in buggies that face the pusher.[32] This means that outward-facing strollers are isolating for babies and could have repercussions on their development.

Second-hand strollers are easy to come by for free or very cheap, but you do need to check that the brakes are in good working order, the handles are at the right height for pushing, the frame is strong enough for your child, and that there is no obvious damage to the wheels, harness and straps.

When choosing a stroller, whether second-hand or new, bear in mind that while the bigger, more solid structures can give baby a lot of space to sit and lie comfortably, they can be a pain to use on public transportation.

Wear your baby

Baby carriers, also called slings, have become popular in the US but choosing one that suits you can also be a minefield. They are worth the effort, though, because they come with the added benefit of increasing parental interaction, which helps with baby's development. Dr Susan Zeedyk, who did the research on parent-facing strollers, says: 'Slings keep a baby close to a parent's body, and thus in constant reassurance. This is why many parents choose to use them. Giving slings away to families living in "vulnerable circumstances" would probably make a great health intervention.'[33]

Other research has found that babies who spent more time close to their mothers were more content to be separated from them at 13 months; they cried and whined less when with a stranger and behaved as if they were more secure.[34]

Before you buy a baby carrier, join a local sling meet and practice trying on slings with experienced babywearers, using helping hands and a doll. When your baby arrives and you're ready to go out and about, you can hire a sling from your local sling library or sling meet to find one that suits you best, or through an online service if you don't have a local group. You can even have a consultation with a babywearing expert over Skype, although these are usually not free. When you know you're comfortable with the sling you've been using, then you can look to buy the same model second hand from a local seller or online. Aside from the websites listed previously, also try babywearing expert websites (see Resources) and official groups on social media where parents often sell their used slings – for example, Babywearing FSOT on Facebook.

You can also watch sling tutorial videos online to check that you're babywearing in the right way. What you want is a sling that keeps the newborn baby snug and supported against your chest, or an older child supported against your body. As a general rule, a newborn baby worn on the front should feel secure in the sling and his or her head should be close enough to kiss.

Types of sling

The different types of sling are as follows.

Wraps, which come in both stretchy and woven varieties, are basically just very long pieces of fabric that you wrap in a specific way around you and your baby. *Stretchy wraps* are made of a stretchy material that keeps its shape; these wraps can be left tied on so that baby can be inserted and removed from the sling without having to untie it and tie it again. However, due to the nature of the fabric, most parents find that stretchy wraps are not supportive enough for babies aged six months or more. A stretchy wrap needs to be used with several layers around the baby to ensure adequate support, which can make wearing it uncomfortable in hot weather.

Woven wraps are diagonally woven cloths, which give the fabric the ideal amount of stretch and support. They are the most versatile form of carrier available, as they automatically adjust to the size of the carried child. They can be used from birth to toddlerhood and beyond, and can be worn on the front, hip and back and tied in many different ways. There are many tutorials available online, for free, on official babywearing websites, to teach you different ways of wrapping your sling.

Mei tais are Asian-style carriers consisting of a shaped piece of fabric with four straps. One set of straps is tied around the parent's waist and the other around their shoulders, and the fabric forms a pocket for the baby. They can be worn on the front, hip and back. As the weight is spread on both shoulders and hips through the straps, they can be comfortable to use with older babies and toddlers.

Soft structured carriers are a mix between a mei tai and a rucksack: the body is similar to a mei tai but this type of carrier has a structured waist and padded shoulder straps which can fasten with buckles or straps. They can be easy and comfortable to use. Some are unsuitable for a newborn but can be modified with inserts and straps to accommodate a little baby, while the upper weight limit allows you to carry a pre-schooler.

Ring slings are pieces of cloth with two rings sewn at one end. The free end is looped through the rings, forming a pouch for the baby, with the tail of the fabric hanging down. They are worn over one shoulder. A newborn or toddler can ride on your hip in it, and they can also be used for front and back carries. Unpadded ring slings can be easier to adjust, and it can be easier to breastfeed a baby in one of these because of the position.

Pouches are also worn over one shoulder. They are made of one folded length of material that forms a pocket for the baby and is worn over the body like a sash. Unless they are adjustable, they need to be exactly the right size for you, so the same pouch cannot be used with two parents of very different sizes.

Unfortunately these is no scientific research available into the benefits of different slings, but as there is research that supports babywearing, it's worth focusing on getting a sling that suits you and clearly soothes your baby.

Forward-facing carriers

Some carriers are forward-facing and these are often criticized for causing potential hip growth (dysplasia) issues. According to a *Which?* review, however, there are no published medical studies that suggest that front-facing baby carrying causes hip and spinal problems.[35] The only types of baby carrier that have been shown to cause hip and back damage to the baby are Native American papooses and Inuit cradle boards. Incorrect swaddling is also emerging as a cause of hip dysplasia.[36]

The Royal College of Midwives in the UK emphasizes that proper support is most vital when your baby is unable to support the weight of his or her head, and they recommend that you do not use the forward-facing position before your baby can hold his/her head and shoulders up unaided.

There is an interesting article arguing against forward-facing carriers on the Ergo Baby website, but, while this piece claims to be a science-based view, it does not give any citations.[37] It's probably fine to wear your baby facing outwards from time to time, but you'll miss out on the benefits of interaction linked to parent-facing strollers when you do so.

The greenest options

There are many locally made, handmade slings, including upcycled slings, which require minimal manufacture, little or no shipping (if the cloth material was sourced from the US) and little or no packaging. Ask at your local sling meet or search social media websites for small handmade sling companies, and you'll probably be supporting parents who run a small business as well. If you sew and want the most inexpensive, eco-friendly sling possible, buy a length of fabric and sew one yourself. Any sling, if used to replace a pushchair or pram, is likely to have much less of an impact on the environment in terms of manufacturing and materials used, and it can be reused or upcycled when it comes to the end of its lifespan. At present, society has little use for a stroller that has reached the end of its lifespan, so it ends up buried in a landfill site.

Car seats

If you drive, or if your baby occasionally goes in someone else's car, you'll need a car seat (or booster seat) for your baby, as per US law, although the exact details vary so find the information you need based on the state you live in through the GHSA website.[38] This is the one area where there are real reasons for buying the item new. Working out which type of seat can be confusing, so read the informative overview on *Parentdish* to make sure you know the type of seat you need to get hold of.[39]

Again, Dr Susan Zeedyk's research applies to this area, as newborn car seats tend to be rear-facing. Although new models are available that are parent-facing, these are not yet commercially available in the US. Therefore, Dr Zeedyk recommends taking time to interact with your baby while driving, for example, by singing along to a music CD together. Keeping driving trips to a minimum will lower your environmental impact significantly as well.

There are pressures on parents to buy certain brands of car seat, as if buying the cheapest model means that you are endangering your child's life. In fact, if it's on sale in the US, even a cheap car seat has been through the same rigorous testing that the most expensive model went through.

The reason behind the advice that car sears are bought new is because a car seat that has already been in an accident may not be fully functional. One way to get around this problem is by getting a used car seat from a family member or friend, so you can be confident that it is in working order. This is probably **the**

greenest option for obtaining a car seat. Keep it in good condition and you can also pass it on when you're done.

Other essential items

Over time it will become apparent that some items make your life easier as a parent – a baby monitor, for example, which can be picked up easily second hand, as most models are efficient at alerting you to when a sleeping baby or toddler wakes up.

Another possible essential item is a high chair, which is easy to obtain second hand or for free and then pass on to another parent. Go for a basic, non-fabric-coated, non-fancy model made of wood, plastic and/or metal, because the ones with fabric on them make cleaning food stains difficult and there's no point buying an expensive model that will inevitably be covered in mess. All your child needs to be able to do is sit in it safely at dining-table level so that s/he can reach food and see you.

Another potential item is a baby bath, which can be obtained second hand in many areas in the US and Canada, though for the first few days a baby can be cleaned using the top-and-tail method. After this, a gentle rinse in an adult bath with mum or dad or in a tub in the sink is also fine.

Nurseries

Decorating a baby's nursery can be an expensive business, but babies don't need lots of expensive items.[40] What they do need is a healthy planet to live on and an environment that isn't full of toxins and waste. By reusing materials and buying certified sustainable products, you can make a real difference to the effect you have on the environment, and save yourself money too.

Choose eco-friendly

This information on VOCs is from the UK government website NI Direct and, because it is so thorough and concise, it's worth repeating in full:

'Most paints contain volatile organic compounds (VOCs), which can be harmful to humans, wildlife, plants and even building materials. When you are choosing a paint, finish or preservative, try to find the one with the lowest impact possible for the job you are doing:

- Check the label and choose the lowest VOC product you can
- If you have the choice, choose a product without a hazard warning on the label
- Try not to buy more paint than you need
- Look for the European Ecolabel for indoor paints, which means that they don't contain certain heavy metals – like lead or mercury – and are manufactured with reduced solvent emissions and waste byproducts.'[41]

A note on wood

If you plan to buy new products made of wood for your baby's nursery, and can't find them made of reclaimed wood, then buy certified wood and use sustainable timber and wood products instead. Look for labels from the Forest Stewardship Council (FSC), the Programme for the Endorsement of Forest Certification schemes (PEFC) or other forest certification schemes.

Paints, finishes and preservatives must be disposed of properly, as they can be toxic. Never pour paint or other chemicals down the drain, as hazardous chemicals can get into the environment. The **greenest option** is to give leftover paint away for free: list it on your local Freecycle and Freegle groups and in the 'Classifieds' section of your local newspaper, and offer it on social networking sites. Failing that, donate unwanted paint to Community RePaint, which is a network of projects that distributes unwanted paint to charities, community projects and people living on low incomes.

Finally, pass it on

When your child is finished with specific items, there are various options for dealing with them in an environmentally responsible manner. If you plan to have more children, keep clothes to reuse on them. If you have time, patch up clothes that need a little TLC, or ask a willing friend who sews to do this for you. For clothes that are beyond being reused, bag them up and take them to your local clothes collection bank for recycling into other products, or cut them up and use them as washcloths. Or you can be altruistic and give them away to friends who are expecting babies, or to charity shops. Clothes that are in good condition can be sold in bundles online, or sold at a car boot or jumble sale. Be even greener and give a percentage of the money you make away to a tree-planting charity: a healthy planet with clean air to breathe is arguably the most essential thing you can provide for your baby.

Summary

- Aim to buy baby essentials second hand where possible
- Clothes swaps and second-hand clothing bundles bought online are great options
- Look for eco-friendly credentials when you do need to buy them new
- Make your main sleeping area safe for bedsharing even if you don't intend to take your baby to bed with you
- Invest in glass baby bottles instead of plastic if you need them
- Invest in steel tableware instead of plastic
- Buying second-hand clothing is a safer option than buying new clothes that have been chemically treated
- If you do need to buy new clothes, buy organically certified and as sourced as local to home as possible
- If buying them from abroad, look for the official fair-trade symbol
- Your baby will not need an indoor hat

- It's okay to buy baby shoes second hand
- Try babywearing: attend sling meets or meet a local sling seller to try one out before buying
- Invest in a good sling and your child will benefit. Second hand is fine, or buy a new one that was locally made
- If you do buy a stroller, aim for a parent-facing model
- Choose eco-friendly products for nursery renovation and sustainably certified wooden products
- Pass used items on to other parents.

1 http://www.whattoexpect.com/preconception/preparing-for-baby/work-and-finance/what-babies-really-cost. aspx 2 Market Watch, nin.tl/babyproductsecrets 3 Which?, nin.tl/usedbabyequipment 4 DEFRA, nin.tl/ greenlabelsguide 5 *Inj Prev* 2000;6:291-292, nin.tl/bedfallinjuries 6 CMAJ. 2006 Jun 20; 174(13): 1861–1869, nin.tl/ suddeninfantdeath 7 *Scientific American*, nin.tl/green-nursery 8 NHS, nin.tl/NHSonSIDS 9 La Leche League International, nin.tl/safesleep7 10 *Mother Jones*. nin.tl/scaryevidence 11 Cochrane, nin.tl/breastfeedingpain 12 Ibid. 13 *Guardian*, nin.tl/parentssplashout 14 Greenpeace, nin.tl/closetmonsters 15 Sense About Science, nin.tl/ toxicclothes 16 http://www.treehugger.com/style/are-these-unethical-fashion-brands-hiding-in-your-closet. html 17 *Scientific American*, op cit, nin.tl/green-nursery 18 PNAS, vol. 103 no. 12, Sasha B. Kramer, 4522-4527, nin. tl/reducednitrate 19 Soil Association, nin.tl/organiccottonreport 20 UNCTAD, nin.tl/organicproduction 21 WHO, nin.tl/pesticidepoisoning 22 World Health Stat Q. 1990;43(3):139-44, nin.tl/pesticide-problem 23 Am J Ind Med. 2004 Jan;45(1):14-23, nin.tl/acuteillness and JAMA. 2005 Jul 27;294(4):455-65, nin.tl/school-pesticides 24 Sense About Science, nin.tl/impactdebate 25 Glenisk, nin.tl/glenisk-biodiversity 26 Reuters, nin.tl/merinowooltrumps 27 Acta Paediatr. 2010 Nov;99(11):1630-4, nin.tl/skincontact 28 UNICEF, nin.tl/babyatnight 29 *Guardian*, nin.tl/ barefootbest 30 Vox topics, 9 May 2014, nin.tl/barefootbullshit 31 Free Our Kids, nin.tl/secondhandshoes 32 Suzanne Zeedyk, nin.tl/buggiesandbrains 33 Suzanne Zeedyk, op cit, nin.tl/buggiesandbrains 34 'Early Days' Timbs, O, 01/88, *The Lancet*, taken from 'Three in a Bed', p67, Jackson, D, 1989 35 Which?, nin.tl/babyslingsafety 36 International Hip Dysplasia Institute, nin.tl/dysplasiacauses 37 Ergo Baby, nin.tl/whichdirection 38 http:// www.ghsa.org/html/stateinfo/laws/childsafety_laws.html 39 Parent Dish, nin.tl/seatconfusion 40 Net Mums, op cit, nin.tl/parentsspending 41 NI Direct Government Services, nin.tl/greenerdiy

8 Travel

Slow or Mindful Travel... Walking... Cycling: types of bikes... Public transport and carbon impacts... Driving... Lift share... Join a car club... Change your driving habits... Choose a cleaner vehicle... Choose a cleaner fuel... Flying: the carbon costs... A note on carbon offsetting

Transport accounts for 27 per cent of total greenhouse-gas emissions in the US, making it the second largest contributor of US greenhouse-gas emissions after the electricity sector and therefore one of the most important lifestyle choices you can make in terms of your impact on the environment.[1] Greenhouse-gas emissions from transportation have increased by about 16 per cent since 1990.

The main thing you can do to reduce the carbon footprint of your travel is to drive less by committing to walking or cycling for short distances instead of driving, opting for public transportation for longer journeys and having regular car-free days. If this sounds impossible to you in our car-based culture, consider the fact that half of Paris decided to take a mandatory day off driving in 2015.[2] Building better rail and bus links is also essential as a long-term plan to tackle travel emissions.

Slow or Mindful Travel

Slow Travel has become popular over the last few decades, as more people come to see that the journey is as much of an enjoyable learning experience as the destination itself, and choose to shun the sudden jet-setting that changed the way we travel when flights became so financially cheap.[3] Also, taking slow journeys even just across the town you live in can be a potentially rich developmental experience for children, and taking the slower (than personal vehicles) option of public transport can help to teach patience, social skills and expose a child to different first-hand experiences, whereas sitting in a car seat looking out the window offers little or no hands-on stimulation.[4]

Walking

Walking benefits your health as a form of exercise that is good for your heart,[5] and also through higher energy levels, higher stamina levels, reduced stress levels, decreased levels of illness and an improved feeling of wellbeing.[6] Studies have also found that walking relieves stress and contributes to mental wellbeing, particularly nature walks in groups.[7]

Walking with a stroller is also a good form of exercise, and various 'buggy-fit' groups that are aimed mainly at mothers have popped up as a way of combining exercise with socializing. In these groups parents are usually led by a personal trainer through power walking while pushing their babies in strollers and doing stretches and exercises. These groups usually take place in parks and can also help to provide social groups for mums and motivation to exercise, all achievable with baby in tow.

Another way to cover short distances with your baby is to babywear. The benefits of carrying your baby in a sling are covered in Chapter 7 but, to summarize, wearing your baby in a sling allows you to connect with your baby in a way that forward-facing strollers generally don't allow.

There's also much to be said in favor of older children walking instead of being strapped into strollers and car seats. Roads are dangerous – in 2014, 32,675 people were killed in motor vehicle crashes on US roadways, and 2.3 million people were injured[8] – but since they can't be avoided altogether, it's considered to be better to teach road safety sooner rather than later.[9] You can achieve this by walking more and crossing roads together safely.

Children also benefit from being exposed to nature and from being able to interact with the world around them rather than looking out at the world from strollers and car seats. Spending more time outdoors has many benefits for children, including giving them the time to wander and play in a different way to indoor environments. Read more about encouraging outdoor play in the chapter titled 'Entertainment'.

Finally, walking of course has no manufacturing costs involved, though it may want to make you eat a bit more than usual!

Cycling

Cycling has many benefits besides being a form of exercise and nice way to get around. It's also a very energy-efficient method of travel, much more so than walking, in terms of energy expended per mile covered.[10] Also, the more people cycle on the roads, the safer roads have been found to become for all road users.[11]

Types of bikes

Cycling with your children is a great way to introduce them to road safety and eco-travel. There are many options for traveling on a bicycle with your child, but the three main types of carriers are: rear-mounted child bike seats, front-mounted child bike seats and bike trailers.

Rear-mounted child bike seats,
age: 6 months to 5 years

These are the most widely used bike seats. They fit over the back wheel of your bike and will usually have a high back and raised sides, leg guards and a harness. They are also easy to get hold of second hand, although it's worth getting any second-hand cycling equipment looked over by a professional when you buy it.

With rear-mounted child bike seats, younger children are well supported if they want to fall asleep while you're cycling, and you can use the seat to carry shopping when you don't have your child with you.

Front-mounted bike seats, age: 1-5 years

With this type of seat, your child sits in front of you and your arms go around the child seat to hold the handlebars. Your vision of the road needs to be clear, so front-mounted seats are more compact than rear-mounted seats, which can be useful when going on train journeys because they take up less room.

Front-mounted bike seats allow you to have closer contact with your child; plus your child is always visible and has a great view of the world. However, these seats are more popular in mainland Europe and therefore harder to find in the US, perhaps because a child sat in this position will bear the brunt of any bad weather, and cannot nap in the front-seat position.

Child bike trailers, age: birth-6 years

With a child bike trailer, you tow your child behind you in an enclosed carriage. The trailer has two large wheels and a long hitching arm that fastens to your bike. Your child is seated and strapped in inside the zipped, weatherproof and ventilated compartment, which has fabric or plastic windows so he or she can see out. (For bikes that don't come with these, you are usually able to buy them separately from the manufacturer.) Bike trailers are lightweight, spacious inside, comfortable, have room for books and toys, and can hold more than one child. Bike trailers tend to be expensive, even second hand.

Any trailer used on the road should have a tall pennant and rear lighting so that it is clearly visible to motorists.

Other bikes for adults with children

This is not an exhaustive list, but it gives you an idea of the main options on offer. If you can find a willing local bike store manager, or join a local parenting group for cyclists, you might be able to have a go on one of these models before committing to buy one. It's worth checking whether there's a cycling group in your local area and joining in.

Cargo bikes, age: birth to adult

Cargo bikes, freight bicycles, carrier cycles, freight tricycles, cargo bikes, box bikes, and cycle-trucks are all designed specifically for transporting loads – including small people.

Box bikes, age: birth to -adult

The 'Bakfiets', which is Dutch for box bike, allows you to carry up to four children, and is popular in continental Europe. A standard Bakfiets is 8 feet long with a 25-inch-wide box, so it isn't easy to store away, but the design is meant to be tough enough to store outside. Box bikes are heavy but are designed to last a lifetime with little maintenance.

The original model has a single gear, fine for the flatness of the Netherlands, whereas export versions now have 8-speed hubs or equivalent, so keep that in mind if you buy a second-hand model from abroad.

Tagalong bike trailers, age: 4 to 9

A tagalong is a third wheel attached to a frame extension fitted with handlebars that often attaches to the adult bike with simple clamp. It enables a child to pedal (or not

pedal), but not steer. Children can help the cycling process by adding pedal power when going uphill. A tagalong is suitable for children aged between four and nine or ten.

Tagalongs can be installed and removed easily, making them good for storing and transport. There are a number of tagalong-style devices that hook up a child's existing bike to the adult's bike. Make sure the affixing hitch is super-strong. Early versions of this style of tagalong – which sometimes come on to the second-hand market – are unsafe. Look for a super-strong hitch.

Child back tandems, age: 6 to -adult

Child back tandems are built to fit a child on the back. The second rider's pedals are connected to the main rider's pedals, meaning the child will have to pedal at the same time and at the same speed as the adult on the front. Little feet are prone to slip off the rear pedals but the captain will still be pedaling, so most child stokers have their feet strapped in with toe-straps or clip-in pedals and shoes. Child back tandems tend to be expensive and many not be practical for as long as other bike options.

Trikes with child seats, age: birth to 4 years

These are purpose-built, child-carrying tricycles. Most carry two children in rear or forward-facing seats, with space for luggage in the tray below. Unlike a bicycle with a child seat, trikes don't present problems of balance. A trike is heavier and slower than a bike, but is probably no slower than a bike plus trailer.

Another thing to consider when you buy your bike is whether you might want an electric model, which will be more expensive but may be worth the investment if you live in a hilly region and struggle to cycle additional weight without a bit of extra help, or live a long distance from where you want to cycle to.

Use your head: buy a bike helmet

There is much debate over whether people should have to wear cycle helmets,[12] thanks to a study that found that compulsory helmet laws in various Canadian provinces achieved only a 'minimal' effect on hospital admissions for head injuries related to cycling – possibly because drivers who see people cycling with their heads protected are less likely to drive carefully around them.[13] However, even if it makes no difference to reduced injury rates, the risk of not wearing a helmet while cycling is still significant, as a severe head injury can occur from any fall and this can be a life-changing event.[14]

There is no US law stating that a cycle helmet must be worn. It is best not to take a baby who can't support his or her own head on a bike, because until this time s/he won't be able to wear a cycling helmet. Ideally, your baby should also e able to sit well and unaided before sitting in a bike seat. Unless you happen to know someone with a cycle helmet that properly fits your child, you will have to buy one new. Think of it this way: any car journey that is avoided through cycling instead will quickly negate the environmental consequences of buying a new cycle helmet.

Public transportation

Buses

Greyhound buses offer an extensive national bus service in the US.[15] Other options vary state by state but they include Megabus, BoltBus, Lux Bus, Vanoose, Tripper Bus and Red Coach, which are assessed usefully by a travel guide available online.[16]

A report commissioned by Greener Journeys concludes that if drivers switched just one car journey to bus or coach *once a month*, it would mean one billion fewer car journeys and a saving of two million tonnes of carbon-dioxide emissions.[17] It also estimates that the best-used bus services in major urban centers may be reducing carbon emissions by 75 per cent or more, when comparing the emissions from bus operations with the emissions that bus passengers would generate if they used cars instead.

In addition, although some people cite speed as a reason to drive, buses have actually been found to reduce congestion due to being able to carry more people, which can shorten journey times and lead to a 10 per cent reduction in travel time.[18] For example, the installation of a bus lane along the A259 in Brighton, UK, led to the 12X bus service cutting its journey by 26 minutes.[19]

Trains

According to the International Energy Agency and International Union of Railways,[20] road users worldwide account for about 71 per cent of transport emissions, while aviation accounts for 12.3 per cent and railway companies contribute to less than 1.8 per cent.

A study by researchers at the International Institute for Applied Systems Analysis (IIASA) and Center for International Climate and Environmental Research (CICERO) recommends reducing emissions and climate impact by choosing train and coach travel over driving alone, driving large cars and flying.[21]

Long distance rail travel in the US is possible with a little planning, and Amtrak passenger train service runs between many states, with both long and short distance options. [22] There is also the option of a renowned 3,000-mile rail journey right across the country, for those after a scenic luxury holiday.

In addition to this, on a train or bus you can interact with your child to pass the time usefully, for example by reading a book to ease frustration. Taking the train makes more sense than getting stuck in traffic with children due to congestion.

Choosing to take the bus, coach and train over driving is generally the greenest option for travelling long or short distances with children.

Driving

The impacts of driving are far-reaching, as driving in a personal vehicle:
- drives climate change – road transport accounts for 27 per cent of total US emissions of carbon dioxide
- impacts air quality – air pollutants from transport include nitrogen oxides, carbon monoxide and hydrocarbons
- increases noise pollution
- uses resources – vehicles have a major impact on the environment through their construction, use and eventual disposal, and
- has an impact on local pollution levels and quality of life.[23]

Also, driving impacts us in ways that we don't necessarily realize – for example, research found that a street that wasn't a through-route for vehicles was more likely to be one where people knew their neighbors and helped out local elderly people.[24] Other research suggests that driver behavior has a substantially negative impact on places that are often assumed to be quiet streets, but are used for racing through.[25] One researcher argues in favor of developing towns differently in order to avoid the focus on roads: 'Who wants their child to be at risk of harassment, such as engine revving, tailgating, beeping, verbal abuse or worse, being driven at? Most adults aren't that keen on it either. So modal filtering could be a key part of creating streets for everyone, where motors can access homes and shops, but don't dominate.'[26]

Lift share

The IIASA-CICERO study found that a 1000-kilometer trip alone in a large car can emit as much as 250 kilograms of carbon dioxide, while a train trip or carpooling in a small car could emit as little as 50 kilograms for each passenger.[27] IIASA researcher

Jens Borken-Kleefeld states that: 'Traveling alone in a large car can be as bad for the climate as flying, but driving with three in a small car could have an equally low impact as a train ride'.[28]

Lift sharing is therefore an excellent way to lower your carbon footprint, and if you already have a couple of children then you're already competing with rail travel in terms of emissions. For lone journeys to work it's fairly easy to set up lift shares if you commute a regular distance at similar times and can pick colleagues up *en route*. You can also alternate driving to work with colleagues who live near you. List car journeys on lifeshare.com and ridester.com.

Join a car club

If you're considering buying a vehicle and only drive occasionally, joining a car club could be a great option for you. It requires virtually no interaction with other people so may be ideal for hermits too. Sign up online and you can access a car in your area (again online), book it and gain access with a swipe card (as the keys are kept inside the car) all without leaving your seat. Membership is monthly but rental rates can be per day or per hour and it works out much cheaper than owning a car as you don't have to pay out for annual insurance, MOT tests, year-round parking costs, and so on. Find your nearest Car Club at www.carclubdirectory.com.

Change your driving habits

According to the Energy Saving Trust, by changing the way you drive you could reduce your fuel consumption by up to 15 per cent, save hundreds of dollars in fuel a year and reduce carbon-dioxide emissions by as much as 400 kilograms of CO_2 a year.[29] They recommend altering:

- The health of your vehicle. A car that is serviced regularly and has proper tuning, tire pressure, brakes and fuel consumption is more efficient and saves fuel. When your tires need replacing, consider *low rolling resistance* replacements.
- The loads you carry. Roof racks add drag and other unnecessary weight increases fuel consumption, so ditch any unnecessary weight before you drive anywhere.
- The way you drive. Driving smoothly decreases fuel consumption, whereas racing starts and sudden stops use more. Use higher gears when traffic conditions allow: shift up at 2,500 rpm for gas-fueled cars and 2,000 rpm for diesel cars, as a vehicle traveling at 37 mph in third gear uses 25 per cent more fuel than it would at the same speed in fifth gear.[30]
- The speed you travel. Emissions are lowest at around 50 mph and much higher above 70 mph.
- The way you wait. If you're stuck in traffic or stopping for more than a minute, running the engine unnecessarily uses fuel needlessly. Switch it off.
- The noise you make. Reduce the volume of your car stereo or close your car window in residential areas, and avoid sounding your horn or revving your engine.
- The energy you use. Air conditioning and on-board electrical devices increase fuel consumption, so only use them when really necessary.
- The people you carry. Lift share as often as possible.
- The times you travel. Aim not to drive at busy times as congestion uses more gas.

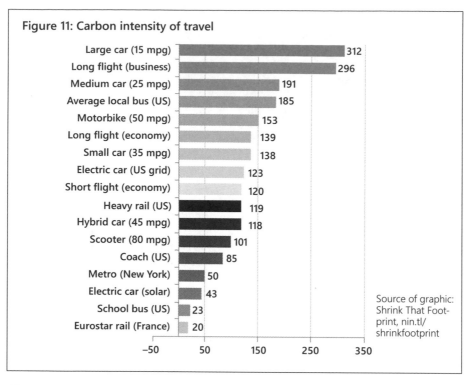

Figure 11: Carbon intensity of travel

Mode	Value
Large car (15 mpg)	312
Long flight (business)	296
Medium car (25 mpg)	191
Average local bus (US)	185
Motorbike (50 mpg)	153
Long flight (economy)	139
Small car (35 mpg)	138
Electric car (US grid)	123
Short flight (economy)	120
Heavy rail (US)	119
Hybrid car (45 mpg)	118
Scooter (80 mpg)	101
Coach (US)	85
Metro (New York)	50
Electric car (solar)	43
School bus (US)	23
Eurostar rail (France)	20

Source of graphic: Shrink That Footprint, nin.tl/shrinkfootprint

Choose a cleaner vehicle

One way to make your driving greener is to invest in the more eco-friendly option for a vehicle to begin with, which will be the most fuel-efficient models, a small car, or an electric car (see Figures 11 and 12). The rule of thumb is that the smaller the car you pick, the smaller its impact on the environment will be. Large cars like 4x4s and Sports Utility Vehicles (SUVs) are the most environmentally polluting vehicles available and SUVs are also more likely to lead to road accidents and fatalities.[31]

However, buying a new car to change your habits will cancel out the carbon you will save by doing so, because the manufacturing process and use of raw materials is so environmentally costly, so follow the second-hand rule for purchases as usual.[32] If you must buy a new car, cleaner choices are now available. Electric, hybrid, gas (LPG) and biofuel vehicles are better choices for the environment than standard models.[33] Although diesel cars emit less carbon dioxide than gas vehicles, they release more local environmental pollutants that are harmful to health and are implicated in many deaths in at-risk groups. You can check the carbon-dioxide emissions and fuel consumption of new cars through an online car fuel guide.[34]

Other factors to consider when choosing a car are:
- **Size:** a smaller car will save you money and reduce pollution.
- **Fuel options:** if you mostly drive on freeways then a diesel car could be the best option for lowest carbon emissions. If most of your driving is urban then a hybrid car has lower emissions of local pollutants.

- **Health**: look for a used car with a good service history to ensure it has been well maintained.
- **Bonus features:** many vehicles now are available with stop-start technology that automatically stops the engine when the car is stationary, and starts it again very quickly when you're ready to move off. This saves fuel and reduces both emissions and noise.

Choose a cleaner fuel

As might be expected, there is a wide range of varying opinions relating to the green properties of different fuels, and many of these are complete untruths told by vested interests.[35]

Biofuels

Biofuels are produced from the oil of crops such as oilseed rape, sunflowers and soybeans, and from waste cooking oils. They are usually sold in blends containing up to five per cent gas or diesel and they are not completely carbon neutral (because of the energy used to grow and process them). Biodiesel is a type of biofuel that is often called 'green diesel'.[36] However, there is a strong argument for biodiesel being

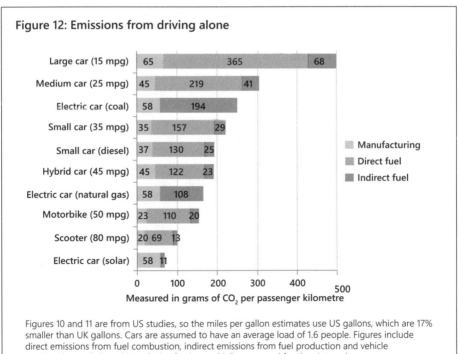

Figure 12: Emissions from driving alone

Large car (15 mpg): 65, 365, 68
Medium car (25 mpg): 45, 219, 41
Electric car (coal): 58, 194
Small car (35 mpg): 35, 157, 29
Small car (diesel): 37, 130, 25
Hybrid car (45 mpg): 45, 122, 23
Electric car (natural gas): 58, 108
Motorbike (50 mpg): 23, 110, 20
Scooter (80 mpg): 20, 69, 13
Electric car (solar): 58, 11

Legend: Manufacturing, Direct fuel, Indirect fuel

X-axis: 0, 100, 200, 300, 400, 500

Measured in grams of CO_2 per passenger kilometre

Figures 10 and 11 are from US studies, so the miles per gallon estimates use US gallons, which are 17% smaller than UK gallons. Cars are assumed to have an average load of 1.6 people. Figures include direct emissions from fuel combustion, indirect emissions from fuel production and vehicle construction emissions. No radiative forcing multiplier was used for the air travel.
Sources of data: DEFRA, EIA, EPA, GREET 1.8, Chester & Horvath Source of graphic: Shrink That Footprint, nin.tl/shrinkfootprint

Source of graphic: Shrink That Footprint, nin.tl/shrinkfootprint

environmentally unsound, because dedicating areas to bioenergy production has been found to impact food supply,[37] and bioenergy production is an inefficient use of land that does not reduce greenhouse-gas emissions.[38]

Straight vegetable oil (SVO) or post-consumer vegetable oil

Many people believe that a very green option is to use vegetable oil or a 100-per-cent post-consumer vegetable oil as a fuel. SVO is new, unused vegetable oil while post-consumer oil has been used and therefore needs filtering before reuse. Using waste oil keeps it from going to landfill sites so that is much greener than buying oil new for running a vehicle. However, research has found that the use of SVO will lead to reduced engine life caused by the build-up of carbon deposits inside the engine.[39] The same problem occurs through using different oil blends. So although it's a green option in the short term, it may cause your vehicle some damage and shorten its lifespan. It's thicker than diesel so it often needs pre-warming before it can be put into the cylinders.

Diesel

Diesel engines are more economical than gas engines, which means they also have lower carbon-dioxide emissions, so on this basis some people argue that diesel is a green fuel option. However, diesel engines emit particulates that harm local air quality and human health and hydrocarbons that are carcinogenic – to a greater extent than gas engines.[40] Diesels also produce several times more nitrogen dioxide than gas-fueled cars, which irritates the lungs of people with breathing problems. And of course, most diesel comes from petroleum so there is still the oil-extraction problem. These points make diesel one of the least eco options.

Electric vehicles

Electric vehicles (EVs) are a complex issue because how green they are comes down to where you live and how you drive. EVs do not produce any emissions when they are driven, but emissions are produced from electricity generation and one study by scientists in EV-friendly Norway has found that in some circumstances electric cars can have a greater impact on global warming than conventional cars due to the lithium battery production.[41] If you plan your routes beforehand and use only renewable energy to recharge your car, this could be a greener option for you. The time of day the batteries are charged also makes a difference because night-time electricity is less dependent on coal.[42] Shrink That Footprint has a very thorough breakdown of this complex topic on its website.[43]

Hybrid vehicles

Hybrid vehicles use a gas engine along with a battery and are very fuel efficient without any compromise on performance. In addition to 'full' hybrids, 'micro' hybrids are also available where the electric motor does not provide power to propel the vehicle, but allows the gas engine to stop when the vehicle comes to a halt. Micro cars are usually cheaper than full hybrids, and in urban areas produce significantly less carbon dioxide, local air pollution and noise.

Hydrogen

Hydrogen uses a fuel cell instead of a battery, which puts it on par with the electric car, environmentally speaking.[44] Hydrogen's only emission is water,[45] and some manufacturers are either producing or trialing cars powered by hydrogen, but there are hurdles such as the expense of making hydrogen-powered vehicles, producing hydrogen sustainably, and infrastructure for refueling: hydrogen is currently only available in a few locations.[46]

Gasoline

Gasoline is a petroleum-derived liquid that is used as a fuel in internal combustion engines, and the price of oil is high in environmental terms because drilling for oil releases greenhouse gases, burning it produces carbon dioxide, and oil spills cause phenomenal environmental damage, to name a few points.[47] Gas, like diesel, is still one of the worst offenders.

There is no such thing as a 'green' fuel, although hydrogen might be a good option if it becomes widespread, and electric cars can be much cleaner if recharged using clean energy. The focus for a green parent, then, is on avoiding the least clean options of diesel and gas, lift sharing regularly, and changing the way you drive. Whatever type of car you need, there will be class-leading models, and you can find out what these are at green-car-guide.com

Flying

Aviation is the fastest-growing source of anthropogenic greenhouse gases according to research, as well as the least environmentally friendly method of travel, whether you're only going a short distance, or going on an international flight.[48] The figures

Table 3: Carbon-dioxide emissions per passenger

Return journey	Time by plane (hours)	Emissions by plane (kg/CO_2)	Time by train (hours)	Emissions by train (kg/CO_2)	Emissions reduction by taking train
London-Paris	3.5	244	2.75	22	91%
London-Edinburgh	3.5	193	4.5	24	87%
London-Nice	4	250	8	36	85%
London-Amsterdam	4	136	Overnight (incl ferry)	27.2	80%
London-Dublin	4	174.8	8 (incl ferry)	46.8	73%
London-Tangier	5	435	48 (incl ferry)	63	85%

Source: The Man in Seat 61, nin.tl/trainvsplane

can be misrepresented because flying is often used to travel huge distances so it's difficult to compare to driving as you rarely drive a small car 2,000 miles overnight. In addition, airplanes put their combustion products (such as NOx) out at an altitude where they may be many times worse as greenhouse gases than at ground level. There are resources available to help you to plan trips abroad without flying, such as The Man in Seat 61, who combines public transport with ferry travel to advise on plane-free travel across the world.[49]

As a rule of thumb, any trip by air is more damaging than one overland, with the possible exception of driving a large car over a long distance alone. Car journeys consume broadly the same carbon as a flight would over the same distance, so if they are shared with others they fare better environmentally. New Internationalist summarizes some of the key points about flying on its website.[50]

Thankfully we're becoming more aware of the polluting nature of aviation, which has helped to lead to a recent resurgence in local holidaying, also called the 'staycation'.

A note on carbon offsetting

Every time you drive or fly on a plane, the vehicle emits carbon dioxide that will stay in the atmosphere, warming the planet for thousands of years. As demonstrated by Figure 11, flying is one of the most carbon-heavy options for travel, so there are companies that offer you the option to 'carbon offset' the emissions from your flight, often by paying to have trees planted to soak up your contribution of carbon dioxide. However, when the trees die, the carbon is released back into the atmosphere, so while you may feel good about this method of offsetting your emissions, in reality it's not going to make the world a cleaner place for your children.

Carbon offsetting cannot lead us to a status of carbon neutrality. It has been called a distraction and a delusion and compared to 'offsetting' the impact of having an affair – check out the Cheat Neutral website for a funny, satirical look at this logic.[51]

Some carbon-offsetting proponents argue that schemes have moved well beyond the limit of planting trees and now also support clean-energy projects,[52] but this highlights another problem with carbon offsetting which is that it's almost impossible to prove 'additionality' – in other words to prove what would have happened if the project had never existed. So you might be paying to offset but the reductions achieved by a project might not be *additional* to what would have happened if you hadn't coughed up.

Eco tourism?

Some people genuinely argue that flying is good for economically poorer countries that thrive on tourism because, for example, wildlife conservation only takes place if people from overseas are paying to see that wildlife.[53] This is a weak argument. As emissions rise and the Earth heats up, these countries have been identified as the ones that will suffer the most from climate change.[54]

If you do have to fly...

...then one thing you can do to reduce your environmental impact is to take less luggage with you, because the heavier the load a plane carries, the more fuel it burns;[55] so much so that a Japanese airline asks passengers to empty their bladders before boarding to decrease the amount of fuel burned by the plane.[56]

Pledge for a better future

Some people choose to commit to not flying by taking a pledge. The Flight Pledge Union allows you to make a 'gold' pledge not to travel by air for a year except in an emergency.[57] Some eco-conscious people choose to take vows never to fly again, although it may not be forever, because solar flight technology has really taken off (!) in the last few years. Who knows what the future holds for the aviation industry?

Summary

- Use 'slow travel' as a rule of thumb
- Choose to walk or cycle short distances instead of driving. Babywearing while walking benefits your baby and there are many different types of bicycle available to parents
- Commit to using public transport for longer distances
- If you are going to buy a car, buy it second hand rather than new. Look for a smaller and cleaner model and consider fuel options when doing so
- Hybrid cars and electric vehicles that are recharged using renewable energy are cleaner options
- Commit to driving less. Try having regular car-free days, once a week, for example
- Get your car serviced regularly and follow the rules for greener driving
- See if you can car share with a colleague who lives locally and sign up for car sharing for longer journeys
- Opt for 'staycations', travel closer to home, use Skype more to stay in touch with people abroad, and take the Flight Pledge.

1 http://www3.epa.gov/climatechange/ghgemissions/sources/transportation.html 2 *Independent*, nin.tl/privatecarban 3 *Hidden Europe*, nin.tl/slowtravelmanifesto 4 *Guardian*, nin.tl/better-brain 5 NI Direct Government Services, nin.tl/walkingtowork 6 *Hidden Europe*, op cit, nin.tl/slowtravelmanifesto 7 University of Michigan, nin.tl/walkoffdepression 8 http://www.nhtsa.gov/NCSA 9 Brake, nin.tl/braketheroad 10 *Popular Mechanics*, nin.tl/bikefacts 11 *Popular Mechanics*, nin.tl/bikefacts2 12 Road CC, nin.tl/helmet-debate 13 *BMJ* 2013;346:f2674, nin.tl/helmetlegislation 14 NHS, nin.tl/head-injuries 15 https://www.greyhound.com/ 16 http://www.budgettravel.com/feature/6-best-budget-bus-companies-in-the-us,7430/ 17 Greener Journeys, nin.tl/more-buses 18 Eddington Transport Study, nin.tl/eddingtonstudy 19 GOV.UK, op cit, nin.tl/roadstats 20 Railway Handbook 2012, nin.tl/railhandbook 21 Phys.org, nin.tl/travel-choices 22 http://www.seat61.com/UnitedStates.htm#.VncffLaLTIU 23 Environmental Protection UK, nin.tl/car-pollution 24 World Transport Policy & Practice , 17 (2). pp. 12-30, nin.tl/driventoaccess 25 *Guardian*, nin.tl/cyclesaferoads 26 Department for Transport, op cit, nin.tl/railtrends 27 Phys.org, op cit, nin.tl/travel-choices 28 International Institute for Applied Systems Analysis, nin.tl/footprintstudy 29 Energy Saving Trust, nin.tl/drive-smarter 30 NI Direct Government Services, nin.tl/greenercars 31 Oak Ridge National Laboratory, nin.tl/suvimpact 32 *Progress in Organic Coatings*, Volume 43, Issues 1-3, November 2001, Pages 193-206, nin.tl/autopaints 33 Environmental Protection UK, op cit, nin.tl/car-pollution 34 For example: carfueldata.direct.gov.uk 35 *Guardian*, nin.tl/greenest-cars 36 US Department of Energy, nin.tl/vegoilfuel 37 Proc Natl Acad Sci U S A. 2006 Jul 25; 103(30): 11206-11210, nin.tl/biofuel-report 38 *Guardian*, nin.tl/biofuelsnotgreen 39 Paper number 016051, 2001 ASAE Annual Meeting, nin.tl/fuelblend 40 BBC, nin.tl/dieselbadnews 41 *Journal of Industrial Ecology*, Volume 17,

Issue 1, pages 53-64, February 2013, nin.tl/el-vehicles **42** BBC, nin.tl/envirofriendlycars **43** Shrink That Footprint, nin.tl/mythdebunked **44** Live Science, nin.tl/greenautotech **45** BBC, nin.tl/future-fuel **46** For example: carfueldata.direct.gov.uk **47** For Dummies, nin.tl/fuelimpact **48** Legal Aspects of Carbon Trading, October 2009, nin.tl/carbon-regs **49** seat61.com **50** *New Internationalist*, nin.tl/reduceflying **51** cheatneutral.com **52** climatecare. org/our-projects/ **53** E.g. Environmental journalist Anna Shepard in her Eco Worrier column for *The Times.* **54** *Guardian*, nin.tl/climate-impacts-poor **55** Oxford University Environmental Change Institute, nin.tl/ calculatingcarbon **56** *Telegraph*, 2 Oct 2009, nin.tl/toiletbeforeboarding **57** flightpledge.org.uk

9 Green your home

Chemicals to avoid... Alternative products you can buy or make... Hair products... Personal cleaning products... Toothpastes... Skincare products... Sun block... Laundry detergents... Tips for going green at home...

In Chapter 7 we looked at potentially dangerous chemicals that are found in new children's clothing, and the debate surrounding whether or not they impact child health. With toiletries we know for certain that what you put directly onto your baby's skin is absorbed by it to varying degrees,[1] but there are still many toiletries which are advertised and sold as being safe for babies and young children that contain small amounts of potentially dangerous chemicals. While using one product with these chemicals in it is probably fine, using several different toiletries containing them may not be worth the risk. In addition, it is also important to consider the environmental impact of using these chemicals.

Which chemicals should you avoid?

Here are the common suspects.

Endocrine disruptor compounds (EDCs) have been found by a recent study to be costing Europe £470 million a year through their impacts on male reproductive health,[2] and a series of reports by 18 of the world's foremost experts estimates the health costs of exposure to EDCs to be between £113 billion ($180 billion) and £195 billion ($310 billion) in Europe alone.[3] Lower IQ, adult obesity and five per cent of autism cases have also been linked to exposure to endocrine disruptors found in food containers, plastics, furniture, toys, carpeting and cosmetics, according to an expert study.[4] EDCs are suspected to be associated with altered reproductive function in males and females, increased incidence of breast cancer, abnormal growth patterns and neurodevelopmental delays in children, changes in immune function,[5] and other serious health impacts for mammals, birds, fish and humans.[6]

The European Commission has compiled a 'priority list' of 118 EDCs based on their persistence in the environment or production at high volumes, 60 of which humans are probably exposed to. The full list can be viewed online, but the 12 worst offenders to avoid are listed as: 2,2-bis(4-(2,3-epoxypropyl)phenyl)propane, carbon disulphide, 4-chloro-3-methylphenol, 2,4-dichlorophenol, 4-nitrotoluene, o-phenylphenol, resorcinol, 4-tert octylphenol, tetra BDE, oestrone, 17b-oestradiol, and 17a-ethinyloestradiol.[7]

Good retailers should promote their products as being EDC-free, but when in doubt, it's worth asking manufacturers directly and boycotting until you gain answers.

Glycol ethers are used as solvents and in cleaning compounds, liquid soaps and cosmetics. Short-term exposure to high levels of the glycol ethers in humans results in serious health problems, as does long-term exposure.[8] The release of some glycol ethers into the air through the manufacturing process can also induce health effects through inhalation and ingestion for employees.[9] Avoiding products with the ingredients 2-butoxyethanol (EGBE) and methoxydiglycol (DEGME) can help reduce exposure to glycol ethers.

Microbeads are tiny bits of plastic that are used in body scrubs, shower gels and toothpaste. They are thought to be safe in terms of human health. However, when they enter water systems they create a plastic build-up that coats the floor of the lake, choking out plant life. Some creatures mistake them for fish eggs and ingest them, filling their bodies with plastic and starving to death. The small fish who eat the plastic are eaten by progressively larger fish, all of whom begin to accumulate the plastic.[10] Not only do microbeads impact fish and marine life, but the plastic can act like a sponge for pollutants like motor oils and pesticides, so toxins could work their way into bloodstreams all the way up the food chain into the fish eaten by humans.[11] There are websites available[12] that list the common products that contain microbeads, or you can email the manufacturers individually to find out. Facial scrubs almost always contain them.

Phthalates are added to polyvinyl chloride (PVC) products to impart flexibility and durability. A report by the American Academy of Pediatrics found that infants exposed to infant-care products, specifically baby shampoos, baby lotions, and baby powder, showed higher than normal levels of phthalates in their urine, but further research is still under way to determine how damaging this may be to babies and children.[13] The worst offenders appear to be diethylhexyl phthalate (DEHP) and diisononyl phthalate (DINP), so look out for these on labels of ingredients.

Triclosan is an antibacterial and antifungal agent that is often added to hand washes. It is also found in toothpastes to help prevent gingivitis, mouthwashes, shaving creams and deodorants. Exposure to triclosan has been associated with antibiotic resistance,[14] and the American Food and Drug Administration is reviewing triclosan use based on the latest science and states that it does not have evidence that triclosan in antibacterial soaps and body washes provides any benefit over washing with regular soap and water.[15] There's really no good reason not to give this one the boot from your home altogether.

Sodium lauryl sulphate (SLS) is a detergent that can cause contact dermatitis or eczema and is found in hand washes, shampoos, shower gels, toothpastes, bubble bath solutions and other baby products.[16] Contrary to what some people believe, no link has been found between SLS and cancer – and SLS is actually the least of your worries in terms of chemicals to avoid.[17]

After reading this list you're probably feeling scared and worried about exposing your baby to these harmful chemicals. The next section on alternative products may help you avoid them.

Alternative products you can buy or make

Although you can't completely eradicate your baby's exposure to harmful chemicals completely, you can limit the number of dangerous chemicals in your home by opting for clearly labeled, green toiletries instead. Lush Cosmetics is a widely available retailer that is committed to not using EDCs and other chemicals, although the brand often comes under fire from consumers for using SLS. However, as mentioned previously, SLS is the least of your worries.

Hair products

The UK-based organization *Ethical Consumer* lists the following shampoos as highly ethical with scores of 20 out of 20: Essential Care, Green People and Yaoh organic. It gives 19 out of 20 to: Caurnie vegan, Faith in Nature, Honesty, and Pure Nuff Stuff.[18] All these shampoos are available in the US online or through health stores.

'No poo' is a recent trend of adults giving up using shampoo altogether, and some are trying it with their children as well. The idea behind no poo is that hair is self-cleaning and that shampoo strips hair of its natural oils, although there is no evidence to back up this theory.[19] Some people choose to 'no poo' for life, while others do it as a form of detox; the rules aren't set in stone. A common homemade alternative to commercial shampoo appears to be baking soda with a vinegar rinse, while others use castile soap, or make up their own recipes.[20]

Not washing your hair won't harm you, but it does get dirty. We secrete an oil called sebum to protect the protein structure of the hair, but that same oil collects dirt and scalp flakes, which can get itchy and may not be practical for babies and children.

Personal cleaning products

Instead of being washed in a bath, a newborn baby can be 'topped and tailed',[21] in other words, wiped from the top down using cotton wool and water, and an older baby only needs clean, warm water to bathe in.[22] Toiletries are not recommended for babies at all because their skin is so delicate. It can be fun to use bubble-bath products in your child's bath-time but these usually contain SLS, which can cause skin problems. Many manufacturers sell 'baby talcum powder' but this has been suspected of leading to tiny airborne particles damaging a baby's developing lungs.[23]

When your child is old enough to need soap for cleaning grubby stains, *Ethical Consumer* lists the following products as highly ethical, with scores of 20 out of 20: Badger Baby bath soap, Essential Care soap and Yaoh liquid soap. It gives 19 out of 20 to: Bio-D handwash, Caurnie soaps, and Faith in Nature soap and handwash.[24]

Toothpastes

Fluoride is a naturally occurring mineral found in water in varying amounts, and in some countries it is added to drinking water and toothpastes to help protect populations against tooth decay.[25] Anti-fluoride activists argue various reasons for avoiding fluoride altogether, none of which have been proven by science.[26] In fact, fluoride at low concentrations has been found to be safe, and fluoridation is supported by many organizations including the World Dental Federation, the World Health Assembly and the World Health Organization.[27].

Even when fluoride is added to drinking water, it is in very low concentrations, with one expert, the Chair of Population Oral Health at the University of Melbourne, commenting that: 'In hotter climates where people drink more, the recommended level can drop to around 0.7 parts per million. As a comparison, the amount of fluoride in children's toothpaste is 400 to 500 parts per million. In regular toothpaste, it's 1,000 parts per million.'[28]

The only health implication of overuse of fluoride, particularly for children, is a condition called dental fluorosis, which causes flecks on the teeth or in severe cases pitted or discolored teeth.[29] This condition is rare but provides a good reason to teach your child to spit toothpaste out rather than swallowing it. Supervise children's brushing, and use only a smear of fluoride toothpaste until three years old, then a pea-sized amount until they are seven years old.[30]

Ethical Consumer lists Green People vegan toothpaste as highly ethical with a score of 20 out of 20, while Weleda toothpaste scores 18.[31]

Skincare products

Babies generally don't need to have their skin moisturized with lotions unless they suffer from dry-skin conditions like eczema, although following daily lotion-applying routines with babies has been found to reduce the onset of eczema later on.[32] Some parents swear by coconut oil or olive oil as a safe alternative to commercial moisturizers for a baby or child. There is no scientific research available on this topic. However, if you need to use moisturizing cream and natural oils aren't sufficient, *Ethical Consumer* recommends the following lotions based on ethical and environmental credentials, all of which are available in the US online or through health stores : Badger skincare, Essential Care and Yaoh organic hemp all score 20 out of 20, while Caurnie, Faith in Nature, Honesty and Pure Nuff Stuff all score [19.33]

Green People is a brand that avoids harmful chemicals and sells organic diaper cream, baby balm and dry-skin lotion (greenpeopleus.com). Weleda Baby Calenda Baby Lotion is also worth looking out for (usa.weleda.com). Lush Cosmetics is another option for buying baby lotion. Unfortunately all of these alternative green products are expensive, but they are worth investing in to protect your baby or child from known harmful chemicals. As more of us choose to buy them, the prices will drop, so this is a real case of voting with your purse or wallet for positive change.

Environmental Working Group's Skin Deep Cosmetics Database site rates popular cosmetics and personal-care products with hazard scores on a scale of 0 to 10, depending on their toxicity.[34]

Sun block

Infants under six months should be kept protected from direct sunlight by staying in the shade at the sunniest times of day and wearing protective clothing, especially around midday, because baby skin is delicate. Parents are advised to cover exposed parts of their child's skin with sunscreen, even on cloudy or overcast days, and use a sun protection factor (SPF) of 15 or above that is effective against UVA and UVB.[35] *Ethical Consumer* lists the following sun blocks as highly ethical and eco-friendly: Badger sunscreen and Yaoh organic hemp sun block score 20 out of 20 and Green People sun lotion and Pure Nuff Stuff sun cream score 19.[36]

Laundry detergents

A thorough review compared four different types of detergent alternatives, which were soap nuts, laundry balls, washing pellets and laundry magnets, to washing with conventional compact powder detergent, and found that in general the tested products had as good washing effect as water alone:[37] 'Conventional compact detergent showed significantly better cleaning effect at all tested soil types. However, the results also indicate that water alone already has a substantial cleaning effect.'

The research summary outlines that: 'It is possible that replacing regular detergent with an alternative laundry product might be positive, as long as no other contradictory changes in laundry process are made and the consumers receive satisfactory clean laundering results of their only slightly soiled laundry.' However, other washing detergents were not tested.

To summarize, ordinary conventional compact detergents did work significantly better for cleaning a few specific stains. For example, 'the soil-removal efficiency was increased on average by 35 per cent, varying from 3 to 66 per cent depending on the soil and fabric type, when adding 1/5 of regular detergent to wash'. However, there was little difference generally between the effectiveness of normal detergent and the specific eco-friendly alternatives tested.

So instead of buying the fancy washing alternatives that were tested in this study, use green laundry detergents. You can help to keep your carbon footprint down and save your baby from harsh chemical exposure by using a green laundry detergent such as Bio-D, Faith in Nature, ECOS or Sodasan, which scored 20, 20, 18 and 17 respectively for eco-credentials and ethical concerns in *Ethical Consumer's* assessment.[38]

Tips for going green at home

In terms of ingredient-reading and keeping the biggest toxic chemicals out of your home, clever marketing can catch you out. It's therefore worth doing your own research or sticking to the brands and products recommended in this chapter. The following pointers should also help you to green your home.

Make your own products. Perhaps the best and cheapest way to know exactly what goes into your baby's toiletries is to make your own. This will also reduce packaging waste. For cleaning your home, vinegar and baking soda can be used to clean almost anything, and tea-tree oil is a natural disinfectant, although it can cause skin irritation so wear gloves when you use it.[39] Mix in a little warm water with these and you've got yourself an all-purpose cleaner.

Buy certified organic products. Look for Soil Association certification. Also, don't fall for the 'natural' label, as the words 'natural', 'all-natural', 'hypoallergenic' and 'organic' are not regulated terms.

Improve indoor air quality. The air inside your home can be 10 times more toxic than the air outside.[40] Although ozone pollution is most often associated with outdoor air, the gas also infiltrates indoor environments like homes and offices. Because so many people spend as much of 80 to 90 per cent of their time indoors, indoor air pollution has been ranked as one of the world's greatest public health risks.[41] Keeping windows open as often as possible allows fresh air in, but adding plants to your shelves will also make a difference. The data on plant-mediated indoor air quality come from experiments conducted by the US National Aeronautics and Space Administration (NASA).[42] They found the top 10 plants for removing chemicals to be:

1 Areca palm
2 Lady palm
3 Bamboo palm
4 Rubber plant
5 Dracaena
6 English ivy
7 Dwarf date palm
8 Ficus
9 Boston fern
10 Peace lily.[43]

In addition to this, a research team recently published the results of a new study of the effects of three common houseplants on indoor ozone levels.[44] The scientists chose snake plants, spider plants and golden pothos plants for the experiment because of their popularity (mainly due to their low cost, low maintenance and rich foliage) and their reported ability to reduce other indoor air pollutants. The data revealed that ozone concentrations were reduced in chambers that contained plants to similar degrees.

So instead of buying an air purifier, which doesn't reduce levels of all indoor air pollutants (and some types can actually aggravate problems with allergies such as asthma), ask on your local Freecycle site for some free spider plant babies to pot yourself at home.

Remove your shoes. Children spend much more time than adults playing on floors and are much closer to them as crawling and toddling babies. Research has found that people bring lawn pesticides into their homes on their shoes.[45] Taking your shoes off and wiping your feet on a door mat or other carpeting before entering are therefore important pollutant-reduction measures.[46] Less dirt also means less sweeping, mopping, and vacuuming, which means less work, water, energy and fewer chemicals.

Choose nontoxic, recyclable packaging. You can never go wrong with glass because it's recyclable and has no danger of leaching toxins into the product inside. Lush Cosmetics is a worldwide brand that takes back used plastic containers to reuse them. Simply save them up and return them to any Lush store.

Summary

- Check the children's toiletries you buy for chemical offenders. If in doubt, change brands or contact the manufacturer directly
- Use reputable consumer guides to work out which products to use instead
- Avoid bubble baths and talcum powder
- Buy organic products where possible
- Consider making them yourself in the long run to reduce packaging
- Fluoridated toothpaste for children is safe and recommended
- Use eco-alternative washing powders – they are just as effective but less harmful
- Always fill the washing machine to its full capacity to avoid wasting water and energy unnecessarily
- Improve indoor air quality by growing plants in pots in the house
- Instigate a shoe-free home rule.

1 *Huffington Post*, nin.tl/skincare-health 2 Nordisk Ministerråd, 2014, nin.tl/cost-of-inaction 3 *Huffington Post*, op cit, nin.tl/skincare-health 4 *Journal of Clinical Endocrinology & Metabolism*, Volume 100, Issue 4, nin.tl/exposurecosts 5 WHO, nin.tl/edc-report 6 *Environmental Health Perspectives*, nin.tl/dev-effects 7 European Commission, nin.tl/substancesofconcern The full list is at nin.tl/substances-annex 8 US Environmental Protection Agency, nin.tl/glycolethers 9 *Environmental Health Perspectives*, Volume 112, Number 17, December 2004, nin.tl/air-toxics 10 IFL Science, nin.tl/microbead-ban 11 *Scientific American*, nin.tl/groomingproducts 12 For example, http://beatthemicrobead.org/images/pdf/RED%20UNITED%20STATES.pdf 13 American Society of Pediatrics, nin.tl/plasticizertoxicity 14 *Clinical Infectious Diseases*, Volume 45, Issue Supplement 2, nin.tl/antibacterialsoaps 15 US Food and Drug Administration, nin.tl/triclosanadvice 16 J Clin Periodontol. 1994 Nov;21(10):717-9, nin.tl/triclosanprotects 17 Treehugger, nin.tl/ecomyth 18 Ethical Consumer, nin.tl/shampooguide 19 Natural Parenting Tips, nin.tl/nopoohair 20 Ibid. 21 Baby Centre, nin.tl/bathingnewborn 22 NHS, nin.tl/washingbaby 23 EWG, nin.tl/saferproductstips 24 Ethical Consumer, op cit, nin.tl/shampooguide 25 The Conversation, nin.tl/fluoridetoothdecay 26 *Guardian*, nin.tl/anti-fluoride 27 WHO, nin.tl/oralhealthfluoride 28 The Conversation, op cit, nin.tl/fluoridetoothdecay 29 NHS, nin.tl/fluorideintro 30 British Dental Health Foundation, nin.tl/aboutfluoride 31 Ethical Consumer, op cit, nin.tl/shampooguide 32 *Wall Street Journal*, nin.tl/bathingtoomuch 33 Ethical Consumer, nin.tl/skincare-guide 34 nin.tl/skindeep/ 35 NHS, nin.tl/childsunsafety 36 Ethical Consumer, nin.tl/sunscreensguide 37 *H&PC Today*, Vol. 7(4) October/December 2012, nin.tl/alternative-laundry 38 Ethical Consumer, nin.tl/laundryguide 39 *Journal of Antimicrobial Chemotherapy*, Volume 45, Issue 5, pp639-643, nin.tl/timekillstudies 40 Treehugger, nin.tl/indoorairpollution 41 *Environ Health Perspect*. 2011 Oct; 119(10): a426–a427, nin.tl/healthierair 42 NASA, nin.tl/pollutionabatement 43 *Environ Health Perspect*. 2011, Oct; 119(10): 1426-427, nin.tl/top10houseplants 44 Science Daily, nin.tl/cutozone 45 Natural Resources Defense Council, nin.tl/ourchildrenatrisk 46 Treehugger, nin.tl/leaveshoes and Science Daily, nin.tl/keepoffgrass

10 Play, toys and entertainment

Fewer toys may mean better mental health... Environmentally friendly ways to get toys... Which toys are best?... Go the extra green mile: upcycle and invent... In praise of books... Social and interactive entertainment... The case for free play... Encouraging 'wild time'

In Chapter 1 we looked at Material Parenting and why it's important to avoid this as aspiring green parents. But how can the modern parent avoid the consumer culture of parenting, and what options are there for low-carbon methods of entertainment?

Research indicates that physical exploration of objects and materials is vital for brain development in babies, as it builds a model for understanding the world.[1] However, when it comes to obtaining items to facilitate this sort of learning, it can come at great cost to the environment: the figures are staggering. The United States leads the world in the production of waste, producing a quarter of the world's waste despite the fact that its population of 300 million is less than five per cent of the world's population, according to 2005 estimates.[2] It is sadly ironic that the toys we give our children to make them happy are polluting the planet they need to live on and the air they need to breathe.

Do babies need so many toys?

Parents tend to go all-out and buy numerous things to occupy and educate their children. These include various types of noisy, bright toys and also so-called essentials like baby swings, baby rockers and bouncers, to name just a few items. While a second-hand bouncer will help to give your arms a rest and may soothe an unsettled baby's tummy, it is no substitute for a parent and you may find that your baby dislikes being strapped into a bouncer far away from mum and dad anyway. All any baby really wants is to be held close and interacted with. Babies crave loving arms, familiar voices, interactive games, socializing and being exposed to lots of different, normal things. In order to attain these things, virtually no products are needed. Some parents feel guilty when they forgo buying masses of items for their children, but no amount of toys you buy can be a substitute for the time and attention you give to your baby.

There's a strong argument that children do not need a large number of store-bought toys, or commercial toys at all. To a newborn baby everything within reach is a toy, although they are more interested in human faces at such a young age.[3]

Recent research has shown that infants learn best from unexpected experiences that challenge their innate knowledge of the world by surprising them and sustaining their interest, which shows that babies as young as 11 months already have sophisticated expectations.[4] How can we meet these as green parents?

Babies are fascinated by all objects, not just brightly coloured plastic toys, and they love different experiences and textures that are typically not found in the toys that are aimed at them. That's part of the reason behind why they want your shiny phone and metal musical house keys so badly. There is a growing range of wooden items available for babies now and these are a good option for moving away from, if not eliminating entirely, plastic toys, since plastic is made of oil and requires an intense manufacturing process, and even BPA-free plastic toys may not be safe for mouthing. Also, there is also a strong argument for avoiding PVC (vinyl) toys completely because they can contain phthalates. Although some types of phthalates are banned from children's teething toys in the US because children can absorb the toxic chemicals through their mouths, they are still found in normal toys for children.[5]

Aside from obvious items that are not baby friendly, there is no harm in letting your baby play with the odd metal key, wooden spoon, and so on, so long as they're not small enough to be a choking hazard. Put them in a bowl with a variety of textures, for example scraps of old clothes or old towels, felts, velvets, even ceramic and glass, and natural materials such as sticks, pine cones and leaves.

You may feel reluctant to do this because these are not brand new shiny toys and to some degree considered to be 'dirty' items. But remember that chapter on plastics and how they may not be safe for eating off? Be afraid of toxic chemicals entering curious mouths, but don't be afraid of exposing your baby to dirt – their immune systems can handle it.

Fewer toys may mean better mental health

Rates of anxiety and depression among children and adolescents were far lower during the Great Depression, during World War Two and during the Cold War than they are today. The changes seem to be more to do with the way young people view the world than with the way the world actually is. We know that anxiety and depression correlate significantly with individuals' sense of control or lack of control over their own lives, and that people who believe that they are in charge of their own fate are less likely to become anxious or depressed than are those who believe that they are victims of circumstances beyond their **control**.[6] You might think that the sense of personal control would have increased over the last several decades, as society has become more individual-based, but the opposite has occurred instead. Sounds a bit like environmental apathy in the face of impending climate disaster, doesn't it?

The most recent evidence for the sharp generational rise in young people's depression, anxiety, and other mental disorders comes from a recent study headed by Dr Jean Twenge. Twenge assessed a variety of mental disorders in the US in older students from as far back as 1938, and younger adolescents from 1951. The results are consistent with other studies that point to dramatic increases in anxiety and depression in children, adolescents and young adults over the last five or more decades.

Twenge's theory is that these increases in anxiety and depression are related to a shift from 'intrinsic' to 'extrinsic' goals. Intrinsic goals are those that have to do with one's own development as a person, such as becoming good at a personal hobby and developing a meaningful philosophy of life. Extrinsic goals, on the other hand, are those that have to do with material rewards and other people's judgements. They include goals of high income, status and good looks. Twenge cites evidence that young people today are, on average, more oriented toward extrinsic goals and less oriented toward intrinsic goals than they were in the past. For example, a poll conducted annually of college undergraduates shows that most students today list 'being well off financially' as more important to them than 'developing a meaningful philosophy of life,' while the reverse was true in the 1960s and 1970s.

Twenge suggests that the shift from intrinsic to extrinsic goals represents a general shift toward a culture of materialism, transmitted through television and other media. Thus, encouraging children to have intrinsic goals is a key way to help children take control of their futures and save their planet, instead of relying on material possessions to bring them happiness and fulfilment (which doesn't work).

A note on cultural differences

A recent study examining temperamental differences between American and Dutch babies found that babies born in the Netherlands are more likely to be happy and easier to soothe as they approach a year of age.[7] American infants, on the other hand, were found to be more active and vocal. To some degree, the results of the study reflect American and Dutch parents' differing cultural values, as American parents often emphasize the importance of stimulation and early independence, whereas parents in Holland are more likely to incorporate children into daily activities at home, placing strong value on the importance of rest and regularity.

This appears to be why Dutch babies demonstrated greater expressions of happiness during routine activities and were easier to calm or soothe when upset. Study co-author Maria Gartstein observed that: 'I was struck by how little Dutch parents use toys when they play with their children, relative to US parents.'

Environmentally friendly ways to get toys

Let's be realistic. Although you may be able to reduce the number of toys in your home, you also need to keep the kids occupied sometimes when you're not able to interact with them properly, and research shows that children with educational toys and books grow up more stimulated.[8] There are plenty of ways to avoid buying new toys however, one of which is to join a local toy share scheme. They usually work by members paying a small fee or putting down a deposit to borrow from a library of toys, then exchanging these toys for different ones when the kids tire of them. This is a great way of teaching children to look after toys as well, since they belong to a community of sorts. If you don't have a scheme like this in your area, consider contacting your local children's center about it or finding a group of like-minded parents to set one up together.

A good way to declutter unused toys is periodically to hide away toys that aren't being played with. Rotating toys can generate new interest in them, but when this doesn't work you can donate them to worthy causes without feeling guilty about your baby losing out.

Free toys can be obtained through the websites Freecycle and Freegle and second-hand toys are easily picked up from charity shops and garage sales.

Which toys are best?

- Climate Counts uses a scale out of 100 and 22 criteria to determine if companies have:
- measured their carbon footprint
- reduced their impact on global warming
- supported (or suggested intent to block) progressive climate legislation
- publicly disclosed their climate actions clearly and comprehensively.[9]

Of the toy companies covered in this section, Climate Counts have assessed 13, one of which scored zero out of a possible 100 points (the higher the better) and three of which scored 11 points or under. The highest marks went to Hasbro and Lego. Toy companies clearly have a long way to go in addressing their climate-change impacts.

Hasbro	73
LEGO	70
Mattel	16
Chicco	0

In contrast, the UK-based organization Ethical Consumer *has an excellent breakdown of different toys that foster specific types of learning and are available in the US and Canada. These include the following:*

Construction and creative toys help to foster inventiveness.[10] This is a key area where toys can be a great learning aid, so long as they allow some flexibility. In terms of ethical rating, including impact on the environment, Ethical Consumer *recommends the following brands: Brio toys, Crayola creative toys, Etch a sketch, Happy Mais creative toy, Maya Organic wooden toys, Plasticine and Sticklebricks. All of these toys scored 14 out of 20 so they're not ideal companies to support, just not as bad as some of the others that are out there.*

Board games and puzzles are great for teaching logic and science. A summary of games for improving executive function is provided by a writer in *The Atlantic*.[11] Ethical Consumer recommends Orchard toys, games and puzzles with 15 points out of 20, while Lanka Kade jigsaws, Ravensburger board games and jigsaws and Rummikub score 14. Again, these are not as eco-friendly as we'd like them to be, so buying second hand is a good option.

Toy cars, buses, trains and planes are common childhood toys and great ways of normalizing types of transport. Some green parents choose to limit the amount of cars and road vehicles and planes that their children play with, preferring to give them toy bikes and trains for imaginative play instead, but using planes and cars is also a useful way of teaching that they are not environmentally friendly options. Ethical Consumer gives 14 out of 20 to Battle Deck cars, Brio toys, Holz wooden toys, Maya Organic wooden toys, Plan wooden toys, Smoby toys, Solar Speedsters build-your-own vehicles and Thomas & Friends.[12]

Try to buy only toys that are likely to be stimulating while allowing room for creative play – in other words, toys that can be played with in multiple ways (as described above).

Go the extra green mile: upcycle and invent

Even if crafting isn't your thing, you're missing a trick if you don't modify or upcycle broken toys. You can also be inventive and create new toys from scrap materials that you already have at home, which is also known as 'junk modeling'. These are great ways to teach your child the value of an item, the work that goes into it, patience while it is made and how to make your own things rather than always having to buy them. Ideas include upcycling worn-out clothes into texture quilts, jars and bottles into lanterns, outgrown socks into sock puppets, toilet rolls into space rockets. There is no end to this list. Search Pinterest for 'upcycled children's items' to bring up a wide range of inspiring ideas. Increasingly, companies are starting to follow the 'closed loop' or upcycling path, and supporting them is another way to avoid contributing to further environmental degradation.[13]

The greenest options are to reduce the number of new toys you bring into your home, buy them second hand instead, and make your own with your child. Get toys free when you can, but don't go overboard. Swap toys with friends and consider setting up an informal toy-sharing group.

If you do buy new toys, or have family members who would prefer not to buy second hand, recommend that they:
- avoid toys that are made of plastic or PVC
- choose toys that don't need batteries or electricity
- look for a Forest Stewardship Council (FSC) label on wooden toys to be sure that the wood was produced in way that hasn't harmed the environment
- look for items that were made with recycled materials.

Also, you can always keep new toys and space them throughout the year, or keep them to 'regift' them to others. This idea has really taken off in the US, where people pass gifts to one another through regiftable.com. Pop in and take a look at the lovely regifting stories on the website. Rehoming is also a great way to ensure that an unwanted gifts reaches hands that really need that item.

In praise of books

There's a lot to say in favor of books. Reading should not be underestimated as a valuable bonding, educational, stimulating activity, and researchers have found that children of well-off families hear an average of 2,153 words an hour versus 616 in less well-off families.[14] The latter group is described as having a 'poor linguistic diet'.

According to a report by Common Sense Media, there is a strong correlation between actions that parents model and how often their children read. For example, among children who are frequent readers, 57 per cent of parents set aside time each day for their child to read, compared to 16 per cent of parents of children who are infrequent readers.[15] The love of reading can set a child up for life, and it begins early with child surrounded by books who is read to and learns to associate reading and books with enjoyment. It doesn't cost you or the environment to attain this goal, as libraries are generally well stocked with children's books.

Social and interactive entertainment

It's good to focus on interactive activities that are enjoyable for all parties involved, rather than worrying about ticking boxes regarding learning. In any case, what we assume to be educational for small children may not be, as with many classes aimed at babies learning languages. Neuroscientist Patricia K Kuhl found that language delivered by television, audio book, internet or smartphone doesn't actually teach infants it, as only children who have been exposed to the new language through human interaction are able to discriminate between sounds.[16]

In addition to attending parenting groups and child-friendly events, it can be nice to do a led class with your baby, for example a regular music, yoga or dance class. This can be a nice way of bonding and interacting that you wouldn't necessarily think to instigate otherwise. On top of this are Sling Meets for babywearing enthusiasts, cloth diaper groups, green parenting groups (I've never heard of these but you could set one up, take along this book and start a conversation!), and other activities for nourishing parental minds without all the focus being on play for the baby.

You'll end up spending plenty of time together at home when you need less busy periods of time to interact and bond together, and this is when you'll want to get out your repertoire of games and songs to do with baby. I'm not saying that you have to entertain your baby non-stop – babies can and do entertain themselves for short periods of time (longer when they're up to mischief), but some parents struggle with the confidence to interact with their babies, which is why they might reach for loud, bright, highly stimulating toys to help them out. Instead, you can teach yourself new habits like singing to your baby, offering a massage, or do a simple clapping routine to a nursery rhyme on a CD. You don't need to know lots of these things as babies love repetition, but you may want to learn several for your own mental wellbeing!

If you're not much of a singer or struggle to remember which games to play, there are lots of other options. Children's music can be streamed online now and there is no end to nursery rhymes and traditional songs for those rainy afternoons. I recommend Putumayo sing-along CDs for children to introduce them to the music of different world regions through age-appropriate songs, and anything by the children's musicians Raffi and Poco Drom to help inspire a love of nature (and good music).

So skip the overly educational classes, CDs and videos, and choose enjoyable interaction-based entertainment instead, with led classes if you enjoy them personally.

A note on screen time

We covered this in Chapter 1 but it's worth repeating here that screen time is not to be feared, but a resource that can be used in a healthy way at home. The updated AAP guidelines advise teaching 'healthy concepts of digital citizenship' and are worth viewing in full on their website.[17] As children get older they can be taught media literacy through watching programmes together, which can help to counter the power of marketers and consumerism.

The case for free play

It's no secret that children today are overscheduled and overwhelmed. While free play has declined, school and school-like activities (such as lessons out of school and adult-directed sports) have increased, and children today spend more time in school than ever before. They take more tests and do more homework, and even outside of school children now spend more time in settings where they are directed, protected, catered to, ranked, judged and rewarded by adults. In all of these settings adults are in control, not children.[18]

Research has found that the more time children spend in structured, parent-guided activities, the worse their ability to work towards self-directed goals and develop self-control.[19] What's the solution to this? Free play. Put simply, free play is unscheduled, unsupervised playtime and it is one of the most valuable educational opportunities we give our children. Boston College psychology professor Peter Gray studies the benefits of play in human development. In his book *Free to Learn*, he discusses how play supports the development of executive function, and particularly self-directed control:

'Free play is nature's means of teaching children that they are not helpless. In play, away from adults, children really do have control and can practice asserting it. In free play, children learn to make their own decisions, solve their own problems, create and abide by rules, and get along with others as equals rather than as obedient or rebellious subordinates.'[20]

The value of free play, daydreaming, risk-taking, and independent discovery is a hot topic at present, and a new study by psychologists at the University of Colorado has demonstrated how important these activities are in the development of children's executive functioning.[21] The study's authors looked at the schedules and play habits of six-year-old children, specifically how much time each of them spent in less structured, spontaneous activities like imaginative play and reading on their own initiative, rather than in structured activities that were organized and supervised by adults, including lessons and homework. They found that children who have more free play have 'more highly developed self-directed executive function', while the more time kids spend in structured activities, the worse their sense of self-direction and self-control is. It's important to note that adult-led activities do play an important role in teaching children, but that the issue lies in the lack of balance. According to the school leader development organization Optimus Education, this balance means one-third adult-directed activities, and one-third child-initiated activities.[22]

Also, a leading researcher in the field of cognitive development says that when children pretend, they're not just being silly – they're doing science.[23]

For more on this topic, I recommend the thorough review 'Free Play in Childhood', which looks at the history and science behind play, links between play and brain development, and ways to incorporate free play into the English teaching curriculum.[24]

Encouraging outdoor play/'wild time'

In a 2005 study, the American Medical Association stated: 'Children will be smarter, better able to get along with others, healthier and happier when they have regular opportunities for free and unstructured play in the out-of-doors.'[25] Project Wild Thing, a British documentary about children and nature exposure directed by David Bond, argues that British children have never been more disconnected from the natural world, as the roaming distance that children play from their home has shrunk by 90 per cent in 30 years with time spent playing outside down 50 per cent in just one generation.[26] Richard Louv takes this argument further in his book *Last Child in the Woods*, where he coins the term 'nature-deficit disorder'.[27]

In addition, recent research has found that children who spend less time outdoors are much more likely to develop myopia (shortsightedness). As an article in the scientific journal *Nature* explains, 'After studying more than 4,000 children at Sydney primary and secondary schools for three years, they found that children who spent less time outside were at greater risk of developing myopia... A stronger effect was found at a school in southern Taiwan, where teachers were asked to send children outside for all 80 minutes of their daily break time instead of giving them the choice to stay inside. After one year, doctors had diagnosed myopia in 8 per cent of the children, compared with 18 per cent at a nearby school.'[28]

Screen time is often blamed for the surge of myopia in our children, but researchers conclude that: 'Children who spent more time outside were not necessarily spending less time with books, screens and close work. "We had these children who were doing both activities at very high levels and they didn't become myopic," says [Kathryn] Rose (head of orthoptics at the University of Technology, Sydney). Close work might still have some effect, but what seemed to matter most was the eye's exposure to bright light.' Not to allow children daily outdoor play is shortsighted indeed.

One study found that adults who spent their childhoods filled with unstructured play in nature, including some that 'was not environmentally sensitive by adult standards; rather, it included manipulation of the environment through war games, fort building, role playing of stories in popular children's adventure books and movies, and the like', became dedicated to nature and conservation.[29]

Since the parents or parents-to-be reading this are mainly green-inclined, I don't think I need to spend a vast amount of time arguing that we need to allow children to spend more time playing outdoors in natural areas with few restrictions. Even simply being in outdoor green spaces has been found to have benefits for mental health and wellbeing, but children benefit in myriad ways, as outlined by various reports by Children & Nature Network, which compiles the relevant scientific data on the topic.[30]

But even for the most committed green parent there are barriers. Busy roads, perceived fears of dangers, lack of green spaces on our doorsteps, health-and-safety worries, the widespread commercialization of play and entertainment: the list goes on. Hence Project Wild Thing has coined the term 'Wild Time' to encourage outdoor play and has a free app to help children to engage with the great outdoors. You can also join The Wild Network to get involved.

For families lucky enough to have access to a garden or who are involved in community or local-authority play schemes, the Forestry Commission produces a practical guide on using natural materials to build play areas which 'stimulate the imagination and sense of adventure'.[31] There are also forest schools cropping up around the US, opportunities to do nature trails and other outdoors-based activities for young people to join in with. And, of course, local parks are there to be used by small but active legs and are usually easily reached by walking or a short cycle ride.

A note on education

Thanks to some of the research mentioned in this chapter, there is an ongoing discussion between parents, educators and governmental officials regarding the way we teach our children and what they learn in schools. This has led to many alternative schools emerging in the US which tend to focus more on free play and child-led learning than mainstream schools. However, such options are not ideal for or available to everyone, so don't be put off by criticisms of mainstream schooling. Yes, they do tend to focus too heavily on adult-led structured learning, but there is a lot you can do with your child to balance those strict learning schedules with opportunities for free play, outdoor play and child-led learning. Take small steps towards these achievable actions – they're great excuses to take part in creative projects, travel to new places and spend more time outdoors – and they will benefit the whole family.

Summary

- Don't buy large amounts of toys. Consider going 'toy-free' with your baby and providing ordinary items as toys instead
- Focus on obtaining specific educational toys that can be played with in different ways
- Choose sustainably made toys and avoid plastic
- Consider joining or setting up a toy library with friends
- Buy books second hand and make good use of your local library
- Upcycle worn-out clothes, broken toys and other household items into new ones
- Choose enjoyable interaction-based entertainment over educational classes
- Avoid screen time for under-twos

- Give gifts of experience-based things rather than material possessions
- Regift new items that your baby doesn't want to play with
- Make space for free play over structured activities
- Encourage outdoor play.

1 John Brierley, nin.tl/givemeachild **2** http://www.forbes.com/2006/05/23/waste-worlds-worst-cx_rm_0524waste.html **3** PNAS, nin.tl/contrastpolarity **4** *Science 3* April 2015: Vol. 348 no. 6230 pp. 91-94, nin.tl/observingunexpected **5** BBC, nin.tl/chemicalban **6** *Psychology Today*, nin.tl/declineofplay **7** EurekAlert!, nin.tl/dutchbabies **8** *Guardian*, nin.tl/better-brain **9** Climate Counts, nin.tl/comparingcompanies **10** Ethical Consumer, nin.tl/toysguide **11** *The Atlantic*, 16 July 2014, http://nin.tl/familygamevalue **12** Ethical Consumer, nin.tl/toycarguide **13** *New York Times.* nin.tl/upcyclingevolves **14** The Atlantic, nin.tl/word-gap **15** Common Sense, nin.tl/children-reading **16** Proc Natl Acad Sci U S A. 2003 Jul 22; 100(15): 9096-9101, nin.tl/foreign-language-effect **17** http://www.aappublications.org/content/36/10/54.full **18** *Psychology Today*, op cit, nin.tl/declineofplay **19** Front. Psychol., 17 June 2014, nin.tl/structuredtime **20** The Atlantic, nin.tl/freeplaybest **21** See 16. **22** Optimus Education, nin.tl/rightbalance **23** *Smithsonian* magazine, nin.tl/playgood **24** Play England, nin.tl/earlychildrenplay **25** Arch Pediatr Adolesc Med. 2005 Jan;159(1):46-50, nin.tl/resurrectingfreeplay **26** projectwildthing.com **27** *Guardian*, 5 Jun 2010, nin.tl/climbtrees **28** *Nature*, 18 Mar 2015, nin.tl/myopiabooming **29** Quote from: *Slate* nin.tl/kidsrunwild Original study requires membership: nin.tl/developmodel **30** Children & Nature Network, nin.tl/childandnature **31** Forestry Commission England, nin.tl/simplefunideas

Resources and further reading

1 The science of green parenting

Books

La Leche League International, *Sweet Sleep: nighttime and naptime strategies for the breastfeeding family*, Pinter & Martin, 2014.
Jean Liedloff, *The Continuum Concept*, Penguin, 1989.
Jonathan Mugan, *The Curiosity Cycle*, Mugan Publishing, 2014.
Barry Schwartz, *The Paradox of Choice: why more is less*, Harper Collins, 2005.
Margot Sunderland, *The Science of Parenting*, Dorling Kindersely, 2008.
Jared Diamond, *The World Until Yesterday*, Penguin, 2013.
Sue Gerhardt, *Why Love Matters: how affection shapes a baby's brain*, Routledge, 2014.
James J McKenna, *Sleeping with Your Baby: a parent's guide to cosleeping*, Platypus, 2007.

Websites

Attachment parenting: askdrsears.com
Juno magazine: junomagazine.com
Safe Sleep Seven leaflet: nin.tl/safesleepseven
'The Tyranny of Choice', TED talk by Barry Schwarz: nin.tl/Schwartzonchoice

2 The green birth

Books

Ina May Gaskin, *Spiritual Midwifery*, Book Publishing Co, 2002.

Websites

Birthright International: birthright.org
DONA International (doula association): dona.org
Evidence-Based Maternity Care: childbirthconnection.org
Freedom for Birth film: freedomforbirth.com
'Love, Breathe, Just Doula', TED talk by Ginny Phang: nin.tl/TEDPhang
Pinter & Martin Publishers: pinterandmartin.com
The Birth Survey: thebirthsurvey.com
The Farm Midwifery Center: thefarm.org

3 Diet and nutrition, part one: the science of milk

Books

Kate Evans, *The Food of Love: the easier way to breastfeed your baby*, Soft Skull Press, 2009.
Gabrielle Palmer, *The Politics of Breastfeeding*, Pinter & Martin, 2009.

Websites

Human Milk 4 Human Babies: nin.tl/humanmilk4
La Leche League USA: lllusa.org
Human Milk Banking Association of North America: hmbana.org

4 Diet and nutrition, part two: weaning

Books

Gill Rapley & Tracy Murkett, *Baby-Led Weaning*, The Experiment LLC, 2010.
Marlene Zuk, *Paleofantasy: what evolution really tells us about sex, diet, and how we live*, WW Norton, 2014.
Felicity Bertin & Anna Walton, *Yummy Discoveries: Worry-Free Weaning*, Robert Hale, 2014.

Websites

My Wish: Protect Our Oceans, TED talk by Sylvia Earle: nin.tl/TEDEarle

5 Vaccines

Websites

Centers for Disease Control and Prevention, cdc.gov
Gavi, The Vaccine Alliance: gavi.org
Voices for Vaccines: nin.tl/thousandvoices
Skeptical Raptor blog on Big Pharma: nin.tl/profitsconspiracy

6 Diaper science: getting to the bottom of it all

Books

Ingrid Bauer, *Diaper Free: the gentle wisdom of natural infant hygiene*, Plume, 2006.
Chris Goodall, *How to Live a Low Carbon Life*, Routledge, 2010.

Websites

Real Nappies USA: realnappiesusa.com

7 Baby essentials

Books

La Leche League International and Diane Wiessinger, *Sweet Sleep: Nighttime and Naptime Strategies for the Breastfeeding Family*, Ballantine, 2014.

Leo Hickman, *The Final Call: investigating who really pays for our holidays*, Eden Project Books, 2008.

Susan Linn, *The Case for Make Believe: saving play in a commercialized world*, New Press, 2009.

Websites

Bikeability: nin.tl/bikeability3levels
Climate Counts: climatecounts.org
Ecos organic paint: ecosorganicpaints.com
The Campaign for a Commercial-Free Childhood: commercialfreechildhood.org

8 Travel

Books

Max Glaskin, *Cycling Science*, Frances Lincoln, 2013.

Carl Honoré, *In Praise of Slow*, Orion, 2005.

Richard Louv, *Last Child in the Woods; saving our children from nature-deficit disorder*, Atlantic, 2010.

Alain de Botton, *The Art of Travel*, Penguin, 2014.

Websites

Go Car Share: gocarshare.com
Lift Share: liftshare.org
Plane Stupid: planestupid.com
Project Wild Thing: projectwildthing.com
Responsible Travel: responsibletravel.com
The Man in Seat Sixty-One: seat61.com
Zip Car: zipcar.com

9 Green your home

Websites

Bio-D: biodegradable.biz
Lush Cosmetics: lush.com
Plastic Free Seas: plasticfreeseas.org
Plastic Soup Foundation: plasticsoupfoundation.org/en

10 Play, toys and entertainment

Books

Peter Gray, *Free to Learn: why unleashing the instinct to play will make our children happier, more self-reliant, and better students for life*, Basic Books, 2015.
Jay Griffiths, *Kith: the riddle of the childscape*, Penguin, 2014.

Websites

Adbusters Buy Nothing Day: adbusters.org/campaigns/bnd
Children & Nature Network: childrenandnature.org
Freecycle: freecycle.org
Poco Drom: pocodrom.com
Project Wild Thing: projectwildthing.com
Raffi: raffinews.com
Rethinking Childhood: rethinkingchildhood.com

Other recommendations

Books

George Marshall, *Don't Even Think About It: Why our Brains Are Wired to Ignore Climate Change*, Bloomsbury USA, 2015.
George Monbiot, *Feral: Searching for Enchantment on the Frontiers of Rewilding*, Penguin 2013.
Marc Bekoff, *Ignoring Nature No More: The Case for Compassionate Conservation*, University of Chicago Press, 2013.
Jay Griffiths, *Wild: An Elemental Journey*, Penguin, 2008.

INDEX

Page numbers in **bold** take you to chapter summaries.